REDISCOVERING FRANK YERBY

Rediscovering FRANK YERBY

CRITICAL ESSAYS

Edited by Matthew Teutsch

UNIVERSITY PRESS OF MISSISSIPPI / JACKSON

Margaret Walker Alexander Series in African American Studies

The University Press of Mississippi is the scholarly publishing agency of the Mississippi Institutions of Higher Learning: Alcorn State University, Delta State University, Jackson State University, Mississippi State University, Mississippi University for Women, Mississippi Valley State University, University of Mississippi, and University of Southern Mississippi.

www.upress.state.ms.us

The University Press of Mississippi is a member of the Association of University Presses.

Copyright © 2020 by University Press of Mississippi
All rights reserved

First printing 2020
∞

Chapters 1 "Focus on Yerby: Transforming Teaching and Research at Paine College" and 8 "Finding the 'Necessary Anguish': Frank Yerby's 'The Tents of Shem'" contain copyrighted materials from Paine College. Reprinted by permission.

Chapter 4 "'I Ain't No Man!': Blackness, Wartime Masculinity, and the Protest Tradition in Frank Yerby's Short Fiction" uses materials from the Yerby Collection, Howard Gotlieb Archival Research Center at Boston University. Reprinted by permission.

Chapter 6 "*Pirates of the Caribbean* in Frank Yerby's *The Golden Hawk*" is reprinted with permission. The essay originally appeared under the same title in *Southern Quarterly* vol. 55, no. 4, 2018, pp. 92–112.

Library of Congress Cataloging-in-Publication Data

Names: Teutsch, Matthew, editor.
Title: Rediscovering Frank Yerby : critical essays / edited by Matthew Teutsch.
Other titles: Margaret Walker Alexander series in African American studies.
Description: Jackson : University Press of Mississippi, 2020. | Series: Margaret Walker Alexander series in African American studies | Includes bibliographical references and index.
Identifiers: LCCN 2019058805 | ISBN 9781496827821 (hardback) | ISBN 9781496827838 (trade paperback) | ISBN 9781496827845 (epub) | ISBN 9781496827852 (epub) | ISBN 9781496827869 (pdf) | ISBN 9781496827876 (pdf)
Subjects: LCSH: Yerby, Frank, 1916–1991—Criticism and interpretation. | African American authors—Criticism and interpretation. | American Literature—20th century—Criticism and interpretation. | BISAC: LITERARY CRITICISM / American / African American
Classification: LCC PS3547.E65 Z86 2020 | DDC 813/.54—dc23
LC record available at https://lccn.loc.gov/2019058805

British Library Cataloging-in-Publication Data available

CONTENTS

INTRODUCTION
- VII -

FOCUS ON YERBY
Transforming Teaching and Research at Paine College
- 3 -
Catherine L. Adams

CIRCLING THE BOUNDARIES OF THE TRADITION
The Strange Case of Frank G. Yerby
- 27 -
Guirdex Massé

Frank Yerby and His Readers
- 47 -
Donna-lyn Washington

"I AIN'T NO MAN!"
Blackness, Wartime Masculinity, and the Protest Tradition in Frank Yerby's Short Fiction
- 68 -
Veronica T. Watson

OVERSTUFFED AND UNDERCOOKED
The Film Adaptation of Frank Yerby's *The Foxes of Harrow*
- 89 -
Matthew Teutsch

PIRATES OF THE CARIBBEAN IN FRANK YERBY'S *THE GOLDEN HAWK*
- 106 -
John Wharton Lowe

Contents

VICTIM'S GUILT
Frank Yerby's *Speak Now* and the "Politics" of Miscegenation
- 127 -
Gene Andrew Jarrett

FINDING THE "NECESSARY ANGUISH"
Frank Yerby's "The Tents of Shem"
- 147 -
Stephanie Brown

A CAMUS FOR THE COMMON FOLK
Yerby, Religion, and Existentialism
- 163 -
Anderson Rouse

ACKNOWLEDGMENTS
- 183 -

CONTRIBUTORS
- 184 -

INDEX
- 187 -

INTRODUCTION

FRANK YERBY PUBLISHED THIRTY-THREE NOVELS THROUGHOUT HIS career, which extended from the 1940s to the 1980s. He was the first African American author to have one of his works adapted to the big screen. He won the 1944 O. Henry Memorial Award for his short story "Health Card." He rubbed shoulders with luminaries of the Chicago Renaissance. He expatriated to France in 1955 then settled in Spain until his death in 1991, linking him to expatriate authors such as Richard Wright, James Baldwin, and Chester Himes. He published stories and poetry while attending school at Paine College and Fisk University in the 1930s. Yet, he has become nothing more than a footnote in African American and American literary studies. How does an author who was so successful over so many decades all but disappear from the literary landscape?

The consensus seems to be that Yerby has fallen to the wayside because he does not neatly fit into established literary categories. The son of a Scots-Irish mother and an African American and Seminole father, Yerby constantly pushed back against those who sought to label him. During an interview with James L. Hill in 1977, Yerby asked, "[I]s a black writer a writer who writes about black themes?" (215). If that is the case, according to Yerby, then "the white Frenchman Guy de Maupassant, who wrote stories defending Blacks in France, is a black writer, and brown-skinned, kinky-haired mulatto Alexander Dumas who never wrote a *word* about Blacks in his life, was a white writer" (215). Gene Andrew Jarrett makes clear that we "must remain fully aware of the fluidity and contestability of racial identity," and Yerby does just that when he asks how we define a black writer (5). After questioning how we define and categorize various authors such as Joseph Conrad and Vladimir Nabokov, Yerby concludes by stating, "I reject adjectives. Adjectives, which are the enemy of nouns, don't mean anything" (216).

For others, especially during the Black Arts era, they saw Yerby as nothing more than a pulpster peddling stereotypical images to a predominantly white audience. Critics disparaged him for not overtly addressing issues of racism and social oppression in his work; however, these issues resided underneath the surface, within the pages of novels that focused on white characters and their lives. Not until *Speak Now* (1969), Yerby's twenty-third novel, did he feature a black protagonist. The novel runs counter to most of Yerby's "costume novels" because it forefronts discussions of race and oppression rather than having them in the background. *Speak Now* was the first novel I read by Yerby, and it served as a meaningful entry point for me into his oeuvre. Upon finishing *Speak Now*, I backtracked and read *The Foxes of Harrow* (1946), discerning the ways that Yerby subversively deconstructs the moonlight and magnolia myth of the Old South and the social construction of race. Following *The Foxes of Harrow*, I moved around: *The Dahomean* (1971) and its follow-up *A Darkness at Ingraham's Crest* (1979), *The Saracen Blade* (1952), *The Old Gods Laugh* (1964), *Gillian* (1960), *Tobias and the Angel* (1975), and more. As I read, I began to discover that Yerby was much more than "the prince of pulpsters," as Robert Bone described him in his 1958 *The Negro Novel in America* (176). I began to see Yerby, rather, as "the debunker of myths," as Darwin Turner described him in 1968.

Critics and artists such as Arna Bontemps and Langston Hughes heralded Yerby's success with his debut novel *The Foxes of Harrow*, a novel that sold over five hundred thousand copies in the first few months after its release. However, they did hope that the success of *Foxes* would lead Yerby away from the "costume novel" formula and toward issues directly affecting African Americans. Hughes even brings up Yerby's success in "Matter for a Book," one of his Jesse B. Simple stories. In the story, Simple and the narrator discuss Jackie Robinson and his career as the first African American player in Major League Baseball. The narrator tells Simple that he wishes individuals would notice and praise other black accomplishments, not just those in the sports arena. He asks Simple, "You, for instance, have you ever bought a book by a Negro writer?" (61). Simple responds by telling the narrator that his partner Joyce is the cultured one. He mentions that he saw her reading "a book about some vixens" (62). The narrator interjects that the book is Yerby's second novel, *The Vixens* (1947). The narrator proceeds to tell Simple about Yerby's success, and Simple proclaims, "It is good when a colored man writes a book" (62). While he does not diminish Yerby's accomplishment, the narrator comments that books can have a negative effect: "Colored books can be bad, too" (62).

Almost twenty years later, Hughes would make a similar assertion in the introduction to *The Best Short Stories by Black Writers, 1897–1967* (1967). Hughes includes Yerby's 1944 O. Henry Award–winning short story "Health

Card" in the collection. In the introduction, Hughes touches on how Yerby's fame at that time surpassed that of Richard Wright, James Baldwin, and Ralph Ellison: "But none has become really rich, except Frank Yerby who, after 'Health Card,' put the race problem on the shelf in favor of more commercial themes. His historical romances have wonderful moviesque titles like *The Golden Hawk* and *The Saracen Blade*, but there are no noble black faces among their characters when brought to the screen. Black faces seldom sell in Hollywood" (xi). To achieve this fame, however, Yerby "put the race problem on the shelf." Like Hughes, Blyden Jackson in his review of *The Foxes of Harrow* comments that Yerby had tapped into a "winning formula," possibly even speculating that Yerby told himself, "It is possible as never before, to get rich quick with one novel. No Negro has ever turned the trick, and nobody really believes that any of us are quite ready or lucky to bring it off. But I understand the winning formula, and I can work it—now" (650). For many, Yerby's decision to focus on financial success over addressing issues affecting African Americans eliminated him from any critical discussion within academia. As Turner points out, if scholars read Yerby, they do so in private because "he has refused to fit comfortably into any of the cherished stereotypes" of black authors (569). Consequently, critics pushed Yerby aside. Turner continues by asking, "Who looks for myths, archetypes, ironies, absurdism, existentialism, or complicated personae in a writer so transparent that ordinary people read him voluntarily? And why read a writer whom everyone can understand?" (569).

Even within his interviews Yerby maintains that in his work he abandons social issues that affect African Americans. Yerby discusses his views on the novel in his 1977 interview with Hill. He sees the novel as addressing individuals and characters, not social problems. Answering critics who maligned him for not confronting racism, Yerby states, "You're going to sit down and tell a novelist to help solve the race problem, and my answer to that is *merde alors*! It can't be done. And it's not even a novelist's job. A novelist's jobs is to write novels, not political trash" (215). While Yerby, on the one hand, claims that his novels focus on individuals and not on political causes, he also makes clear that literature can affect individuals' views and beliefs. Earlier in the same interview, Hill asks Yerby about his criticism of the South in his costume novels: "As you were writing novels about the South, were you consciously including that criticism?" (211) Yerby begins his response by noting that, while he admires Baldwin, he felt that Baldwin and others "were preaching to the converted" and thus not reaching the audience that needs to change. Yerby wanted to reach those who still needed to be converted: "And

I was trying to get to the bigots; I was trying to get to the nigger-haters. I got some of them, and I actually received letters that indicated that I made some of that kind of people think, you know" (211).

Yerby's work, in various ways, confronts racism, specifically the social construction of race that works to uphold white supremacy. His work does not fall into the protest literature of Wright and others. Instead, Yerby's work directly targets the constructions of whiteness that "the bigots" he tried to reach firmly believed. In this manner, he follows in a long tradition of African American artists such as Paul Laurence Dunbar, Charles Chesnutt, and George Schuyler. In his interrogation of the social construction of whiteness, Yerby examines the effects of racism on the perpetrators, something Toni Morrison would call upon critics to do in *Playing in the Dark*. She encouraged critics not just to study the effects of "racist policy and attitudes" on those affected by it but also to study "the impact of racism on those who perpetrate it" (11). Using characters ranging from Stephen Fox in his debut novel to Kathy Nichols in *Speak Now*, Yerby illuminates the effects of racism on the perpetrators and works to deconstruct whiteness. The "literature of white estrangement," as Veronica Watson argues, "critically engages Whiteness as a social construction . . . mak[ing] visible the unseen, unspoken, and unevaluated nature of Whiteness" (5). Again, Yerby consistently deconstructs whiteness throughout his career, especially in his historical novels set in the ancient, medieval, or colonial periods such as *The Saracen Blade* or *The Golden Hawk*.

Recently, critics have started to reexamine Yerby's life and work, challenging the long-held notion that he composed nothing more than popular fiction for financial success. Scholars such as Gene Andrew Jarrett, Stephanie Brown, Veronica Watson, Mark Jerng, John C. Charles, Maria Christina Ramos, and I have drawn upon the foundations laid by James L. Hill, Maryemma Graham, and others. However, this influx of critical work on Yerby typically focuses either on his early novels, such as *The Foxes of Harrow* and *The Vixens*, or on his biography and his ambivalence toward addressing the "race issue" in his writing. Others, such as Bruce A. Glasrud and Laurie Champion in "The Fishes and the Poet's Hands: Frank Yerby, A Black Author in White America" (2000), examine Yerby's earliest publications, specifically his poems and short stories. While focusing on the above-mentioned aspects of Yerby's work, these scholars all make a case for including Yerby and his writing in the classroom and in the African American and American literary canons. This collection of essays adds to the body of scholarship by considering a wider range of Yerby's work.

Rediscovering Frank Yerby: Critical Essays explores multiple aspects of Yerby's life and career. Ultimately, each contributor addresses the ambivalence that underlies Yerby's comments in his interview with Hill about how he sees his role as an author. Although the essays here do not definitively resolve these ambiguities, each of the writers works through the contradictions that Yerby himself repeatedly expressed throughout his life. In addition to these discussions, the contributors explore a myriad of topics: pedagogy and teaching Yerby; reading Yerby in relation to the Harlem Renaissance and the Chicago Renaissance; the reaction of Yerby's readership to his work; the ways that Yerby addresses issues of masculinity and patriotism in his short stories; the film version of *The Foxes of Harrow*; the transnational aspects of his third novel, *The Golden Hawk*; how Yerby engages race and identity in *Speak Now*; Yerby's continued work within the protest novel tradition; and religion and its construction throughout Yerby's work.

Catherine Adams's "Focus on Yerby: Transforming Teaching and Research at Paine College" chronicles the ways that Yerby's alma mater, Paine College, celebrates his life and work, most notably by incorporating Yerby into the classroom and having students participate in recovering some of his early works. Along with detailing the ways that Paine College incorporated Yerby into its curricula, Adams details methods that could be applied at other institutions. Guirdex Massé's "Circling the Boundaries of the Tradition: The Strange Case of Frank G. Yerby" places Yerby's work, especially his poetry and short stories, within the artistic milieu at the end of the Harlem Renaissance and the beginning of the Chicago Renaissance. Massé argues that Yerby circled major literary movements and trends in African American literature from the 1930s and 1940s. While Massé places Yerby in conversation with both Harlem Renaissance and Chicago Renaissance authors, Donna-lyn Washington's "Frank Yerby and His Readers" examines Yerby's readership and reception over the course of his career. Drawing upon the work of Elizabeth McHenry and Janice Radway, Washington asks us to consider how Yerby's desire both to target a white readership and to distance himself from writers such as Wright and Baldwin caused critics to malign his novels.

Veronica Watson's "'I Ain't No Man!': Blackness, Wartime Masculinity, and the Protest Tradition in Frank Yerby's Short Fiction" explores how Yerby's short stories detail the psychological effects of racism on the black psyche. Notably, Watson examines both published and unpublished wartime stories, showing how these stories explore the intersections of race and masculinity in wartime and postwar America. My essay, "Overstuffed and Undercooked: The Film Adaptation of Frank Yerby's *The Foxes of Harrow*," examines how the 1947 film adaptation of Yerby's debut novel sought to counter David O. Selznick's 1939 adaptation of Margaret Mitchell's *Gone with the Wind*. Although it ultimately failed in countering the myths that Mitchell's novel and film adaptation perpetuated of the Old South, I argue that the adaptation does contain some moments that push back against the mythological narrative of the Old South; however, these fleeting moments do not prove effective in relation to the entire film. John Lowe's "*Pirates of the Caribbean* in Frank Yerby's *The Golden Hawk*" details the ways that we need to think about Yerby's third novel as a transnational text that engages with the Circum-Caribbean. Lowe argues that *The Golden Hawk* shows Yerby's career-long attempt to counter the narrow focus of social protest writing by presenting a transnational, cosmopolitan, and diasporic vision of black life in his novels.

Gene Andrew Jarrett's "Victim's Guilt: Frank Yerby's *Speak Now* and the 'Politics' of Miscegenation" examines Yerby's twenty-third novel. Jarrett proposes *Speak Now* as an important entry point into Yerby's oeuvre because of its explicit discussion of the social construction of both race and human identity. *Speak Now* highlights how Yerby engages with racial politics throughout his career. Stephanie Brown's "Finding the 'Necessary Anguish': Frank Yerby's 'The Tents of Shem'" counters the longstanding thought that Yerby completely abandoned the "protest novel" after publishers rejected his first manuscript, "This Is My Own." Twenty years after that rejection, Yerby attempted to publish another "protest novel," "The Tents of Shem"; however, publishers rejected it as well, in 1963 and 1969. Brown reads this unpublished manuscript as an important link between Yerby's early career of "costume novels" and his later career of expressly addressing issues of race in novels such as *Speak Now* and *The Dahomean*. Anderson Rouse's "A Camus for the Common Folk: Yerby, Religion, and Existentialism" looks at Yerby's views on religion throughout his oeuvre. Specifically, Rouse examines Yerby's work in relation to Albert Camus and to black existentialist thought, arguing that we need to think about Yerby as a philosopher for the masses.

As scholars, we cannot continue to ignore the impact of Frank Yerby on the African American and American literary landscape. His fingerprint extends across this landscape, as evidenced by the number of books he published, the frequency of his books appearing online for sale, discussions of his texts online, and references to him by authors such as Stephen King, George R.R. Martin, and Thomas Mullen. Yerby's impact cannot be diminished. *Rediscovering Frank Yerby: Critical Essays* works to rectify the misunderstandings of Yerby's work that have relegated him to the sidelines of African American and American literature by bringing his work into conversation with that of his contemporaries such as Richard Wright, Dorothy West, and James Baldwin. This move does not diminish some of the problematic aspects of Yerby's work, specifically his representations of women and his repeated comments on his role as an author. Ultimately, *Rediscovering Frank Yerby: Critical Essays* marks the beginning of a reexamination of "the prince of pulpsters" and "the debunker of myths" in African American and American literature.

BIBLIOGRAPHY

Bone, Robert. *The Negro Novel in America*. Yale University Press, 1958.
Hill, James L. "An Interview with Frank Garvin Yerby." *Resources for American Literary Study* vol. 21, no. 1, 1995, pp. 206–39.
Hughes, Langston. "Introduction." *The Best Short Stories by Black Writers: 1899–1967*, Little, Brown and Company Inc., 1967, pp. ix–xiii.
Hughes, Langston. "Matter for a Book." *Simple Speaks His Mind*, Simon and Schuster, 1950, pp. 60–64.
Jackson, Blyden. "Silver Foxes." *Journal of Negro Education*, vol. 15, no. 4, Autumn 1946, pp. 649–52.
Jarrett, Gene Andrew. *Deans and Truants: Race and Realism in African American Literature*. University of Pennsylvania Press, 2007.
Morrison, Toni. *Playing in the Dark: Whiteness and the Literary Imagination*. Random House, 1992.
Turner, Darwin T. "Frank Yerby as Debunker." *Massachusetts Review*, vol. 9, no. 3, 1968, pp. 569–77.
Watson, Veronica T. *The Souls of White Folks: African American Writers Theorize Whiteness*. University Press of Mississippi, 2013.

REDISCOVERING FRANK YERBY

FOCUS ON YERBY

Transforming Teaching and Research at Paine College

CATHERINE L. ADAMS

WHAT IS POSSIBLE IF WE DARE TO DISMANTLE SOME OF THE ACADEMIC hierarchies and treat our classrooms like millennial and postmillennial think tanks for the production of new knowledge? For example, "great works" in the western academy usually refer to canonical writings produced by mostly dead white men. However, at a Historically Black College or University (HBCU) like Paine College, we can redefine what are the "great works" in new and organic ways. We chose to read Frank Yerby's writings as canonized by the Paine College community. The much-needed concentration of critical attention to Yerby gave the college a challenge and opportunity to develop a critical voice that included twenty-first-century learners in important ways that may serve as a model for other learning communities.

As a college professor of Africana literature and literary history, teaching both local writers and little-known writers alongside canonical writers has become a hallmark of my pedagogy and student training. Upon my arrival at Paine College in Augusta, Georgia, in 2011, a humanities colleague, Anthony Neal, suggested he and I examine the work of Frank Yerby.[1] Yerby was certainly local. He was born and raised in Augusta, he earned his high school diploma from Haines Institute, and then he earned his first degree in English from Paine in 1937.[2] Yerby is well known in Augusta and Georgia literary circles for his prolific career as a writer who published thirty-three popular novels. However, in 2011, his poetry, short stories, and novels were little known to students at Paine and even African American and American literary scholars beyond those local and regional circles. Save the work of scholars such as Darwin T. Turner, James L. Hill, Maryemma Graham, Veronica Watson, Gene Andrew Jarrett, Stephanie Brown, Robert A. Bone,

Bruce A. Glasrud, and Laurie Champion, the lack of critical insights into Yerby's work presented some challenges—though not insurmountable—to teaching Yerby. From 2012 to 2016 the focus on teaching Yerby and his work at Paine College transformed the teaching and learning of literary content and research methods for undergraduate students and ultimately created a larger critical conversation on Yerby's work among scholars beyond local and regional enthusiasts.

Spanning more than half of the twentieth century, Yerby's work has sporadically emerged as fertile ground for teaching and research at Paine College. The archives at Paine include correspondence between Yerby and his editor Bob Cornfield at Dial Press, programs, and articles. The articles document Yerby's early connections to his former English professor Emma C. W. Gray, Paine College's president E. C. Peters, and later reconnections that began with President E. Clayton Calhoun (the last white president of Paine College) in the mid-sixties. Yerby's connection to Paine seemed intimate in the correspondence with Presidents Lucius H. Pitts (the first African American president of the college) and Julius S. Scott Jr., who conferred upon Yerby an honorary doctorate degree of humane letters at Paine's commencement in 1977.[3] Yerby was also interviewed by James L. Hill, an English professor at Paine from 1968 to 1971, and Maryemma Graham, a former Paine College student whose father, William L. Graham (class of 1929), served as registrar, professor, and vice president at the college. Yerby's work was celebrated in 1987 with a three-day symposium directed by Vivian U. Robinson and featuring presentations by Hill, Graham, and William W. Hill Jr.[4] After Yerby's death in 1991, the college would document its remembrance of its famous alumnus under the first woman president, Shirley A. R. Lewis, with tributes in the *Inkwell Collective*, a campus literary publication, and at the 25th Annual Conference on the Black Experience (COBE) in 2006.[5] Additionally, Yerby's childhood home was reconstructed on the campus under the meticulous care of alumnus Roscoe Williams (class of 1958), who served as executive assistant to two presidents—Lewis and George C. Bradley.[6] Finally, in conversations with Paine alumni, faculty, and staff, iterations of the Paine community read Yerby's work, and some faculty assigned his novels in literature courses as was done in the spring semester of 2012. Seventy-five years after Yerby's graduation from Paine, students were charged with learning of Yerby's complicated reception and reputation and viewing Yerby's literary legacy on their own terms—as generations of students had done before them.

The suggestion to explore Yerby transformed into a multiyear engagement largely because of the community of faculty, administrators, and alumni where, according to Maggie Berg and Barbara K. Seeber, collegiality matters (77). Berg and Seeber capture the decreasing social support on many college campuses when they write "in academic culture, it's mind over matter; we are expected to 'rise above' whatever is ailing us; and rather than help each other, we're taught to compete with each other" (85). However, at Yerby's alma mater, I found that interdisciplinary and multilateral collaboration offered "the promise that ideas will be preserved and nurtured rather than dismissed" (86). The length of time it took for some actions to materialize proved invaluable as it allowed deliberation with Neal, colleagues in the English program, such as Marva Stewart and Elizabeth Sicilano, and even other division chairs, such as Lawanda Cummings in Social Sciences and Teri Burnette in Media Studies. Many of those conversations happened in our offices during and after normal business hours, over dinners in our homes and local restaurants, as well as during scheduled meetings regarding Yerby projects. We shared resources, expertise, and insights that were foundational to the work that followed. With enthusiastic support from Emily Williams, then the dean of the School of Arts and Sciences, Neal received funding from the Georgia Humanities Council and the National Endowment for the Arts (NEA) to get the proverbial ball rolling with a symposium on Yerby hosted at Paine in 2013. We also had the support of a standing Yerby House Committee made up of faculty, administrators, and alumni, which met several times a year to discuss the usage of the Yerby House and the development of Yerby-related projects.[7] Lastly, the countless conversations with my colleagues in the humanities, social sciences, media studies, and the provost's office led to a proposal to "Focus on Yerby" that was generously funded by the General Board of Higher Education and Ministries (GBHEM) of the United Methodist Church for planning and implementation of projects from 2014 to 2016.[8] Our work with students was greatly enhanced by the ability to bring speakers to the campus, fund student and faculty travel, and acquire originals and copies of primary sources related to our focus on Yerby.

While Yerby deserves greater focus from as many perspectives as there are interested scholars, my decision to revive the teaching of Yerby at Paine was rooted in a necessity to impact and inspire a new generation of students to read, write, and research the school's most famous literary alumnus. According to Maryellen Weimer, "learner-centered transformative change in teachers and students often involves a synergistic relationship" (443). In my role as instructor and director of the Yerby Scholars, I employed a learner-centered approach where students worked with faculty as coresearchers in the unearthing of Yerby materials and the development of critical perspectives. For example, from the first group of readers, students were encouraged to select Yerby novels of interest and then report their selection process to the group. Two of these students extended their interest in Yerby into larger research projects of their own design during the following year. Later, even when students were assigned a particular topic or text, they all were encouraged to draw on familiar theories, landscapes, and experiences to inform their analyses. The approach empowered the students—through struggles and successes—to produce original research on Yerby.

Additionally, in my literature courses, the reemerging study of Yerby was informed by an approach in Africana Studies which revolves around intensive study of intellectual genealogy. According to Greg Carr,

> The challenge for African intellectual work and workers remains the same as that for all knowledge work and workers: to ask and answer the fundamental questions of human existence and to leverage answers by drawing first on the most familiar, richest and most accessible deep well of human experience, namely the one native to the cultural arc out of which one emerges as a human being and as a custodian to the received inscriptions of the group, as a "representative thinker." (180)

In other words, how might students at Paine use their own knowledge, experience, and investigations of historically black institutions, of Augusta, of Georgia, and the American South to reposition Yerby into a genealogy of thinkers on race and inequality?[9] How might we unpack some of the complications of Yerby's life and work as a self-exiled writer who penned many texts seemingly outside of his own cultural grounding? How does Yerby's early approach to and then avoidance of black protest influence the learning of students at his undergraduate alma mater? How might students understand the importance of black educators and institutions as nurturers of a young writer like Yerby—who as a student published poems and stories in literary organs years before his most celebrated short story, "Health Card," appeared in *Harper's Magazine* in 1946? And finally, how might studying Yerby provide a model for the grounding of curricula at HBCUs, as outlined by W. E. B. Du Bois, in the condition of and work of people of African descent (95)? In contrast to seeking a "universal" system of learning, this grounding "in the group life" would enable the university to "become not simply a center of knowledge but a center of applied knowledge and guide of action" (96). While searching for answers to these critical framing questions, it is important to note that Yerby's name was not new to the students on campus in 2011. In fact, the words he penned in the 1930s for the Paine College Hymn are read and sung weekly at student-led assemblies and annually at college ceremonies. His name was familiar; his literary legacy was not. With that said, the study of Yerby as a way to transform teaching, research, and learning was both a natural fit and a previously undocumented endeavor.

After the development of a learner-centered approach and culturally based framing questions, this study looked to the scholarship of teaching and learning to inform the research methodology of documenting pedagogy and learning. In *Literary Learning: Teaching the English Major* (2011), Sherry Lee Linkon writes,

> I see research on students' learning as fitting into two of the three standard categories of faculty work: scholarship and teaching. Analyzing students' understanding, investigating their difficulties and evaluating strategies for effective teaching involve intellectual processes and strategies that are similar to what I do in literary research, though with a focus on students' texts rather than literary works. Making this part of my research agenda not only integrates two core parts of my professional life, it also contributes to the ongoing critical discussion about teaching and learning in our discipline and across higher education. (106)

Linkon's work served as a guide for the close reading of students' work, and it informed the development of assignments, the gathering of data, and the interpretation of assessments. Moreover, from 2012 to 2016, adjustments were made from one student cohort to the next based on student outcomes at the end of a semester or an academic year. The results were dynamic in the coverage of Yerby's literary works and in the expansion of the research curriculum for English majors at Paine College.

This essay attempts to capture some of what is possible when scholars work with students as coresearchers on an organic research agenda. In the first section, "Undergraduate Literary Analysis of Yerby," I introduce ideas from the analytical essays completed by the first group of students who studied Yerby in 2012. At that early stage, we were just beginning to piece together critical mentions of Yerby by his contemporaries and other literary scholars—many of which were not favorable. Nevertheless, students—in defense of their famous alumnus—made up their own minds about Yerby's novels. In the section "The Development of Yerby Scholars," I describe the four cohorts of students who engaged in at least one semester of research and academic presentation of Yerby's writings. The first cohort focused on Yerby novels, online resources, and the college's archival material on Yerby. The second cohort shifted to a focus on Yerby short stories accessible either online or in the campus archives. The third cohort explored Yerby's experiences and writings while he was a student at Paine and Fisk. The fourth cohort focused on materials in the Yerby Collection at Boston University. These cohorts mined campus resources, local resources beyond the campus, and digital resources in ways that expanded their own understanding of Yerby as well as the understanding of academics and enthusiasts who attended their presentations. In the final section, "A Campus Focused on Yerby," I conclude with some of the ways in which the study of Yerby, as representative thinker and exemplar, spilled over into other curricular (and extracurricular) projects at Paine.

UNDERGRADUATE LITERARY ANALYSIS OF YERBY

As a young man born and raised during the Jim Crow Era in Augusta, with a mother who was Scotch-Irish and father who was African American, the complications of navigating a life as a writer in the United States sent Yerby out of the country into self-imposed exile.[10] According to James L. Hill, "like other African American expatriates—Richard Wright, Chester Himes, and James Baldwin—Yerby left the United States to escape the psychological burden of racism and find refuge from racism in a foreign land ..." ("Frank" 398). However, for students at Paine, Yerby's expatriation was, obviously, closer to home. They became engaged in the critical reception of the 1944 publication of O. Henry Award–winning "Health Card," which seemed like a promising start for Yerby's career. One student, Jameelah, observed, "As a poet and short story writer, he was accepted into the canon of African American literature early in his career. His work appears in anthologies including: Arna Bontemps's *American Negro Poetry* (1963), Langston Hughes's *The Best Short Stories by Negro Writers* (1967), and John Henrik Clarke's reprint *Black American Short Stories: A Century of the Best* (1993)" (2).[11] Students found that initially one could find Yerby amongst other African American canonical writers; however, only a few critics granted him this position.

In fact, after the rapid release of his first five novels—*The Foxes of Harrow* (1946), *The Vixens* (1947), *The Golden Hawk* (1948), *Pride's Castle* (1949), and *Floodtide* (1950)—Yerby's white protagonists and mostly white cast of major characters relegated his work to nothing more than brief mentions in critical texts. Faithful fans continuously read his novels, but literary critics seemed uninterested in Yerby's novels because they didn't place Africans in America (or elsewhere) at the center of the story. For example, critics in the 1950s such as Hugh M. Gloster opined, "Writing entertaining romances for big-money profits, Frank Yerby has produced in rapid succession five novels that are ideologically and esthetically unimportant but nevertheless noteworthy as the first series of best-seller triumphs by an American Negro writer in the field of general fiction" (370). Similarly, Thomas D. Jarrett stated, "Even though Yerby made an auspicious beginning in *The Foxes of Harrow*, a semi-historical romance, he has moved away from the realm of true historical fiction and has repeatedly employed a rags-to-riches theme, cemented with triangular romances and bits of historical material. Certainly, from a viewpoint of socially significant literature he cannot be given serious consideration, although few would deny that he is a gifted storyteller" (90). A decade later, Darwin Turner wrote, "Scholars no longer read Frank Yerby. Or if they do, they refuse to admit the fact publicly. They have reason to ignore him, for he has refused to fit comfortably into any of the cherished stereotypes" (569).[12]

With this daunting reception in mind, during the spring semester of 2012, the first group of students—English majors in their junior year of study at Paine—tackled some of the complications regarding Yerby's critical legacy. Each student was assigned the reading of a Yerby novel of their own choosing for the "Twentieth Century Black Literature" survey course. The class, consisting of four students, selected for literary analysis the following titles: *A Woman Called Fancy* (1951), *The Serpent and the Staff* (1958), *Speak Now* (1969), and *Western: A Saga of the Great Plains* (1982).[13] Their readings of the novels did not plead with Yerby to address racial inequality overtly, in the same way Yerby's contemporaries did during the Post World War, Civil Rights, and Black Power Eras of the 1940s, 1950s, and 1960s. The lack and inaccessibility of critical work on Yerby required students to derive meaning from Yerby's work using a few published essays, the texts themselves, other similarly situated texts, biographical information about the author, and their own knowledge of themselves and the world around them. For example, one student whom I will call "Maria," used her own understanding of race in America—plus Turner's essay, and Yerby's biography—to analyze *A Woman Called Fancy*.[14] She writes, " Yerby was born into an interracial family. . . .

The majority of Yerby's books are written where the main character is a total outcast, but finds success in an unknown culture.... This was [Yerby's] way of expressing his feelings towards interracial relationships. By having Fancy as a main character, Yerby suggests that it's hard to have African Americans and whites live together in dignity in America" (2). Turner discusses the ambivalence towards interracial families or "the possible amalgamation of certain groups" in Yerby's work (570).[15] In other words, the complications regarding race and interracial relationships from one's own observations and experiences in America, coupled with Turner's reception, were central for students to construct their literary analyses. Maria's essay suggests that Fancy's struggle for acceptance, problematized by the intersection of gender and class, may even be proxies for race.

On the other hand, Jameelah analyzed Yerby's work and reception by coupling Turner's essay with the reading of double consciousness from W. E. B. Du Bois's *The Souls of Black Folk*. For example, she wrote,

> Frank Yerby's literary career was a push and pull of what can only be described best by W. E. B. Du Bois's description of "two warring ideals" in *The Souls of Black Folk*. Yerby was caught between writing for a generation that loved his fiction, and a race that criticized it. Readers must examine an author's true purpose before judging his body of work. Must we assume that all African American authors must write protest literature about the plight of the African American in order [for it] to be considered a work of art? (5)[16]

As she questioned the negative critical reception of Yerby's work, Jameelah demonstrated a high level of synthesis in her reading of a primary source and her incorporation of secondary sources and nonliterary concepts. Faced with what was read as meager and mostly negative criticism, I encouraged the class to decide for themselves what Yerby's value was for twenty-first-century learners. And they did. Furthermore, because students in the course generally believed that greater attention of Yerby's work was overdue, two of the four students in the survey course showed strong interest in extending their examination of Yerby into their senior research projects for the next academic year. This interest reinforced the synergy between my students and me as we planned to access more Yerby material, generate more discussions, and extend the study of Yerby.

THE DEVELOPMENT OF YERBY SCHOLARS

In the English program at Paine College every student completes a course on literary methodology titled "Readings and Research." The course is a prerequisite to the Senior Research Project course offered during the spring. By the end of the spring semester, students complete and defend an undergraduate thesis in the presence of the Humanities faculty. During the fall semester of 2012, a much larger research agenda began to take shape for multiple cohorts of English majors at Paine. The students' short literary analysis papers, completed during their junior year, prepared them for longer research projects and transformed how Paine's methods course was taught. This process evolved into the Yerby Scholars Program at Paine College. The Yerby Scholars were students who committed at least one full semester (most committed two or three) to original research on Yerby's life and writings.[17] Under my direction and nurturing as division chair, students engaged in close reading, archival research, and field work related to the study of Yerby; these methods became essential to teaching literary methods in the English program at Paine.

The first cohort of five student researchers began with a methodical search for published, critical articles and scholarly books on Yerby. They completed online and library searches to locate dozens of the primary and secondary works cited in the bibliography of Bruce A. Glasrud and Laurie Champion's "'The Fishes and the Poet's Hands.'" Students conducted close readings of literary critics who examine Yerby in their monographs, such as Robert Bone's *Negro Novel in America* (1958), Gene Andrew Jarrett's *African American Literature beyond Race* (2006), and Lawrence Jackson's *Indignant Generation* (2011). They also read articles from local and regional newspapers housed in the college's special collections, chronicling Yerby's literary milestones and few returns to Augusta.[18] Additionally, one student, Kyle, in preparation for his senior project, read James L. Hill's dissertation on Yerby. The result was a cohort of student researchers who were better trained in literary research methods than previous groups of English majors at the college and better acquainted with Yerby's work and reception than most American and African American literary scholars.

In February 2013, the students' knowledge—and ability to demonstrate said knowledge—of Yerby's legacy was repeatedly put to the test. Yerby Scholars participated in a symposium that marked the return of Hill and Graham to Paine College, where they presented their work on Yerby to the twenty-first-century learners on campus.[19] The three-day event also included a faculty and student pair cofacilitating a movie screening and discussion of the 1947 adaptation of *The Foxes of Harrow*, a student panel presenting an analysis of "Health Card," and a student panel presenting research collected from the campus archives. In March 2013, Eugene Stovall, author of *Frank Yerby: A Victim's Guilt* (2006), traveled to Augusta for an annual literary festival sponsored by the Augusta-Richmond County Public Library. The festival featured an annual Yerby Literary Award, and in 2013, it included a roundtable discussion by junior and senior Yerby Scholars in the Yerby House on Paine's campus. Soon after the literary festival, a Yerby Scholar, Jameelah, presented the preliminary findings from her senior project as a part of a student panel at an Africana Studies conference held on the campus of Howard University. In April, Jameelah and Kyle presented findings at the campus-wide research day. Presentations and question-and-answer sessions provided students incremental opportunities to demonstrate their content knowledge. These opportunities translated into very strong project defenses: the 2013 spring semester ended with five successful defenses of thesis projects. Two cohort members continued to study Yerby, and three other members used the methods learned while researching Yerby to complete other literary projects.[20]

Three semesters of continuous work on Yerby laid the foundation to expand research projects and plan for more involvement in critical discussions on Yerby. However, during the 2013 fall semester, the research agenda had to be amended to accommodate the absorption of new students; Paine College's secondary education program closed, and education students were preparing for a last semester of education coursework, followed by a semester of student teaching. These students were now required to enroll in previously unneeded 300- and 400-level courses in the English program, such as the "Readings and Research" and "Senior Research Project," to earn their degrees in English, History, or Math. They had to trade the tools and rituals of one program for another. As director of the Yerby Scholars, I needed to maintain the integrity of the new research curriculum; build on the foundational work the first cohort had already completed; and quickly establish trust with the new majors. I decided to shift the focus from Yerby's novels to his short stories.[21]

During the fall semester, six students enrolled in the course for literary methodology, and two students made commitments to develop and complete research projects based on Yerby's short stories. One student researcher, Mychaelj, compared and contrasted Yerby's protest short stories with the similarly themed protest stories of Richard Wright, specifically Wright's

"Long Black Song."[22] Students in any African American literature course in 2013 would likely be familiar with the *Norton Anthology of African American Literature* and possibly familiar with Wright's "Long Black Song," originally published in *Uncle Tom's Children* (1938). According to Mychaelj's understanding of Yerby's purpose in "Health Card" and Wright's purpose in "Long Black Song," "Yerby and Wright were writers who were not quiet" about racial inequality and violence in America (3). In her comparison of themes, both texts "show how African American men had no authority to protect their wives, daughters, or sisters [from] a white man" (8). She added, "If society says that a man must provide for and protect his family, but this man can't protect his wife from a policeman's harassment as they are walking home or from a salesman raping his wife with no care in the world, that man loses all respect" (8). While both stories focus on similar themes, Wright's work is repeatedly anthologized and Yerby's work is repeatedly omitted. From the side-by-side close reading, Mychaelj concluded, "Frank Yerby and Richard Wright produced many works of protest literature. Although Wright's work was more well-known, Yerby's work should be just as familiar" (17). In examining the short stories published by Yerby between 1936 and 1946, the student researcher could clearly recognize Yerby's contributions to the genre of protest literature. What was, and still is, less clear was why Yerby's protest fiction is not often reprinted and included in American and African American literature anthologies.

For the second Yerby Scholar in that cohort, Shanequa, the revised focus on researching Yerby's short stories was an unforeseen opportunity to revisit special collections on campus and to locate a short story not included in the Glasrud and Champion article excavated by the previous cohort. While "Health Card" is Yerby's most famous published short story, the Paine College archives contain 1936 and 1937 editions of the *Paineite*—the campus newspaper—which included two of Yerby's earliest short stories written during his senior year.[23] The Glasrud and Champion article mentions Yerby's "Love Story," which was published in the *Paineite* in February 1937, but not "Salute to the Flag," published in November 1936.[24] Shanequa began with a close reading of "Salute to the Flag" and then added "Health Card" and "The Homecoming." By selecting the three texts, she could craft a research project that questioned Yerby's use of African American military protagonists in each of the short stories. Shanequa used her active participation in the Army ROTC at Paine and also discussions with an uncle who was then enlisted in the armed forces to analyze the texts using reader-response criticism as a way to interpret Yerby's selection of protagonists.[25] Her integration of her own experiences and understanding of military service and racism in the United States—regardless of service or the ultimate sacrifice—reinforced the continuing relevance of Yerby's protest stories. At the end of the academic year, both student researchers successfully completed projects on Yerby. The setback, if any, was that the students expressed a dwindling passion for reading longer texts and synthesizing secondary sources into the literary analysis. During the next academic year, I hoped that examining the college-aged Yerby and how his experiences at Paine and Fisk shaped him might restore some of that lost passion. Broadening the scope of the research agenda to include Yerby's biography meant traveling off the Augusta campus to Fisk University in Nashville.

Skillful, prolific writers like Yerby do not just appear; they are often nurtured in a milieu of teachers, mentors, and peers. As a youth, Yerby was trained at the Haines Institute, which was under the direction of Lucy C. Laney until her death in 1936.[26] During his years at Paine, he was influenced by Emma C. W. Gray's instruction in the English program as well as her direction of extracurricular activities such as the dramatic arts. His training would continue as a graduate student under M. Franklin Peters, Director of Dramatics, and Lorenzo Dow Turner, head of the Department of English at Fisk. And so, in 2014, during the third year of the Yerby research agenda, the lens on Yerby was widened a bit to include some inquiry into classmates and teachers of Yerby during his college years.[27]

The third cohort of Yerby Scholars experienced two significant field trips to gather and document biographical information about Yerby. The first trip was local—to conduct an oral history interview with Ruth B. Crawford, an alumna of Paine and former classmate of Yerby.[28] Crawford majored in social studies with a minor in English. She graduated in 1939 and had an influential career as an educator for almost four decades and as a leader committed to community service in Augusta. Just as Yerby authored the text of the alma mater, as an undergraduate, Crawford designed the Paine College flag which flies from the front porch of her home.[29] In 2014, four students traveled to her home near the college to interview her. When asked what she remembered about Yerby, Crawford recalled, "Frank Yerby was a brilliant scholar—very brilliant—but his social skills were poor." She remembered he was a straight "A" student. She also shared a specific moment in an English class with Yerby:

> Now, I was in his class when he wrote the first poem for *Harper's Magazine*. They had never published anything by blacks before. You have to look at the day and time I was in school. And Miss Emma

C. W. Gray had him to read the poem to us. And she said, "Young man, you're going to be a great writer if you apply yourself and do something for your temper."[30]

Although more than seventy-five years had passed since Crawford and Yerby sat in Gray's classes, Crawford was able to recollect Yerby vividly because of his academic prowess and his social quirks, and she could also recall Gray's encouragement of Yerby.[31] The trip to interview Crawford was designed to collect insights from someone who knew Yerby as a student at Paine College, sharpen students' oral history interviewing skills, and to develop a complete, collective transcription of the interview.[32]

Crawford's first-person accounts of Yerby as a "brilliant student" were also documented in an essay by Gray following the release of his first novel. The essay echoes Crawford's recollections, when she wrote, "Mr. Yerby was an excellent student. He had intellectual curiosity that led him to do the maximum assignments. His name was always on the Dean's List, and he was graduated with the highest average in his class."[33] Importantly, the essay also documents Gray's presence at a critical stage in Yerby's development as a writer—a time when he was creating and sharing his work with the Paine College community and even beyond the campus. Gray notes,

> When he was a seventeen year old freshman in the college here, I noticed that his English themes were always very carefully written and that often he would do more than was required. When he discovered that I was interested in this extra work that he did, he told me that writing was his hobby and began to let me read the products of his spare time. In this way I was able to watch his progress during the four years. And how he did grow! He wrote poems, stories, plays; he wrote for the *Paineite*, for a local magazine, for the dramatic club, and he wrote the Paine Hymn.[34][np]

Gray's nurturing of Yerby's hobby and his intellectual curiosity forged a deep connection between Yerby and Gray. She ended the essay explaining how college affected Yerby's development:

> I believe it is important to remember that during the years spent in college young people are growing and becoming what they are going to be in after years. Frank Yerby put his best in what he did as a college student. He made an excellent scholastic record, worked well on

tasks assigned him, and developed a hobby he planned to use as a life interest. It was inevitable that he would succeed. We are not surprised, but we are justly proud of him.[35]

Gray's words are quoted at length as evidence of the kind of nurturing Yerby received at Paine College in the 1930s. The same kind of relationships continue at the college like those that were forged between Yerby Scholars and faculty as we worked to understand Yerby's legacy and relevance to this new generation.

The second trip was to the special collections at Fisk University in Nashville, Tennessee. It was an overnight trip planned to locate two Yerby short stories: "Young Man Afraid" (1938) and "A Date with Vera" (1938). Both stories appeared in the *Fisk Herald* while Yerby earned a master's degree in English. During the trip to Fisk, student researchers were able to view Yerby's poetry as well as the two short stories. Jessie Carney Smith, then Dean of the John Hope and Aurelia E. Franklin Library, provided copies of the texts that were shared with special collections at Paine College.[36]

As a result of the rich field trips and literary discussions, the third cohort of Yerby Scholars were able to see Yerby as a young writer in training. This may have been the first cohort to think about Yerby not solely as a fully formed, famous writer, but as a work in progress—much like themselves. His vulnerabilities as a student may have even been comforting to one student, in particular, who initially struggled with identifying a viable research project. After two unsuccessful attempts, Teandra allowed me to give her a Yerby topic from an ideas journal I keep. I gave her "The Parable of the Prodigal Son" and Yerby short stories.[37] I told her to begin by reading the biblical parable in the gospel of Luke, followed by Yerby's "Roads Going Down," "The Homecoming," and "My Brother Went to College." Teandra successfully defended a research thesis using biblical allusion to generate framing questions for her study. For example, Teandra wrote, "'The Prodigal Son' raises many questions of why an individual would leave home to go into the world where they have no one" (2). She argued that through Yerby's works, readers can gain a multifaceted understanding of the journey, to understand what it means to be out in the world and to experience evil, and to realize what it means to return home, if return is possible (2). Teandra admitted having difficulty locating sources for her literature review. However, she used the library's online database to locate academic journal articles on the prodigal son. Her project inventively integrated biblical scholars and theologians who enabled her to expand her understanding of the "lost" son in Yerby's work: the "lost" son at the beginning of his journey in "Roads Going Down"; the son who returns home and tries to leave again because he is "lost" during the return in "Homecoming"; and the "lost" son who returns to his welcoming brother, a father figure, in "My Brother Went to College" (19). Despite a rocky start, Teandra completed her own undergraduate journey with successful presentations of her findings at the campus-wide research day event and, as required for all English majors, for the humanities faculty.

The texts and information gathered in special collections at Paine College and Fisk were fruitful for the first three cohorts of Yerby Scholars, but Boston University houses the lion's share of Yerby's papers. Consequently, we assembled a travel team of student and faculty researchers. Student researchers for the travel team needed a minimum grade point average of 3.0 and approval from faculty and administrators to miss three days of classes.[38] For both academic and personal reasons, there were no English majors eligible or able to travel. Refusing to let a field trip to Boston go to waste, the last cohort of Yerby Scholars was made up of two history majors. Though the shift created a vacuum for student literary research, it benefited the study of Yerby for students in the humanities generally. The two Yerby Scholars in the fourth cohort traveled and viewed Yerby's archived papers at the Howard Gotlieb Center at Boston University.[39] The student researchers pored over boxes of Yerby's notes, handwritten and typed manuscripts, correspondence, and the contract from 20th Century Fox for the rights to *The Foxes of Harrow*. The students kept a daily journal of the field trip, and their entries provided useful data for the program. For one of the students, Sharonda, an aspiring lawyer, the research experience tied directly to her career goals. She noted in her travel journal,

> My experience was phenomenal today. The Frank Yerby Archive had a lot of information that opened my eyes to the significance of Frank Yerby as a novelist and Paine College as a school. Frank Yerby made me realize that I am walking on very valuable and historical grounds when I walk on Paine's campus. In his writings, he talked about places in Augusta that we are very familiar with such as "Broad Street," "Walton Way," and so on. The most significant moment of today was actually holding the original copy of the Paine College Hymn. It gave me a lot more school spirit than I had before and it made me appreciate my HBCU even more. The surprise of the day was to be in a setting where information has to be handled carefully because it was years old and we had to wear gloves. I have never been to an archive

before so it was great to see how things work. I found everything that I was looking for today. [np]

For Sharonda, the trip to the Gotlieb Center increased her content knowledge of Yerby, transformed her relationship to Paine, and provided very practical archival experience with rare and old documents.

The second student, Georgina, was an ideal travel team member because during the 2015–2016 academic year she worked as for Special Collections at Paine College, under the tutelage of archivist Alana Lewis. Georgina made observations not only about the content of the Yerby collection but also about the archival processes at the Gotlieb Center and at Paine College. While she appreciated the vast resources of the Gotlieb, she was also critical of the unprocessed boxes she called up from the Mark Fax Collection at the Gotlieb. Fax was a music professor at Paine in the 1930s who put Yerby's words to music for the hymn. Fax's boxes were seemingly untouched since 1986, and documents were unsorted and unfiled in the boxes. Some were bound with staples that had rusted with time. Georgina remarked that under Lewis those boxes so dear to Paine College history would have been processed in a timely fashion, including the removal of staples and the establishment of finding aids. Georgina noted her appreciation of the great finds at the Gotlieb and also an appreciation for her training at Paine College. The results of the trip were shared at the 2015 Conference on the Harlem Renaissance, which featured Jessie Carnie Smith of the Fisk Library as a keynote speaker. Because of the prior introduction to Yerby Scholars in Nashville, Smith also moderated a roundtable discussion with both Yerby Scholars from the fourth cohort—Georgina Lewis and Sharonda Richards—Alana Lewis, and myself.[40] The discussion of the research repositories at the two HBCUs from which Yerby earned degrees was another significant moment for the Yerby Scholars Program and for the conference participants, who attended from across the country.

A CAMPUS FOCUSED ON YERBY

The attention paid to Yerby was not simply contained within programs of study for English and history majors. Using the growing compendium of Yerby materials from the Paine College archives, during the 2014–2015 academic year, selected protest short stories were integrated into the general education curriculum. The stories were embedded in four courses through the campus-wide Quality Enhancement Plan (QEP). The QEP at Paine College sought to assess the critical thinking and writing skills of students and to expose them to "great works" in the exhibition of those skills. The integration of Yerby's work included the following courses: EDU 101: Preparation for Excellent (Freshman Seminar)—"Salute to the Flag"; ENG 101: Composition I—"Young Man Afraid"; ENG 102: Composition II—"A Date with Vera"; and ENG 232: Introduction to Literature—"Health Card." During the 2015 fall semester, faculty piloted the integration of texts, discussion questions, and essay prompts using both the classroom and Blackboard (Paine College's learning management system). This project provided a way to begin to measure the academic engagement of students at the first-year and sophomore levels and the relevance of Yerby's literary work to twenty-first-century learners, regardless of major.

Additionally, Lawanda Cummings, Teri Burnett, and I developed and taught a 400-level Special Topics course that was cross listed as a major elective in English and Psychology and was open to all majors. The course, titled "Black Protest Literature and Social Movements 1930–1970," was offered for both the fall 2015 and spring 2016 semesters, and the first assigned reading was Yerby's "A Date with Vera" as a literary text that employs the trope of "black rage."[41] The Yerby text was the first of several assigned texts that were connected to the history of Paine College and to local protest writings and activities. In March 2016, two students from the fall semester offering, a psychology major and a religion major, presented on a faculty/student panel at an Africana Studies Conference held in Atlanta, Georgia. Two months later, three students from the spring, one psychology major and two religion majors, developed and hosted an event on campus using texts from the course to ground a discussion on #BlackLivesMatter. With this Yerby-related project, upper level students connected Yerby's youthful protest writing to contemporary forms of protest—hashtags, social media posts, and academic writings. Then, just as with the Yerby Scholars, these students publicly presented their findings to the campus and at other academic venues. For faculty who teach at independent HBCUs like Paine College, the Yerby research agenda invites the question, "How might HBCUs centralize the experiences and products of exemplars among students, faculty, and alumni to build curricula that distinguish, in rigorous ways, their students' learning experiences in relation to their counterparts at predominantly white institutions? How might we transform our institutions into places that master the particularities of black experiences as they relate to literature, culture, history, philosophy, social sciences, natural sciences, education, business, etc., and then master the global experiences of the African diaspora in ways that might redefine 'universal' understanding?" Pedagogically, in just four years, the organic study of Yerby proved itself to be worthwhile, flexible, and engaging for teachers and learners. Yerby's life and work is also sturdy enough to act as a bridge to other authors, texts, historical events, and social concepts. The work is worth it for our teaching and for our student's learning.

CONCLUSION

Though some scholars have dismissed Yerby's popular literary oeuvre, he deserves study, especially at his alma mater, Paine College. Those four years of sustained focus on Yerby through teaching, research, and academic engagement meant members of the Paine College community were actively reading Yerby's work and scholarly work about Yerby. In our development of a Yerby Scholars Program, students created projects and presentations that repositioned Yerby's literary contributions among his contemporaries. Students conducted an oral history interview and examined archival materials maintained at Paine College, Fisk University, and Boston University, leading to deeper analysis of Yerby's life and writings. We initiated Yerby-related projects across the curriculum, which affected teaching, learning, and assessment of student outcomes for students at early and advanced levels of study. By establishing Paine College as a locus for Yerby study, students had a stronger, more positive connection to the college and its resources and to the experience of field work. Each year leading up to the centennial celebrations of Yerby's birth in 2016, Paine's annual Conference on the Harlem Renaissance featured panel presentations on Yerby. Students even traveled to conferences on other campuses to present their research. Many of the research presentations were useful preludes to senior research projects required for graduation. Additionally, local and national scholars visited the campus, and their visits augmented the critical discussion of Yerby. Hopefully, through the exchange of academic presentations and scholarly discussions, the students reaffirmed the work of people who write about Yerby—sometimes in isolation. Lastly, students were able find a research niche where they could immerse themselves in work that is of interest to academic communities and to the local Augusta and Georgia reading communities. The efforts to teach Yerby to a new generation of students at Paine College, ultimately, transformed curricula, generated new research, and widely shared the celebration of Yerby's life and work.

NOTES

1. Initially, this conversation was between two new faculty members who began teaching at Paine in the fall of 2011. However, between 2012 and 2016, I served as English Coordinator and Chair of Humanities, which contributed greatly to the ability to adding "Yerby" as an agenda item for discussing curriculum, faculty and student research, and college initiatives even beyond the Humanities division.

2. In 1933, Yerby memorialized the founder of his high school in a poem titled "Lucy Laney," which was printed in a souvenir booklet published by the Institute. In 1949, the public high school A.R. Johnson merged with the private Haines Institute. The school was renamed Lucy Craft Laney Comprehensive High School to "keep the Laney Legacy alive" ("School History").

3. See Frank Garvin Yerby. File, Box 34, Folders 1–39, Special Collections, Collins-Callaway Library, Paine College, Augusta, GA.

4. At the time of the symposium, Maryemma Graham had interviewed Yerby in "Frank Yerby, King of the Costume Novel," 1985; James L. Hill had completed a dissertation titled *The Anti-Heroic in the Fiction of Frank Yerby*, 1976, University of Iowa, under the direction of Darwin T. Turner; and William W. Hill Jr. had completed a master's thesis titled *Behind the Magnolia Mask: Frank Yerby as a Critic of the South*, 1968, Auburn University, under the direction of Eugene Current-Garcia. See Frank Garvin Yerby, Box 34, Folder 1.

5. The theme of the conference was "Race, Representation, and the Arts and a Tribute to Frank Yerby," February 8–9, 2006, Candler Memorial Conference Center, Paine College, Augusta, GA. See Frank Garvin Yerby, Box 34, Folder 1.

6. See Frank Garvin Yerby, Box 34, Folder 6.

7. Between 2011 and 2016, a number of Yerby-related projects were hosted in the Yerby House including faculty-student panels during the 2012 symposium on Yerby, annual roundtable discussions with the Richmond County Public Library Yerby Award nominees, and tours of the house—upon request and by appointment.

8. Paine College is a Methodist institution formed in 1882 by the Colored Methodist Episcopal (CME) Church (now the Christian Methodist Episcopal Church) and the Methodist Church South (now The United Methodist Church). Since its founding, it has received support from both Methodist bodies. ("Biblical Foundation Statement" on Paine College's website)

9. This kind of inquiry is consistent with the vision articulated by Du Bois in "The Field and Function of the Negro College" when he writes, "a university is made of human beings, learning of the things they do not know from the things they do know in their own lives" (*The Education of Black People: Ten Critiques, 1906–1960*, 98).

10. Detailed accounts of Yerby's expatriation differ, but according to an interview with James L. Hill, "In 1952, [Yerby] expatriated to France because, he said, of racism; after remarrying in 1955, Yerby moved to Madrid, Spain, where he lived until his death on 29 November 1991" ("An Interview with Frank Garvin Yerby" 206). See also Hoyt Fuller's interview in *Ebony*.

11. This excerpt was taken from a student essay by Jameelah Jones, titled, "Yerby as Debunker *and* Relevant Black Author," submitted on May 1, 2012, Paine College. Author's personal collection.

12. It is worth noting that critics and educators like Turner who read Yerby's work as subversive influenced their students not to ignore Yerby. For example, there is the body of work by Turner's student, James Hill, including a dissertation, a published interview, articles, and book chapters.

13. Jameelah actually read an uncorrected proof from special collections bearing the one-word title, *Western*.

14. Fourteen former students were contacted and given the option of being referred to by name or by pseudonym. One former student, cited here, left Paine College at the end of Spring 2012. No contact information was available for consent request, so the pseudonym, "Maria," was used. The essay was submitted March 9, 2012. Author's personal collection.

15. Furthermore, in an interview with Paine alumnus and College Historian Mallory Millender, Yerby confirmed his ambivalence when he states, "I have never been an advocate of racially mixed marriages. It makes things much more difficult." Frank Garvin Yerby, Box 34, Folder 6.

16. See also James Smethurst's discussion of writings by Paul Laurence Dunbar and W. E. B. Du Bois as expressions of African American dualism. Particularly, Smethurst query of how one responds to "the problem of being a citizen and yet not a citizen" connects Yerby to this genealogy (29).

17. Tina Marshall-Bradley, who served as Associate Vice President of Academic Affairs at Paine from 2013–2014, suggested the name.

18. See Frank Garvin Yerby, Box 34, Folder 6.

19. The Frank Yerby Faculty and Student Symposium was held from February 13–15, 2013, and was sponsored by the Yerby Committee at Paine College. The event was spearheaded by Anthony S. Neal and funded by the Georgia Council for the Humanities and the National Endowment for the Humanities.

20. Titles of Yerby projects: "Race, Class, and Oppression in Works by Frank Yerby and Walter Mosley" by "Kyle" and "Georgia as a Literary Landscape in Selected Works by Frank Yerby" by Jameelah Jones. Both projects were submitted on April 24, 2013. Author's personal collection.

21. A full set of Yerby's novels is available digitally at archives.org. Both public libraries and college-level libraries usually have a few titles on the shelves. The Collins-Calloway Library at Paine has a full set in Special Collections, and thirty of Yerby's novels are available for circulation. The Yerby House also has a full set on display. Fortunately for the second cohort, four Yerby short stories were located by the previous cohort: "Health Card" (1944), "White Magnolias" (1944), "Roads Going Down" (1945), and "The Homecoming" (1946).

22. Mychaelj Jackson Hicks submitted her research projected, titled "'Treat the Negro Kindly, but Keep Him in His Place': Clashes of Race, Class, and Culture in Protest Short Stories by Frank Yerby," on April 30, 2014, Paine College. Author's personal collection.

23. The *Paineite* was "published five times during the school year by the students of Paine College," according to the masthead. In an April 1935 issue of the *Paineite*, Yerby is listed as an assistant editor. During his senior year, Yerby served as literary editor. Also,

during the 1936–1937 academic year, William L. Graham served as Faculty Advisor and E.C.W. Gray served as Alumni Editor.

24. The article also omits early poems published in the *Paineite* such as "Pine," published in April 1935, and "Conversion," published in 1936 and reprinted in the 1937 Yearbook.

25. The student at Paine wasn't the first to inquire about Yerby's choice of protagonist in "Health Card." In 1944 and 1945, Yerby exchanged letters with Private John S. Cousins, who was then stationed in Augusta, Georgia. Cousins asked Yerby about his use of a "clean, decent young couple" versus the use of "average educated members of the Northern Negro group" to settle some discussions regarding the author's intent. "Frank Yerby." Biographical file. Special Collections, Fisk University, Nashville, TN.

26. In 1936, Yerby authored a poem of tribute to the Haines founder titled, "Lucy Laney." See Frank Garvin Yerby, Box 34, Folder 32, Special Collections, Collins-Callaway Library, Paine College, Augusta, GA.

27. During the 2014–2016 academic years, much of the work and travel for the Yerby Scholars was made possible through funding from the General Board of Higher Education and Ministries (GBHEM) of the United Methodist Church.

28. Student researchers conducted and transcribed the interview under the direction of Catherine L. Adams. The interview was conducted September 18, 2014. Author's personal collection.

29. Crawford's original drawing of the flag is located in "Paine College History." File, Box 147, Item 16.

30. Considering the time frame, it is possible that Crawford is referring to the poems Yerby had published in *Challenge*, not *Harper's*. According to Glasrud and Champion's note, beginning as a seventeen-year-old, Yerby published poems in Dorothy West's magazine, *Challenge*—two in 1934 ("Miracles" and "Brevity"), two in 1935 ("To a Seagull" and "Drought"), and one in 1936 ("Three Sonnets"). The poems and correspondence from Yerby to West are available for online view in the "Dorothy West Papers," Series IV, 9.20.

31. Crawford was asked if she had a favorite teacher, and she said, "I don't know if I really had a favorite. When I came, I resented all of them and loved all of them when I left. . . . Maybe. I respected Miss Gray more. . . . See, Miss Gray said one day to me . . . 'Young lady, you come from a little town where you were that big frog in a little bitty pond, but here at Paine College, you are nothing but a tadpole out in the ocean.' So, Paine College set me straight. It set me straight on the issue of black and white. And it set me straight on the issue of thinking I was important. Now Paine College did that for me, and it will do it for you if you listen."

32. An added bonus was the encouragement that the four female students received from Crawford. She told the students, "I'm glad you all are English majors. I don't care how pretty you are, you always have to open your mouth."

33. See Frank Garvin Yerby Box 34, Folder 39.

34. Frank Garvin Yerby Box 34, Folder 39.

35. Frank Garvin Yerby Box 34, Folder 39.

36. A subsequent return to the special collections at Fisk during the summer of 2015 contributed greatly to this wider ranging project. Apparently, Gray's work in dramatics at Paine, and with Yerby, specifically, influenced his master's thesis, "The Little Theatre in the

Negro College," which included a mention of Gray's organization of the drama club at Paine. Fisk University Archives, Nashville, TN.

37. Teandra Gilchrist submitted a research projected titled, "A Man Must Work to Live in this World: Prodigal Sons in Frank Yerby's Short Stories" on April 20, 2015, Paine College. Author's personal collection.

38. As director of the Yerby Scholars Program, I mandated the GPA requirement and faculty approval.

39. Special thanks to Laura Russo, Manager of Public Service and Donor Relations, and Sarah Pratt, Archivist, at the Howard Gotlieb Archival Research Center. This trip seemed like a lofty dream when I began corresponding by email with Russo in 2012. Once we arrived in 2015, Pratt treated students like the coresearchers that they were, which allowed us to move efficiently through two dozen boxes in two full days.

40. "A Roundtable Discussion with Paine College Yerby Scholars" was held on November 5, 2015, at Paine College.

41. I, along with Lawanda Cummings, wrote about this course for the Faculty Resource Network at New York University.

BIBLIOGRAPHY

Adams, Catherine, and Lawanda Cummings. "Standing on the Box You've Built: Using Technology and Learning Tools to Build Knowledge and Agency Among 21st-Century Students at HBCUs." Edited by the Faculty Resource Network at New York University, Fall 2016.

Berg, Maggie, and Barbara K. Seeber. *The Slow Professor: Challenging the Culture of Speed in the Academy*. Kindle ed., U of Toronto P, 2016.

"Biblical Foundation Statement." *Paine College*, www.paine.edu/web/about/foundational-statements/biblical-foundation-statement. Accessed 6 June 2018.

Carr, Greg. "What Black Studies Is Not: Moving from Crisis to Liberation in Africana Intellectual Work." *Socialism and Democracy*, vol. 25, no. 1, March 2011, pp. 178–91.

Crawford, Ruth B. Personal interview. 18 Sept 2014.

Du Bois, W. E. B. *The Education of Black People: Ten Critiques, 1906–1960*. Edited by Herbert Aptheker, Monthly Review Press, 1973.

"Frank Garvin Yerby." File. Box 34, Folders 1–39. Special Collections, Paine College, Augusta, GA.

"Frank Yerby." Biographical file. Special Collections, Fisk University, Nashville, TN.

Fuller, Hoyt A. "Famous Writer Faces a Challenge." *Ebony*, vol. 21, no. 8, June 1966, pp. 188–94.

Gates, Henry Louis Jr., and Nellie McKay, editors. *Norton Anthology of African American Literature*. 2nd ed., W. W. Norton, 2003.

Gilchrist, Teandra. "A Man Must Work to Live in This World: Prodigal Sons in Frank Yerby Short Stories." Student essay, 20 April 2015. Author's personal collection.

Glasrud, Bruce A., and Laurie Champion. "'The Fishes and the Poet's Hands': Frank Yerby, A Black Author in White America." *Journal of American and Comparative Cultures*, vol. 23, no. 4, Winter 2000, pp. 15–21.

Gloster, Hugh M. "Race and the Negro Writer." *Phylon*, vol. 11, no. 4, 1950, pp. 369–71.
Gray, E. C. W. "Frank Yerby as an Instructor Sees Him." *The Paineite Annual Edition*, Paine College, 1946.
Harris, Shanequa R. "The Military Season of Frank Yerby's Short Stories." Student essay, 30 April 2014. Author's personal collection.
Hill, James L. "An Interview with Frank Garvin Yerby." *Resources for American Literary Study* vol. 21, no. 2, 1995, pp. 206–39.
Hill, James L. "Frank Garvin Yerby." *Writers of the Black Chicago Renaissance*, edited by Steven C. Tracy, Kindle edition, U of Illinois P, 2011.
Jackson Hicks, Mychaelj. "'Treat the Negro Kindly, but Keep Him in His Place': Clashes of Race, Class, and Culture in Protest Short Stories by Frank Yerby." Student essay, 30 April 2014. Author's personal collection.
Jarrett, Thomas D. "Recent Fiction by Negroes." *College English*, vol. 16, no. 2, 1954, pp. 85–91.
Jones, Jameelah T. "Yerby as Debunker *and* Relevant Black Author." Student essay, 1 May 2012, Paine College. Author's personal collection.
Jones, Jameelah T. "Georgia as a Literary Landscape in Selected Works by Frank Yerby." Student essay, 24 April 2013. Author's personal collection.
"Kyle." "Race, Class, and Oppression in Works by Frank Yerby and Walter Mosley." Student essay, 24 April 2013. Author's personal collection.
Lewis, Georgina, Sharonda Richards, et al. "Roundtable Discussion with Paine College Yerby Scholars." Conference on the Harlem Renaissance, 5 Nov 2015, Paine College, Augusta, GA.
Linkon, Sherry Lee. *Literary Learning: Teaching the English Major*. Indiana UP, 2011.
"Maria." "A Woman Called Fancy." Student essay, 9 Mar 2012. Author's personal collection.
Millender, Mallory. "Frank Yerby Lashes American 'Hypocrisy.'" *The Augusta News-Review* vol. 7, no. 3, 12 May 1977, p. 1.
"Paine College History." File, Box 147, Items 15–16, Special Collections, Collins-Callaway Library, Paine College.
"School History." *Lucy C. Laney High School*. www.rcboe.org/Domain/3221. Accessed 6 June 2018.
Smethurst, James. *The African American Roots of Modernism: From Reconstruction to the Harlem Renaissance*. UNC P, 2011.
Turner, Darwin T. "Frank Yerby as Debunker." *Massachusetts Review*, vol. 9, no. 3, Summer 1968, pp. 569–77.
Weimer, Maryellen. "Learner-Centered Teaching and Transformative Learning." *The Handbook of Transformative Learning: Theory, Research, and Practice*, edited by Edward W. Taylor, et al., Kindle ed., John Wiley & Sons, 2012.
West, Dorothy. "Papers of Dorothy West ca.1890–1998." MC 676, Series IV: Editing and Work by Other Writers, 1926–1949, 9.20. Schlesinger Library, Radcliffe Institute, Harvard University, Cambridge, MA.
Yerby, Frank. "A Date with Vera." *The Fisk Herald*, vol. 31, Nov. 1937, pp. 16–17.
Yerby, Frank. "Health Card." *Harper's Magazine*, May 1944, pp. 548–53.
Yerby, Frank. "The Homecoming." *Common Ground*, Spring 1946, pp. 41–47.

Yerby, Frank. "Lucy Laney." *Golden Jubilee Souvenir Booklet, 1886–1936*. Haines Normal and Industrial Institute, 1936, p. 37.

Yerby, Frank. "My Brother Went to College." *Tomorrow*, Jan. 1946, pp. 9–12.

Yerby, Frank. "Roads Going Down." *Common Ground*, Summer 1945, pp. 67–72.

Yerby, Frank. "Paine College Hymn." File. Box 147, Item 15. Special Collections, Paine College, Augusta, GA.

Yerby, Frank. "Salute to the Flag." *The Paineite*, vol. 16, no. 1, Nov. 1936, pp. 4, 13, 23

Yerby, Frank. "White Magnolias." *Phylon*, vol. 5, no. 4, Third Quarter 1944, pp. 319–26.

Yerby, Frank. "Young Man Afraid." *The Fisk Herald*, Oct. 1937, pp. 15–16.

CIRCLING THE BOUNDARIES OF THE TRADITION

The Strange Case of Frank G. Yerby

GUIRDEX MASSÉ

AS A VARIETY OF CRITICS HAVE NOTED, THE PROLIFIC WRITER FRANK Garvin Yerby (1916–1991) occupies a very strange place in the African American literary tradition. While by the time he passed away in Madrid, Spain, on November 29, 1991, he was quite possibly the bestselling African American writer of all time, he remains but a vague shadow in the African American literary canon, as evidenced by the relative lack of scholarly work produced about his life and works. This omission is due in large part to what scholars of American literature have regarded as the author's eventual decision to write financially rewarding, commercially successful fiction, as opposed to literature with more overt social and political resonance. By the midpoint of the twentieth century, as black male writers of his generation such as Richard Wright, James Baldwin, Ralph Ellison, and to a different extent Chester Himes, had achieved some significant critical success, such a body of work for any black writer would inevitably have meant directly addressing the social and ideological conditions that affected black lives. However, although Yerby began his career on a path similar to that of his peers, by the time he published his first novel *The Foxes of Harrow* (1946), Yerby had determined that for himself the route of the "race novel" was an artistic dead end; Yerby's novel is a southern plantation romance in the tradition of Margaret Mitchell's *Gone with the Wind* (1936), featuring a white protagonist and treating issues of race as secondary.

To simply dismiss Frank Yerby as a peculiar case in African American writing is to misunderstand how significant turns in his literary career reflected dominant movements and trends, as well as how formal and thematic innovations and limitations have characterized the trajectory of African American literature from the early 1930s to the 1940s. This period ranges from the tail end of the Harlem Renaissance/New Negro Movement to an era of social realism in African American fiction. This chapter is not so much concerned with reviewing, assessing, or critically analyzing the body of Yerby's work, as it is with delineating the writer's relationship to the black literary tradition at the midpoint of the twentieth century. For, as literary historian Lawrence P. Jackson has rightly noted, a different image of this writer emerges when he is considered not in isolation but in relation to a network and artistic milieu to which he was closely connected (Jackson 12). If the scarcity of information available on Yerby's life renders challenging any critic's ability to firmly delineate Yerby's presence within such a milieu, it remains possible to glean enough of Yerby's early efforts as a writer to broadly illustrate his engagement with the institutional and ideological infrastructures that have informed our understanding of African American writing at the halfway point of the twentieth century. From his early contact with Dorothy West, a key writer of the Harlem Renaissance, to his brief presence in Chicago during a period of great literary and artistic creativity in the 1930s, Yerby's literary trajectory paralleled that of many of his now more prominent peers. This essay seeks to explore some aspects of these engagements and connections in order to provide a perspective on this writer's career—one that does not unjustly relegate him to the margins of African American arts and letters.

AT THE TAIL END OF ONE RENAISSANCE AND AT THE BEGINNING OF ANOTHER

In a letter dated June 1, 1934, a seventeen-year-old Frank Yerby expressed to Dorothy West, the Harlem Renaissance writer and founder of the New York–based magazine *Challenge*, "The idea of a Renaissance in Negro letters appeals to me very strongly; I hope to be in the vanguard of those who will foster such a rebirth. If your magazine is successful, which I believe it will be, it will be the very hub of such a movement." Yerby was then a student at Paine College, a historical black college in his native city of Augusta, Georgia. He had been introduced to *Challenge* by Grace Walker, a fellow Augusta native and acquaintance of Dorothy West. Walker's interest in African American arts and letters had led her to pursue academic degrees at Fisk University and Atlanta University in the early 1930s ("Obituary for Grace Walker Ramsey").

While at Fisk, Walker had been encouraged by no less than the renowned writer and race man James Weldon Johnson to seriously delve into her literary interests. She produced a pioneering master's thesis on "The Negro Novelist" (Price 511). Given her educational background and her remarkable Rolodex of acquaintances, Walker was very well acquainted with the then-unprecedented literary and artistic outpouring emerging from Harlem throughout the 1920s. She would have been an excellent source of information and guidance for a young and eager writer who throughout his college years at Paine College and later Fisk University had been diligently typing away poems, short stories, and plays. In that same letter, Yerby enclosed three poems—"Then tears well up," "Belief," and "Pain"—that he hoped West would deem strong enough to grace the pages of her publication.

While West did not publish the first three poems Yerby submitted to her in his initial correspondence, over the next couple of years, he would succeed in landing five other poems in her journal—"Brevity," "Drought," "Miracles," "Three Sonnets," and "To a Seagull"—marking his initiation into the sphere of national publication. While time would eventually contradict his expressed belief that *Challenge* would "foster a rebirth" in black creative writing, he had all the same accurately summed up West's motivation in founding her magazine. *Challenge* was in effect West's attempt to rekindle the flames of creativity from the 1920s (Sherrard-Johnson 107). For although she was barely a decade older than Yerby, West was a veteran of the Harlem literary scene. Affectionately nicknamed "the Kid" by the genial and ever-wandering Langston Hughes, she, along with her cousin and fellow writer, the poet Helene Johnson, had moved to Harlem from Boston in 1926 in order to pursue their literary careers. Success came early; in that same year her short story, "The Typewriter," placed second in a national writing contest sponsored by the Urban League's *Opportunity* magazine. West proceeded to insert herself into the coterie of writers and artists whose works would come to define the aesthetic ethos and literary practices of the Harlem Renaissance period.

As Arna Bontemps, a contemporary of Yerby's, would note, by the early 1930s the Great Depression had severely limited the ability of black writers and artists to sustain themselves (43). The coterie of writers and artists began to disperse, and along with it, the creative spirit that in the prior decade had made Harlem a dynamic center of black arts. West's cognizance of what was occurring in her immediate social and cultural milieu is reflected in a letter to James Weldon Johnson. The year before coming out with the first issue of *Challenge*, West wrote to Johnson, "Suddenly I am serious and entirely grown up . . . and I know the promise we, the New Negroes, were so full of is enormously depleted. And now, there are newer voices that are younger and surer" (qtd. in Lewis 304). Faithful to these words, West's magazine would attempt in part to bridge the work of Harlem Renaissance writers to that of a younger generation that Yerby himself exemplified.

Between 1934 and 1937, *Challenge* appeared six times. Its indebtedness to the spirit of the Harlem Renaissance can be gauged by simply reviewing its list of contributors, especially in its first couple of issues. *Challenge* included established writers such as Langston Hughes, Countee Cullen, Arna Bontemps, Zora Neale Hurston, Helene Johnson, and Claude McKay. Considering the relative cachet of these names even by Yerby's time, it is fair to assume that if the magazine had indeed augured the kind of rebirth Frank Yerby wishfully anticipated, and Dorothy West had hoped for, any serious discussion of Yerby's career would inevitably consider his work alongside theirs. While several early estimations of *Challenge* by West's peers initially pointed to its promise, the periodical eventually failed as a result of various factors. West struggled to secure adequate financing for her small and independent publication venture. In her "Dear Reader" column in the magazine, West also alluded to the difficulty she experienced in finding material "fair" or strong to justify the magazine surviving past its six issues (qtd. in Sherrard-Johnson 112).

If West's words here may initially temper our appreciation of Yerby's early publication efforts, it is useful to contextualize her remarks. Langston Hughes, in his autobiography *The Big Sea*, recalls a similar situation from his own career. Reflecting upon the publication of his stories in the political and literary magazine *The Messenger*, Hughes explains how fellow writer Wallace Thurman, who briefly served as the magazine's managing editor in 1926, had accepted Hughes's stories even though he considered them bad because they were better "than any others they could find" (234).

What both West and Hughes's words speak to is an often-neglected aspect of how we come to apprehend and value the works of established, "serious" writers. Similar to the image of Athena emerging fully grown from Zeus's head, the gestation period of a writer in the process of becoming is often ignored for a narrative that highlights undeniable individual genius. Here, however, West's and Thurman's respective editorships of different literary organs illustrate a self-conscious project of cultivating talent at moments of possible, but not assured, germination. Yerby's inclusion in West's magazine reflects not only a nod to his literary potential but, given the magazine's stated aims, also an attempt to enlist his creative energy in the service of a new wave of writing.

If West's comments cite her struggles with finding talent as a key reason for *Challenge*'s eventual folding, literary historian Lawrence P. Jackson's brief assessment of West's magazine presents a different perspective on the journal—one that highlights both formal and ideological factors that might have affected its reception. To Jackson, West's publication "seemed mainly interested in cuddling a kind of polite aestheticism" that looked askance at what she deemed "turgid and artificial" investigations of racial and economic issues (31). This statement finds some support in the fact that of the five poems Yerby published in *Challenge*, none addressed a racial theme. However, it is also likely that she considered her own literary organ as providing a niche of sorts for more formally sound literary works; West knew that that more prominent race journals such as *Crisis* and *Opportunity* were not invested in publishing creative writers whose style reflected more modernist literary innovations and aesthetics.

What Jackson's meditations on the formal and ideological qualities of *Challenge* compellingly suggest, however, is a significant change in tone, posturing, and theme in the literature coming from a younger cadre of writers who from the mid-1930s to the 1960s would come to dominate the field of African American letters. Referred to as "social realism" even at the moment of its emergence, this new literary movement was characterized by what Stacy I. Morgan, has associated with a "heightened emphasis on the role of the creative artist as an agent of democratic consciousness raising and social change" (2). This is not to say that Harlem Renaissance writers were unconcerned with the American racial conundrum and with the social and economic issues that affected black lives. A brief overview of one of the movement's key texts/manifestoes, Alain Locke's introduction to his anthology *The New Negro* (1925), illustrates how the eruption of literature, visual, plastic, and performance arts that characterized the Harlem Renaissance was closely aligned ideologically with the politics of racial egalitarianism. However, the African American social realist tradition that was emerging in the 1930s, and in which a younger Yerby would figure in his own way, was much more intimately connected to progressive and radical leftist political ideologies, agendas, and practices. The tradition's literary and artistic purview more explicitly addressed issues of poverty and racism by centering on the experiences of the black urban industrial masses and the rural poor.

While too much is often made of how severe the break was between the Harlem Renaissance and African American social realism, it is useful here to briefly delineate some of the key thematic differences and sites of conflict between narratives of the Harlem Renaissance (1915–1935) and narratives written in the subsequent twenty-five years (1935–1960). These differences are key to understanding Yerby's erasure from the African American literary canon.

In comparing the two different movements, literary scholars Robert Bone and Richard Courage have argued that Harlem Renaissance writers tended to "turn inward, toward heightened ethnic consciousness and a romantic identification with a southern-rooted folk culture," while writers out of the social realist school emphasized literary representations that sought to create "social transformations through the cold-eyed documentation of oppressive social realities" (161). Bone and Courage effectively argue that there was a strong idealist streak in how Harlem Renaissance writers approached black existence. They were often interested in examining the particularity of black culture, whose provenance they associated with folk traditions of the American South, in a romanticized fashion. Jean Toomer's *Cane* (1923), Langston Hughes's *The Weary Blues* (1926), and Sterling A. Brown's *Southern Road* (1932) are texts that clearly exemplify this idea. By comparison, writers of the social realist school were more materialist in their orientation. Their investigations of the folk tended to be more invested in presenting a class paradigm, as opposed to illustrating the particularity of black cultural folkways.

The work of two key intellectual figures associated with these two movements—W. E. B. Du Bois and Richard Wright—allows us to broadly sketch the thematic concerns of these two periods. We will specifically look at W. E. B. Du Bois's trope of "double consciousness," as articulated in *Souls of Black Folk* (1903), and what can arguably be considered a reconfiguration of that trope in much of Richard Wright's work. Both writers provide us with useful conceptual metaphors to explore. Early in "Of Our Spiritual Strivings," Du Bois remarks, "The Negro is born with a veil, and gifted with second-sight in the American world,—a world which yields him no true self-consciousness, but only lets him see himself through the revelation of the other world.... One ever feels his two-ness—an American and a Negro" (8). Du Bois's statement can be understood in three different ways. We can say for one that this passage refers to a social and political reality—and thus a material reality. The African American born within the "veil," a metaphor that symbolizes supposedly discrete racial boundaries which preclude normative interracial interactions, is a second-class citizen who daily experiences exclusion from the mainstream American body politic. From this material reality—social and political exclusion—arises a subjective dimension, or, the raced subject's lived experience of *being* in "a world which yields him no true self-consciousness." The second aspect of Du Bois's statement thus forces us to consider the idea that African American subjectivity undergoes a process of self-alienation—the seeing of one's self through the eyes of others, as well as a questioning of one's identity as an American.

Yet having posited these two realities—on the one hand the social/political, and on the other the subjective and experiential—as inescapable characteristics of African American life, Du Bois suggests one positive outcome; "born with a veil," the raced subject is also "gifted with second sight." Here, the Du Boisian veil assumes a quasi-prophetic quality akin to Nathaniel Hawthorne's metaphor in the short story "The Minister's Black Veil." This third reading of Du Bois's statement broaches the question of agency: that racism as an ideology and a set of practices does not foreclose the raced subject's power of knowledge/knowing. Du Bois appears to propose that "double consciousness" as a state of being and allows for a privileged form of knowing that white Americans are not privy to. This knowledge destabilizes racist ideology insofar as it inverts the economy of its logic, given that "knowing" here belongs to the racially marginalized.

It is worth considering the possibility that the literature produced during the Harlem Renaissance—even more than that of the later, socialist realist tradition—has a wider framework of thematic preoccupation as it broadly engages these three interpretations of Du Bois's statement. The social and political dimension can be accepted as a given, insofar as narratives by black authors that focus on black lives and experiences in the United States generally tend to challenge racist ideologies and discourses. However, the idea of the raced subject's experience of alienation, the questioning of one's identity, and the idea of that subject's agency (arrived through an understanding of "double consciousness") reify themselves in a multiplicity of thematic representations. So for instance, there are a number of works that dramatize the theme of "passing" (e.g., Jessie R. Fausset's *Plum Bun* [1928], James Weldon Johnson's *The Autobiography of an Ex-Colored Man* [1912], Nella Larsen's *Passing* [1929]); the marginal position of the black bourgeoisie (e.g., Jessie R. Fausset's *Plum Bun*, Nella Larsen's *Quicksand* [1928]); black intellectual malaise (e.g., Nella Larsen's *Quicksand*, Claude McKay's *Home to Harlem* [1927] and *Banjo* [1929]); and a search for racial/cultural wholeness (e.g., Jean Toomer's *Cane*, Sterling Brown's *Southern Road*, and Langston's Hughes *The Weary Blues*). Also, at least in the novel form, when compared to the literature of the social realist tradition, more of the Harlem Renaissance works address specifically and at length the conditions of black women's lives.

Lastly, it would be reductive to claim that Harlem Renaissance writings all address the "privileged knowledge" Du Bois's statement implies, but the theme appears more characteristically in works from that movement than in those of the later, social realist tradition. So, for instance, the character of Ray in Claude McKay's novels *Home to Harlem* and *Banjo*, who functions as the intellectual doppelganger of both novels' folk-inspired protagonists (Jake and Banjo respectively), pits black subjectivity against capitalist logic. While Jake and Banjo live happy-go-lucky lives, in some ways even unencumbered by their blackness, Ray's function within the narrative is to articulate a philosophy that provides depth to the otherwise thin representations of both protagonists' bohemian existence. Although in representing Ray, McKay may be accused of relying on essentialist tropes of the black primitive, a significant aspect of what informs Ray's understanding of black subjectivity is an awareness of how the color line prevents the black subject from having full and normative access to society. Ray presents this position of marginality, however, as one that can be productive, insofar as it allows for alternative ways of being and knowing. For Ray himself, this required abandoning respectability and, through his association with Jake and Banjo, committing a form of class suicide.

While Richard Wright's work demonstrates his knowledge of Du Bois's theory of the black subject's ontological position, he reconfigures Du Bois's concept of "double consciousness" in ways that emphasize the material conditions that affect black lives over the forms of consciousness they produce. Wright's approach reflects Bone and Courage's assertions regarding the realist writers' investment in social transformation and in the documentation of injustices, versus the Harlem Renaissance writers' more inward turn. In Wright's last novel *The Long Dream* (1958), the protagonist, Fishbelly, reflects upon the lynching of a young black man (Chris) over a consensual sexual relationship he had with a white woman. Fishbelly's father, Tyree, motivated by fear, responds to Chris's death in a way that leads Fishbelly to realize that if he had been in a similar situation his father could not have protected him. The narrator states, "One thing [Fishbelly] knew: the *real reality* of the lives of his people was negated; the *real* world lay over *there* somewhere—in a place where white people lived, people who had the power to say who could or could not live and on what terms; and *the world in which he and his family lived was a kind of shadow world*" (67; emphasis added). Similar to Du Bois's theorization of the duality of black being, this passage articulates a split between a normative existence (white) and an existence on the margins (black). Wright's passage, however, places more weight on the material conditions of oppression (the "*real* reality") as opposed to the forms of consciousness that this "real" reality produces. Blacks in the racist South, Wright's protagonist tells us, live in a world of shadows deprived of any means of self-assertion. The "real world" is the world of those with power—the world of whites. Here, the idea that residing within the "veil" also generates a certain kind of privileged knowledge is utterly negated. Rather, blacks inhabit a particular existentialist position that demands that they continually compromise their ideal values (i.e., courage, resistance, self-assertion) in order to survive. If it exists at all, the black subject's "second sight" in this sense is fear; fear is what shapes his/her behavior and allows him/her in large part to survive.

Wright therefore adopts a Manichean vision of black life that elevates racial conflict over all other features of black existence, thereby positing limited existential possibilities for black subjects. This perspective is essentially what informs his negative appraisal of Zora Neale Hurston's *Their Eyes Were Watching God* (1937) in *New Masses*. Reflecting on Hurston's representation of the black cultural enclave her characters inhabit in Eatonville, one that barely addresses a white presence, Wright notes, "Her characters eat and laugh and cry and work and kill; they swing like a pendulum eternally in that safe and narrow orbit in which America likes to see the Negro live: between laughter and tears" (16–17). Wright's review ultimately criticizes Hurston's work for dramatizing intricacies of black life without addressing racial strife, for presenting a southern black folk culture that is contained within itself without addressing the racist conditions of oppression that affect black possibility. One can deduce that to Wright, Hurston's narrative setting in that novel examines a "shadow world," while the "real" reality resides outside the scope of the author's literary representation.

Even though his first publications in *Challenge* appeared at the tail end of the Harlem Renaissance, Yerby's peculiar position in the African American literary canon would not so much be affected by having missed that literary movement—which likely would have best suited his literary predispositions—as it would be by his eventual failure to leave a stronger imprint on the social realist school of writing. While critics have typically faulted Yerby's career for turning away from that literary tradition, rarely do they address what may have caused his inability to produce "serious" works. One such factor to consider is the obvious formal and thematic limitations the genre of social realism itself placed on writers whose perspectives on black lives did not altogether mesh with the Wright school of writing. In that vein, we can ask ourselves if Nella Larsen's *Quicksand*, a Harlem Renaissance novel that recounts the experiences of a black female college instructor whose migrations take her to a variety of locales, both elite and humble, would have been published in an era in which critically successful narratives about black lives centered on the plight of working-class male characters confronting various racial slights and injustices.

When we look at some of the short stories Yerby composed before he hit it big, and when we read some of his statements about the early part of his career as a "serious" writer bucking stereotypical representations of black characters, Larsen appears to be an apt comparison. What I would like to suggest is that Yerby's strange erasure from the African American literary canon must be understood in relation to changing literary tastes, the racial dynamics of American literary criticism, and the arbitrary way in which a literary canon defines what kinds of narratives it includes. For while he is often considered a genre writer who exhausted his creative energies in producing historical fiction of no lasting significance, it remains that in the formative stage of his writing career Yerby persistently struggled to perfect his mastery of the social realist genre while attempting to imbue it with narrative elements he found authentic to his own experiences. This period began with his time in Chicago in the late 1930s as a member of the black avant-garde that was giving birth to the African American social realist tradition in writing and would last until the publication of his first popular bestseller *The Foxes of Harrow*.

THE (BLACK) CHICAGO RENAISSANCE AND THE ASCENDANCE OF SOCIAL REALISM

Although not much is known about Yerby's brief time in Chicago in the late 1930s, the significance of the city as a literary hub for writers of any hue would have had a remarkable impact on his evolution as a writer. He moved there in 1938 after earning a master's degree in English from Fisk University to enroll in the English PhD program at the University of Chicago. The university was one of the few elite institutions of higher learning in the United States that permitted the matriculation of black students. It also had the unique distinction of housing a sociology department that was at the cutting edge of research on race and ethnic relations in urban environments, producing such distinguished black scholars as the sociologists E. Franklin Frazier, Horace Cayton Jr., and St. Clair Drake. The work being done in that department did not simply remain within the ambit of the proverbial ivory tower. The Chicago School of Sociology, as that body of scholarship came to be called, also informed the proletarian-focused social realist literature that was emerging, with Richard Wright as its most prominent and successful practitioner.

Outside of the university setting, Yerby would have been acquainted with a number of writers, artists, and intellectuals native to the city, or who had more recently migrated there. Many of them had found work in the Illinois chapter of the Federal Writer's Project (FWP), a Depression-era New Deal program that was an extension of the Works Progress Administration (WPA). Richard Wright, who by the time Yerby arrived in Chicago had already made his way to New York City, had worked for the FWP initially as a field reporter and was later promoted to editorial supervisor as his writing career took off. Other writers employed by the WPA at various times included black poets and novelists such as Margaret Walker, Willard Motley, Fenton Johnson, William Attaway, and Arna Bontemps. As an FWP field reporter, Yerby worked on a project investigating African American religious sects in Chicago under the direction of dancer/choreographer/anthropologist Katherine Dunham, a fellow University of Chicago alum. After Dunham left the project to pursue what would become an illustrious career in dance and choreography, Yerby then began working under her replacement, Jack Conroy, a white radical novelist and editor who counted Wright and Bontemps as close friends and colleagues. Likening him to Wright, Conroy considered Yerby a promising young talent and predicted for him the kind of national success the older writer was then experiencing (Bontemps 45). Around the time that Yerby left Chicago, Conroy's faith in Yerby's writing was exemplified by his willingness to feature one Yerby's short stories, "The Thunder of God," on the cover of *New Anvil*, a literary magazine he edited.

While literary movements and trends are often only discerned in their aftermaths, or at peak moments of their development, Chicago's significance as a hub for black writing in the mid-1930s and onward was essentially announced around the moment it emerged. Arna Bontemps, for instance, a writer who had made his mark with the Harlem coterie of writers in the 1920s, would note in a 1950 *Negro Digest* article that the city of Chicago by the 1930s had become the site of a second black literary awakening. To Bontemps, no other chapter of the FWP had produced talent comparable to the group based in Chicago (Bontemps 46). Similar sentiments about Chicago's literary significance were expressed by Alain Locke, a leading critic of contemporary black arts and letters, and another old guard of the Harlem Renaissance. Upon the publication of Frank Marshall Davis's first collection of poetry, *Black Man's Verse* (1935), Locke would enthusiastically claim that "For the new notes and the strong virile accents of our poetry today, we must shift from Harlem to Chicago" (qtd. in Bone and Courage 162).

Bontemps's and Locke's perspectives on the Chicago literary scene were informed by their respective experiences and awareness of that scene. Bontemps was a member of the South Side Writers Group, an informal collection of writers who for the most part were in the formative stages of their careers. The group began meeting in 1936 at the Wright's instigation Wright. Essentially an autodidact, Wright spent his formative years as a writer and intellectual in Chicago, learning and mastering his craft. He also learned Marxist principles by participating in a variety of different clubs and organizations such as the John Reed clubs. The South Side Writers Group extended, for him, the significance of voluntary organizations in the sharing, pursuit, and elaboration of knowledge for intellectuals seriously committed to the life of the mind, the production of art, and political activism. While neither a creative writer nor a resident of the city, Locke in the 1930s evinced an appreciation for the Marxist inflection appearing in the social realist African American fiction and remained in correspondence with Wright throughout that decade.

Along with more established writers such as Bontemps and Fenton Johnson, other members of the South Side Writers Group included up-and-coming voices such as Margaret Walker, Frank Marshall Davis, Marian Minus, Theodore Ward, and the critic Edward Bland. The early promise of the group was a motivating factor for a failed publishing collaboration that involved Wright, Marian Minus (who was then also a student in the anthropology department at the University of Chicago), and Dorothy West. After *Challenge* folded, the three writers worked to publish *New Challenge*, a journal that would showcase the work of younger writers. The first and only issue was specifically dedicated to the South Side Writers Group. The magazine's most memorable work, however, remains Wright's "Blueprint for Negro Writing," an essay that articulated in manifesto-like fashion the proletarian focus of the emerging social realist movement.

The brevity of Yerby's time in Chicago renders it somewhat difficult to place him in active conversation with other writers and artists present in the city. In his account of the writers working with the FWP, Bontemps, for example, writes that Yerby was a "wraith-like member of [the project]" and that not many people remembered him (Bontemps 45). While this comment appears to marginalize the significance of Yerby's presence in Chicago to the evolution of his career, Bontemps later offers a useful insight that should have us reassess the young writer's eventual literary trajectory in relation to the social realist genre that emerged out of Chicago: "Yerby was not at his best when smarting under insults or boiling with anger. Instead he turned away from the whole contemporary scene" (46). While the focus on Yerby's personality and its connection to the kind of writing he was not able to produce implies a failure of sorts, Bontemps is really deploring the publishing industry's restrictive expectations of the kind of writing it considered marketable from its black writers. In that vein, his assessment of young Yerby's inability to conform to the prevailing social realist literary taste of his time is not presented as the writer failing to live up to the creative demands of producing "serious" literature. Rather, implied is a critique of ideological conditions that limited black literary expression—conditions that have little to do with a writer's ability to explore the full scope of his creative imagination.

It bears noting that Bontemps was better positioned than most to have a sense of Yerby's potential as a writer, especially in light of his friendship with Jack Conroy, the radical white writer and editor. During Yerby's brief employment as a field reporter with the Illinois chapter of the FWP, he submitted the short story "The Thunder of God" for publication in Conroy's *New Anvil*. Bontemps and his peers certainly would have been reading the leftist periodical; thus, it is fair to say that Yerby was a presence in the city in the way that Conroy saw him: as a promising young writer with a lot of potential. It is also reasonable to assume that given Yerby's educational background, professional aspirations, and personal acquaintances, he was part of the creative social milieu that had produced Chicago's black literary awakening.

A DIFFERENT KIND OF SUCCESS—YERBY'S (MISUNDERSTOOD) LEGACY

The significance of Yerby's time in Chicago, if not apparent in the little that is known about his acquaintances, is clearly exemplified in his evolution as a writer from the late 1930s to the mid-1940s. The period between 1938 and 1946 saw Yerby leave Chicago, teach at two different colleges in the American South (Florida A&M and Southern University), work in the defense industry in Michigan and then New York, and finally achieve literary success and personal wealth in 1946 with the publication of his bestselling novel *The Foxes of Harrow*. During this time, Yerby diligently exerted himself to master the social realist genre of fiction that emerged from Chicago. He published a number of short stories that illustrated not only his growth as a writer but also the unique set of preoccupations he brought to the genre. While his 1944 short story "Health Card" is often pointed to as the work most illustrative of his early promise as a "serious writer," other short stories such as "The Thunder of God" (1939) and "White Magnolias" (1944) also provide a good index to Yerby's early style.

Perhaps the weakest of the three stories in narrative form, "The Thunder of God" nevertheless is a compelling read because of Yerby's ability to skillfully present the dynamics of race relations in a small city through his account of a single event. The narrative opens with a black college student recounting his experiences of a flood that occurred in Augusta in 1929. While the story initially appropriates the form of a reflective personal narrative, it becomes clear early on that Yerby is not so much concerned with depicting the narrator's individual reaction to the event as he is with dramatizing the subjugated position of the black community. As a response to the flood, white authorities in the city conscript black men to shore up a levee. As one of the conscripted laborers, the narrator at the end of the story witnesses the conscripted black men ignoring the call for help of a rabidly racist white leader as the Savannah River carries him downstream.

While "The Thunder of God" is relayed to the reader mostly through vivid narrative descriptions, "White Magnolias" is a well-paced narrative that unfolds as a dialogue among four characters. Beth Thomas, the daughter of a well-to-do white southern couple, invites Hannah Simmons, the college-educated daughter of a black doctor whom Beth befriended at an interracial conference, to her home. Yerby's staging of the dialogue among Beth, her two parents, and Hannah adroitly depicts the uneasy scene. Beth's racial liberalism is countered by her parents' prejudice, particularly her Archie Bunker–like father Clinton Thomas, while Hannah calmly maintains a dignified composure. The narrative ends in a symbolic show of interracial friendship. After having explained to Hannah her father's view that the white flowers of the magnolia tree in front of their home represent the beauty of southern womanhood, delicate and refined, Beth breaks off a low-hanging flower from the tree and tears it to shreds.

Yerby's "Health Card" won him the 1944 O. Henry Award, the same honor Wright had garnered five years earlier for the short story "Fire and Cloud." The narrative follows the experiences of Johnny Green, a young black soldier stationed in the South. Johnny learns in a letter that his significant other, Lily, was able to save enough money to come to visit him from up North.

Unwilling to have her boarded in disreputable hotels in the "Black Bottom," he manages to secure a room for her in the home of a Baptist pastor after convincing the pastor's wife that Lily and he are married. As he heads back to camp, he notices a group of white soldiers and policemen asking black women, whom they view as sex workers, for their "health cards." The scene quickly dissolves into a physical confrontation among the women, their black male companions—who themselves are soldiers—the white soldiers, and military police. As punishment for the confrontation, the commanding officer of the camp bars black soldiers from entering the town for a month. After explaining to the colonel his situation, however, Johnny wins a reprieve from the order and is able to meet Lily when she arrives in town. As they head to the preacher's house, two military police officers accost Johnny and Lily, demanding that the latter present them with her "health card." On the brink of a confrontation that would very possibly lead to Johnny's death, the more reasonable of the two officers is able to calm the other down. Lily convinces Johnny to maintain his composure, telling him, "You's all I got" (553). The narrative ends with Lily comforting Johnny as they head to the preacher's house.

All three short stories highlight the weight of racial discrimination on black lives, the workings of the metaphorical Du Boisian veil on the quotidian lives of black subjects. If "White Magnolias" dramatizes the dehumanizing nature of basic interracial social interactions "The Thunder of God" and "Health Card" emphasize the ever-present threat of violence on black bodies. The group of workers in "The Thunder of God," for instance, are threatened with physical harm as they work on the levee, while Johnny in "Health Card" must temper his sense of masculine pride to preserve his life. What is unique about these short stories is how Yerby attempted to reconfigure the black narrative voice of these "protest" narratives. Like Ann Petry, who inflected the social realist tradition with a different set of concerns by focusing upon gendered aspects of black urban experiences, Yerby's stories present more nuances to black experiences of the color line. The narrative voice of "The Thunder of God" is that of an educated young black male who, even as he does not ostensibly occupy the class position of others in the work gang he is conscripted to, stands to experience similar treatment by white authorities. Considering that the first-person narrator of the story functions more as a witness that relates a set of events to the reader than a character around which a plot unfolds, his presence is actually not necessary. Yerby could easily have adapted a third-person narrative perspective that focused on the city's working-class characters, a narrative device that would have conformed to social realism's tendency to explore the experiences of working-class subjects. However, framing the narrative through the young narrator's voice challenges the facile association of black southern subjectivity with images of the folk. Yerby's South is a region not only of humble farmers and workers in the service industry who have to navigate an oppressive racial system, but also of a professional class trained at black educational institutions who exist in this same system.

"White Magnolias" can be read as a work of protest fiction that does not adapt a social realist framework but rather fits the mold of a racial uplift narrative. Similar to a narrative of manners, the story relies on the author's ability to convey bourgeois societal conventions, values, and mores. In this specific instance, however, those norms and values derive from competing worldviews. Through witty and at times ironic dialogues, the characters in the story both consciously and unconsciously place into relief important points of contention and misunderstandings. Beth and Hannah's integrationist values are opposed by Beth's parents' strict adherence to Jim Crow principles. And while it is clear that Hannah's education and class background approximate Beth's, Beth's parents are ultimately unable to envision a normative middle-class existence for a black person. Even after hearing of Hannah's level of education, Beth's mother offers her a position as her maid. Near the end of the story, a little abashed by her parents' views, Beth asks Hannah why she would not allow Beth to tell her parents about a fellowship Hannah had earned and of her impressive academic achievements. To this, Hannah simply answers that even after hearing that, Beth's mother "would have still offered [her] a maid's job" (325).

"Health Card," Yerby's most remarkable short story, combines a vivid and terse narrative style with well-paced and pointed dialogue. In but a few pages, Yerby constructs a narrative that encapsulates the physical and psychological pitfalls of life within the veil. The story's unsentimental ending poignantly reaffirms Wright's reconfiguration of Du Bois's vision of double consciousness by negating the possibility that knowing one's marginality affords any degree of agency. Rather, what the ending presents is a commonplace encounter that is nonetheless rife with the potential for fatal violence: a man picking up his wife from a train or bus station. Faced with white military police officers who unabashedly assume that Lily is a sex worker, Johnny finds himself in a situation where he must either betray a universal ideal connected to values associated with normative manhood (protecting Lily's honor) or live up to this ideal and very possibly die. At Lily's urging, he subdues his burning rage but not before saying to himself, "I ain't no man" (553). In this moment,

Yerby's Johnny Green realizes what Wright's Fishbelly in *The Long Dream* acknowledges after observing his father's reaction to Chris's lynching: that "*the world in which he . . . lived was a kind of shadow world*" to the world of those with power (67; emphasis added).

If "Health Card" neatly fits into the stylistic, thematic, and narrative paradigms of the kind of fiction Wright's writings rendered critically popular, it did not do so without posing a specific challenge for Yerby: the problem of black representation. Gene Andrew Jarrett alludes to this problem in a brief discussion of Yerby's decision not to portray Johnny and Lily as a college-educated, northern young black couple. While Yerby notes this decision was partly in response to not having narrative room to flesh out their educational background, at other instances he also indicated how publishing houses were not interested in backing narratives with educated black characters because they did not believe a mainstream readership would find such characters believable. In "Health Card," Yerby skirts this dilemma by inflecting Johnny and Lily's voices with a folksy dialect traditionally associated with those who have not attained a high level of formal education, while scaffolding their representation with indicators of middle-class black respectability. Yerby admits as much by noting to an interested reader, "If I had insisted as I dearly desired to—upon making college graduates out of Johnny Green and Lily I can assure your friends that *Harper's* or no other white magazine would have touched it" (qtd. in Jarrett 149).

Yerby's reflection on his portrayal of Johnny and Lily in his short story stands also as a reflection on why he ultimately gave up composing "highbrow literature." Around the same time he published "Health Card," Yerby was revising a novel he'd written entitled "This Is My Own." Yerby described the novel's protagonist as someone "intelligent and educated—no 'Bigger Thomas' in any sense of the word. He is myself and thousands of my friends and maybe a little bit of all the persecuted minority peoples all over the world" (qtd. in Jarrett 150). Receiving a series of rejections, Yerby eventually burned the manuscript, convinced that publishers were unwilling to take a chance on it because it did not meet expectations of how black characters should be portrayed.

Thus, even with the fair amount of success he eked out as a young, up-and-coming writer working through a tradition that most prominently emerged in 1930s Chicago, by the midpoint of the 1940s Yerby lost faith in the possibility that he could carve out a "serious" literary career for himself that reflected the uniqueness of his voice and perspective on the black American experience. His belief that a literary market that traded in racial myths and stereotypes suffocated black literary expression turned him away from the kind of fiction he had written for nearly a decade in favor of a popular genre, historical fiction, with mostly white characters—a genre that ultimately produced much success.

In the immediate period after publishing his national bestseller, *The Foxes of Harrow*, Yerby was not universally regarded as a writer who had betrayed a higher calling for quick commercial success. According to *Publisher's Weekly*, by the end of 1946 the novel's total sales amounted to 1.2 million copies (qtd. in Jackson 235). Such impressive and historically unprecedented sales numbers for a black writer would lead the prominent literary historian Hugh M. Gloster to declare in a 1948 issue of *Crisis* magazine that Yerby's "chief contribution [was] to shake himself free of the shackles of race and to use the treasure trove of American experience—rather than restrictively Negro experience—as his literary province" (qtd. in Bone 168). The fact that the novel did not feature major black characters seems to have been initially apprehended as a necessary compromise that other writers of Yerby's generation had also made. As literary historian Robert Bone has illustrated, Yerby's example was mirrored by a number of black writers, such as Ann Petry, William Gardner Smith, Chester Himes, Willard Motley, Zora Neal Hurston, and Richard Wright. They all, at one time or another, composed what he referred to as "assimilationist novels," or novels that portray primarily white characters and also avoid racial conflict and an examination of black lives. Bone, however, is quick to point out that unlike Yerby, these writers did try to produce "serious novels of white life," not simply entertainment (168). His parting words on Yerby have followed the writer to and beyond his grave: "All that is proved by Yerby's 'raceless' novels—and they are 'raceless' only in the most superficial sense—is that Frank Yerby is interested in making money" (168).

Yerby's own discussion of his literary practice has not always worked to reform his image among critics. He is reported to have once said to Jack Conroy, the editor who published "The Thunder of God," "You intellectuals go ahead and write your highbrow stuff. . . . I am going to make millions" (qtd. in Mangione 126). Writing to Richard Wright's biographer Michel Fabre in the 1960s, Yerby notes that while he did not know the latter too well, he greatly admired him as a man. However, he did not think he was "influenced by him as a writer, except perhaps negatively" (qtd. in Jarrett 143). Rather, Yerby felt that if Wright's work influenced him at all, "it was to confirm [his] growing suspicion that the race problem was *not* a theme for [him]" (qtd. in Jarrett 143). Two decades later, commenting on the trajectory of his career, he would express to Bill Lyon in *People* magazine that "[writers and critics have] gotten on me for not dealing with racial issues.... But that's an artistic dead-end. I'm glad to have escaped" (Lyon 99).

Putting aside what comes off as a cheeky retort to Conroy, what Yerby articulated about abandoning the kind of writing he was doing in the 1930s and 1940s reflects the limits of social realist fiction that a number of black writers have suggested, especially since the publication of James Baldwin's essay on *Native Son*, "Everybody's Protest Novel." Instead of carving out a critical space for himself where he could present his own theory of what literature is supposed to do, Yerby relied on catchy statements that seemed to reaffirm critics' broad dismissal of his work. However, for reasons that include his early narratives that touch upon key African American literary moments, the unprecedented nature of his later success, and questions we may have about the value of popular literary genres, it may now be time to turn a critical lens on this writer whose literary trajectory has circled the boundaries of the African American literary canon.

BIBLIOGRAPHY

Bone, Robert. *The Negro Novel in America*. Yale UP, 1958.
Bone, Robert, and Richard Courage. *The Muse in Bronzeville: African American Creative Expression in Chicago, 1932–1950*. Rutgers UP, 2011.
Bontemps, Arna. "Famous WPA Authors." *Negro Digest*, June 1950, pp. 43–47.
Dolinar, Brian, editor. *The Negro in Illinois: The WPA Papers*. The U of Illinois P, 2013.
Du Bois, W. E. B. *The Souls of Black Folk*. Oxford UP, 2007.
Hughes, Langston. *The Big Sea*. Hill and Wang, 1993
Jackson, Lawrence P. *The Indignant Generation: A Narrative History of African American Writers and Critics, 1934–1960*. Princeton UP, 2011.
Jarrett, Gene Andrew. *Deans and Truants: Race and Realism in African American Literature*. U of Pennsylvania P, 2007.
Lewis, David Levering. *When Harlem Was in Vogue*. Knopf, 1981.
Lyon, Bill. "Expatriate Writer Frank Yerby Is Grousing Even Though His 30th Best Seller Is Coming." *People*, 30 Mar. 1981, pp. 99–101.
Mangione, Jere. *The Dream and the Deal: The Federal Writers Project, 1935–43*. Syracuse UP, 1996.
Morgan, Stacy I. *Rethinking Social Realism: African American Art and Literature, 1930–1953*. U of Georgia P, 2004.
"Grace Walker Ramsey Obituary." J. Foster Phillips Funeral Home, Inc., 10 Aug. 2018, http://www.jfosterphillips.com/obituary/1167898.
Price, J. St. Clair. "Current Literature on Negro Education." *The Journal of Negro Education*, vol. 2, no. 4, Fall 1933, pp. 509–13.

Sherrard-Johnson, Cherene. *Dorothy West's Paradise: A Biography of Class and Color.* Rutgers UP, 2012.

Wright, Richard. "Between Laughter and Tears." Edited by Henry Louis Gates and K. A. Appiah. *Zora Neale Hurston: Critical Perspectives Past and Present.* Amistad, 1993.

Wright, Richard. *The Long Dream.* Perennial Library, 1987.

Yerby, Frank G. "Health Card." *Harper's Magazine*, vol. 188, no. 5, May 1944, pp. 448–53.

Yerby, Frank G. Letter to Dorothy West. 1 June 1934. Papers of Dorothy West, ca.1890–1998. Editing and work by other writers, 1926–1949. Schlesinger Library, Radcliffe Institute, Harvard U, MC 676, folder 9.20. http://nrs.harvard.edu/urn-3:RAD.SCHL:8500114.

Yerby, Frank G. "The Thunder of God." *New Anvil*, vol. 1, no. 2, April–May 1939, pp. 5–8.

Yerby, Frank G. "White Magnolias." *Phylon*, vol. 5, no. 4, Fourth Quarter, pp. 319–26.

FRANK YERBY AND HIS READERS

DONNA-LYN WASHINGTON

BORN IN 1916 AND RAISED IN AUGUSTA, GEORGIA, FRANK YERBY CLEARLY understood racism in America. He grew up in a country that definitively drew color lines, particularly in the South. Yerby's mother was European (Scots-Irish), his father African American and Seminole. He came from a middle-class home, where his father had a steady job as a doorman; his father believed education was important and sent Yerby to the Haines Institute, a primary school in Augusta. Later, Yerby graduated from Paine College, and then received a master's degree from Fisk University. From a young age Yerby often faced discrimination, as evidenced in a 1981 interview with *People* magazine; Yerby said while growing up in the South that he "was considered black there" (Lyon 99). Continuing, he stated, "When I was young a bunch of us black kids would get in a fight with white kids and then I'd have to fight with a black kid who got on me for being so light" (Lyon 99). Yerby's mixed heritage became an increased point of contention when it came to his writing.

When he was being considered for the Georgia Writers Hall of Fame, Harry Crews reminded the panel that Yerby's parentage should not play a factor in their decision making: "Think of when this man was born he carried in his veins, a mulatto, yes. It wasn't too long before he was born that one drop of black blood made you a nigger. Do any of us have to wonder why he left the noble state of Georgia for France and then Spain, where he stayed, married and died?" (qtd. in Hulett 428). Crews goes on to say that Yerby was a "word man just as all the men and women in the Georgia Writers Hall of Fame are word people" (qtd. in Hulett 428). Finally, Crews gave his personal account of when he was first introduced to Yerby's novels. As a child Crews would hang around the mansion of a rich, white couple. The wife would loan Crews the novels she read. They were all Frank Yerby's books. Crews describes reading those works as being "instrumental with feeding the hot embers already burning in my heart" (qtd. in Hulett 429). As a result of Crews's advocacy, Yerby was inducted to the Georgia Writers Hall of Fame in 2006.

Yerby grew up in the shadow of events such as the "Red Summer" of 1919. After World War I, whites massacred blacks at an alarming rate by lynching and murder. According to Elizabeth McHenry, "race riots broke out in major U.S. cities, including Washington, D.C., all African Americans became subject to ever-stricter lines of racial demarcation, and the tendency of white America was simply to lump all blacks together regardless of their racial heritage, color, or social or economic standing" (262). This is the world Yerby grew up in; yet, he did not write about the black experience right away in his novels. Instead, his novels, starting in 1946, centered on white protagonists until his twenty-third novel, *Speak Now*, in 1969.

Once Yerby became rich from his novels, his fellow black authors offered him little support. Yerby recollects, "They've gotten on me for not dealing with racial issues . . . but that's an artistic dead end. . . . There's no hope for racial harmony in the U.S. and never was" (Lyon 101). Keenly aware of the environment he wrote in, Yerby chose his reading audience and made a conscious decision to write for people who would buy his books regardless of his cultural background. In actuality, few of Yerby's readers cared about his parentage. Yerby wrote over thirty novels and continued writing up until his death in 1991. For decades the buyers of his books were predominantly middle-class Caucasians and teenage girls. Readers obviously bought Yerby's books in droves, leading him to be the first black author to have one of his novels optioned for a film, and perhaps this is why his race remained an open secret. It may also be argued that Yerby was the first prosperous black historical romance writer, although he had referred to these books as "costume novels." Considering his audience, it isn't surprising that his books sold well. After all, the majority of his protagonists are white men, out to seek adventure and to bed as many women as possible. However, his early poems, short stories, and a few of the books written throughout his career delved into the themes of racism on a variety of levels. Still, critics often maligned the novels he wrote, the ones he became wealthy from, because they believed he was avoiding what might have been considered controversial subjects, such as the realities and repercussions of slavery in the United States. Even in Richard Match's *New York Times* book review of *The Foxes of Harrow* he comments on how Yerby avoid using his black identity as a main plot point:

> In this, his first novel, one might have hoped for the ideological intensity, of say, Howard Fast's "Freedom Road," and, indeed, there are some sympathetic evidences of the Negro's deep resentment against

slavery. Mr. Yerby has chosen, however, to concentrate on a conventional historical narrative of passionate amours and gentlemanly swordplay. (118)

W. E. B. Du Bois praised *Freedom Road*, which was written in 1944 and takes place from the end of the Civil War to the end of Reconstruction, for its historical accuracy. However, we do not know how he felt about Yerby's debut novel. We do know, though, what other critics thought. Blyden Jackson describes Yerby's first novel as a film storyboard lacking the depth to explore serious themes. Jackson's acerbic tone is exemplified in his review of *The Foxes of Harrow*. Jackson advises "to go through this book—the way, probably, which should be recommended to divert the pain of readers who hope for several dimensions and a significant attack upon the problems of life in the fiction they essay—is to check the number of scenes which you have seen done over and over so much in the movies that they become stock shots" (650). Jackson goes on to refer to the possible camera angles that could be used. According to Jackson and other critics, instead of making a statement about the horrors of slavery and the plight of black Americans, Yerby was writing to make as much as a profit as possible in both the sales of his book and the optioning of the novel to a film studio. The criticism isn't the same for Yerby's contemporaries, including Howard Fast. The period during Reconstruction saw the end of the horrors of slavery and attempts to bring the nation back together. The United States had trouble coming to terms with dealing fairly with those previously enslaved. Howard Fast's *Freedom Road* has been seen as a clear and realistic depiction of what ex-slaves had to contend with. Fast had been influenced by Du Bois's essays about Reconstruction which countered major discrepancies from historians about the period. In the foreword to *Freedom Road*, Du Bois refers to Fast's use of research for the novel's depiction of slavery's psychological legacy. Fast focuses on the black protagonist Gideon Jackson's journey from being enslaved to becoming a congressman using the timeline from the beginning of Reconstruction to the novel's violent end. The last chapter of the novel deals with the Ku Klux Klan terrorizing Gideon's community. Fast says in the afterword to his narrative that this little-known time in history, though well documented, had to be erased: "Powerful forces did not hold it to be a good thing for the American people to know that once there had been such an experiment—and that the experiment had worked. That the Negro had been given the right to exist in this nation as a free man ... to work out his own destiny in conjunction with the poor southern whites, and that in an eight-year period of working out that destiny he had created ... a truly democratic nation" (263). In most recollections of the period immediately following the Civil War, the lives of formerly enslaved individuals are not included when considering why Reconstruction failed. Eric Foner, in his introduction to Fast's novel, discusses how the description of the Ku Klux Klan in early school textbooks differed from the reality. Foner regards the Klan as a terrorist group whose main agenda was to bring back white supremacy to the southern states by instilling fear through lynchings, murders, and other atrocities. Fast utilized much from Du Bois in researching the time period, giving his work the ring of authenticity. Also, having a black protagonist who is an ex-slave as the central voice of his narrative was paramount in telling the story of this erroneously described period in history. Fast showed what worked during Reconstruction and that blacks were more than idle sheep. They became literate, formed communities, and held political office. The publication of Fast's book dispelled, through fiction, several myths of Reconstruction due to his thorough research and an appendix detailing the sources he used in writing the novel. Blacks and whites worked together during that near decade in history, following the Civil War.

While Du Bois and others praised Fast's work, some diminished Yerby's attempts to highlight and explore the same period. Nick Aaron Ford saw Yerby's second novel *The Vixens*, which also takes place during Reconstruction, as a

> determination to avoid all semblance of racial propaganda [in his] treatment, or lack of treatment, of the Negro's part in the reconstruction of Louisiana. On one occasion he comments in two brief sentences on the honesty of a small group of Negro legislators, led by Oscar Dunn. On another occasion he uses one paragraph to praise the general intelligence of the Negro legislators. But he gives no attention to the records of those legislators.... He passes over with no more than a brief sentence the unusual achievements of such Negroes as ... Pickney Pinchback, Lieutenant and Acting Governor of Louisiana, and T. Morris Chester, Brigadier General in charge of the Louisiana State Guard, who were powerful participants in the great drama of Reconstruction in Louisiana which the novel is supposed to present. (37)

Ford's critique of *The Vixens* is a clearer comparison in respect to the time period. Fast brought the issues of Reconstruction to the forefront, while Yerby incorporated the time period simply to provide a historical setting for his costume romance. Consequently, although it may have been unintentional, Match seems to suggest that Yerby should have capitalized on his being black, to give *Harrow* (set before the Civil War was about to begin) an authentic voice. Unlike Fast, who was white and Jewish, Yerby would not have had to imagine a black protagonist like Fast's. Keeping this in mind it is disturbing to read how Yerby's narrative was not black enough. To be compared to a white author who has a black protagonist in his novel hints at the racism Yerby may have endured from both black and white Americans. It seems that his work has been misunderstood in a variety of ways.

Besides racism, perhaps critics' preconceived notions of what they believed Yerby attempted to do in his novels led to their disappointment in the final products. Yerby said on numerous occasions that his goal was to entertain his readers. He believed his novels gave them what they wanted. Literary critic Blyden Jackson in his review of Yerby's *The Foxes of Harrow* describes Yerby's first novel as "a highly sophisticated and masterful piece of cynical eclecticism" (651). Then Jackson delves into Yerby's significance as a writer: "Yerby has gone to great pains to reproduce with the verisimilitude of infinitely cumulative detail a half-century of Louisiana's past.... Scholars who have a high sense of mission will sorrow somewhat over Yerby's reconstruction.... Yet Yerby has spared no pains to make his canvas correct and rich" (651). There is no doubt that Jackson believed Yerby thoroughly researched his subjects. Also, he saw that Yerby's success as an author meant that he was breaking color barriers. The financial achievement of Yerby's first novel reflects that black Americans did not have to write about racially charged subjects to make money. Still, Jackson came to the conclusion that Yerby was "just an entertainer" and in his criticism warns "that fiction which serves only as entertainment is, at its best, trivial, and at its worst, dangerous. The brand of escapism in *The Foxes of Harrow* seems innocent enough. But the book certainly has no great positive values" (652). True, not all of Yerby's novels dealt with politics, race issues, or were even set in the United States. The research Yerby undertook to accurately display the settings and time periods of his books shows a level of professionalism and dedication towards his craft. Still, some critics of his novels held Yerby to a standard rarely seen by his contemporaries. In Alain Locke's "Reason and Race: A Review of the Literature of the Negro for 1946" he gave the warning that the "best sociological intentions often make the worst dramas and novels" (19). Locke was specifically speaking of books and plays that dealt with race in a one-dimensional manner. Essentially, Locke argues that the "racial situation is not enough by itself; if vivid essential humanity is lacking, no amount of race drama will bring a character to life" (19). Locke also makes a point to say that Yerby's first novel gives him "the right to a vast audience" and how it is "significant to see a Negro author shake free of the conventional confinement to racial themes and strictly serious social objective" (20). However, while Locke praised Yerby's decision to write in what would be considered a nontraditional genre for black authors, he provided a caveat by saying Yerby could provide "a deeper influence when and if he should later choose to write more seriously realistic fiction, whether of Negro life or American life in general" (20). The idea that Yerby should at some time leave the genre that made him rich gets planted early on in his career. Locke even hoped that Yerby's second novel would have "a significant say on the more serious side of black-white relations" (20). Essentially, Locke implies that Yerby must move forward to deal seriously with black issues rather than staying in the safe space of romance novels, or what Locke referred to as a "neutral but rewarding field of entertainment fiction" (20).

Harvey Curtis Webster's review of Yerby's 1954 novel *Benton's Row* in *New Republic* mentions that Yerby's tenth novel was on pace to be as successful as some of his earlier novels, but he continues by pointing out that for all of his success Yerby "has never won a prize and his novels have never been praised by any critic as enthusiastically ... as on the dustcover of *Benton's Row*" (24). For the most part, Webster bemoans Yerby's choice of subject matter. *Benton's Row* is about several generations of the Benton family, from the antebellum period to the beginning of the twentieth century. The novel begins with Tom Benton barely escaping a hanging and concludes with his wife, nearly one hundred years old, looking over what their family has built. Set in Louisiana, the novel covers a one-hundred-year time period and is told in three parts. *Benton's Row* begins with Tom Benton in the Antebellum South taking a man's wife, property, and slaves as his own. According to the book Tom is like any southerner who owns a plantation. He knows "that no amount of kindness could make up to a man the soul-destroying indignity of being owned like a dog" (85). Still Tom, like most of the characters in this novel, "put those disturbing thoughts quickly out of his mind" (85). Part two takes place after Tom Benton's death and focuses on his children: Wade who is described as a coward, Stormy who runs away from home to become a serial mistress, and his illegitimate son Clinton, a Civil War hero. The last section gives an overview of what happens to the future generations of the Benton family. The narrator, Tom Benton's now ninety-six-year-old wife Sarah, reflects on all the wild Bentons and how most of them lost their lives in some reckless way. While Webster bemoans Yerby's choice of subject matter, he mentions how well written Yerby's protest stories were for the Common Council for American Unity's quarterly magazine *Common Ground*. Still, Webster makes an important observation in regard to Yerby's novel:

> All of us are guilty. The publishers and writers and booksellers and editors who consciously or unconsciously put profit before consciences. The teachers who exact the writers of the past and forget the writers of the present. The other teachers who do the reverse. The lazy escapist reader. The critics and reviewers who demonstrate their own cleverness rather than the substance and quality of what they want to write about, who condescend to all but the few the highest brows have chosen, who pay scant attention to merely good novels. (25–26)

The mixed messages Webster admits in regard to how to read *Benton's Row* gives credence to Yerby's stance of only writing to satisfy his readership. For the most part, Yerby's audience seems only to be aware of his success in giving them historical romances, and his readers took his books for what they were—entertainment. Still, Webster goes on to mention the underappreciated writer William Gardner Smith's novel *South Street* (published in the same year as *Benton's Row*) as being a superior work that deserves to be read by mass audiences, yet it does not get the attention of one of Yerby's endeavors. The critiques from all sides, coupled with the expectation that Yerby write the great protest novel may well be the reasons why he became an expatriate in France and eventually lived out the rest of his life in Spain, where even his death was not known for several weeks (Folkart 344). For instance, Alain Locke's "Four Popular Negro Novelists" summarizes Yerby's career up to 1954, and he notes that Yerby is not an "inferior writer. He has rich imagination, a talent for vivid expression, ability to create pity and terror, and an understanding of the suffering of the poor and the oppressed. But it appears that Yerby is satisfied with popularity without greatness" (37). Yet, within this same article, Locke's description of Yerby as a self-possessed author, who despite his ability to write had, at the time "in less than ten years . . . built up for himself a large and—mark you—faithful public. . . . These avid readers are not intellectuals, whose creed is cosmopolitanism. They are masses, poor prey for all the propaganda self-seeking men can concoct" (38–39). We can see how Yerby appears to simultaneously defy and reinforce stereotypes with black characters, specifically in *Benton's Row*. Even though the black descendants of lead protagonist Tom Benton are acknowledged and even buried in the family gravesite they are referred to as being "naturally born to trouble [causing] . . . a mighty heap of crying and hurtfulness and even the shedding of blood . . . specially since the Bentons got the bad habit of getting themselves getting killed off. . . . Even the Benton niggers got the same bad habit" (223). This seems to imply that the negative aspects of both blacks and whites are the only ways in which they can be equal. Still, Locke sees a turn in Yerby's work. After reading *Benton's Row*, Locke describes it as a novel which makes the most "heretical and blood-curdling comments about Southern religion, Southern womanhood, the Old Southern Mansion, planter culture . . . the Southern defense of lynching, and even Southern cooking" (39). Essentially, by the time *Benton's Row* appeared, Locke comments on "race consciousness, that [Yerby] has had it all the while, that it took inner discipline to control himself" (39). Considering what Yerby had to deal with when all he wanted to do was write and have people buy his books, we can understand better why, despite having a rabid readership for most of his career, Yerby has faded into obscurity.

Eventually, Yerby decided to accommodate what he considered to be a bigoted readership that he "believed made up the bulk of the American reading public" (Brown 71). This decision caused him to, according to Langston Hughes, "become really rich . . . after 'Health Card,'" [where it was assumed that Yerby had] put the race problem on the shelf in favor of more commercial themes" (xi). Hughes goes on to say that Yerby's "historical romances, have wonderful moviesque [sic] titles like *The Golden Hawk* and *The Saracen Blade*, but there are no noble faces among their characters when brought to the screen. Black faces seldom sell in Hollywood" (xi). Yerby cultivated an audience for his most famous works tactically, purposefully, and pragmatically.

Conversely, there is a misconception about Yerby's work because it has not been studied broadly on a scholarly level. In regards to the racial conflict, labeling Yerby's work as "'protest' stories . . . does not do justice to the overreaching analysis of racism and discrimination emanating from Yerby's stories" (Glasrud and Champion 16). Writer Stephanie Brown attests to this when she notes the erroneous comparisons of the film adaptation of *The Foxes of Harrow* as merely a poor copy of Margaret Mitchell's *Gone with the Wind* which debuted ten years earlier in 1936 (71–72). In actuality, according to Brown, Yerby was "unique in realizing that literary representations of the period had been inextricably linked to the form of the historical romance" (72). Yerby manipulated his audience with a genre that "challenged the conventions of the historical romance and the assumptions of popular historiography, laying bare the power of fiction to reshape historical fact in the minds of the general public" (72). As a novelist, Yerby sought for his "readers to reevaluate their emotional investment in the hero, heroine, and trajectory of the romance narrative.... Yerby also asked them to reconsider biases and misapprehensions on which their enjoyment of that narrative, which might influence their acceptance of its historical accuracy, was based" (73). Instead of writing about racial conflict in his books, Yerby used what some may perceive as a frivolous genre as a way to subvert the status quo and cause his readers to feel empathy for black Americans. *The Foxes of Harrow* according to Brown is a "biracial book by a biracial writer, not 'raceless' but rather ... profoundly interracial" (74). The reality is that Yerby confronted racism from his first successful novel to his last. When showing blacks in a positive light, Yerby's work "expresses the obvious—that blackness and whiteness are inseparable in American culture—with the overwhelming acceptance of ordinary readers" (Brown 75). His first successful book explores a world where people of mixed race are an integral part of southern, pre–Civil War society and play roles other than enslaved individuals. While Yerby may not have addressed racial conflict in the traditional sense, he did populate his narrative with "light-skinned blacks as a central feature not only of plantation life but also of social life in sophisticated New Orleans, where they are not slaves but rather free blacks who may be tradesmen ... or the paid mistresses of well off white men" (Brown 76).

Yerby goes on to disrupt the traditional plantation narrative of novels like *Gone with the Wind* by contrasting the Stephen Fox's son Etienne with the enslaved Inch. The white Etienne is an ill-educated, alcoholic brute who rapes women while the black Inch is well-read and rises to a position of power during Reconstruction as Etienne falls. Mark C. Jerng, in his essay "Reconstruction of Racial Perception: Margaret Mitchell's and Frank Yerby's Plantation Romances," describes this as making "race readable at the level of informing context in ways that show how the organizing of racial salience structures what can and cannot be done, and how one's actions are evaluated" (60). Jerng emphasizes this point by saying that Yerby's use of the "plantation romance genre ... demonstrates the particular role that it plays in our organization of racial meanings. When, where, and how race is foregrounded or placed in the background ... plays a crucial role in how narratives shape meaning and causality" (59). Therefore, in juxtaposing these two men, in a historical romance, Yerby shows what would be the failure of Reconstruction and propagation of systemic racism. If a white man, on paper, appears to be inferior, skin color is the only thing left to divide him from his black counterpart, keep the black man from claiming his own power, and prevent his equality with said white man. Through these men and other situations in *Harrow*, Yerby addresses racial as well as societal matters. Yerby has Stephen Fox evolve from a young man with a narrow-minded, Eurocentric idea of how he would reshape the South to a white man who has a mature understanding of the best way to see America grow. Towards the end of the novel, Fox lays out to his son Etienne how and why revolutions occur:

> Ye can't have a land like America unless the people—all the people—have a hand in its shaping. And the South has never dealt fairly with the people.... Either ye give the people their freedom—or they will take it, and ye and yours will perish in the whirlwind.... Remember Nat Turner? Remember Haiti? Remember Saint Dominique?... freeing the blacks would not destroy our economy. Slave labor is about the most inefficient there is. (375)

Later, when a delegation of tradesmen comes to ask for Fox's aid in representing their desire not to secede from the union, his speech is akin to that of a practical abolitionist: "When I came to this land, 'twas in my mind to rise in life and everybody else could go hang. But 'tis an old man, I am now, by all the saints, and I know that we've got to rise together or else we fall separately" (376). Throughout his career, Yerby's critics such as Langston Hughes and Alain Locke varied in their reasons for dismissing Yerby's work for its apparent lack of addressing issues of racism. For the most part, they saw Yerby's texts as romance novels and as nothing more than popular fiction, having little value in an academic setting. The novels that made him rich were misguidedly extolled for avoiding racial conflicts. The tension between popular and protest literature led Yerby's works to, as John C. Charles notes, fight with themselves: "*Foxes* is ... a text at war with itself ... [which] expresses both intense longing *and* resentment—longing for the privilege of white masculinity, and veiled resentment of its oppressive effect on black masculinity" (133). Charles goes on to say Yerby's "masculine sympathy is powerful enough to master Scarlett [O'Hara] and her literary forbears, yet insufficient for managing the pain of black male subjugation" (133). This meta-examination of Yerby's text, which uses a white protagonist to prove a point about how slavery continued to hinder black progress after World War II, is an important discussion. Pointedly, Yerby's books are not only for entertainment; there is value in critically analyzing them for a variety of reasons, most importantly, for their genre-bending abilities. A prime opportunity has been missed in allowing Yerby's works to go out of print.

Furthermore, we should consider the research aspect of Yerby's writing. His first five historical romances were book club selections with a distribution of at least one million copies. *Harrow* sold over two million copies by 1951 (Breity). One reason for the novel's popularity may be that Yerby made sure his work was not only entertaining but also accurate. Talking with Harvey Breity in 1951, he notes, "I work as much as eighteen hours a day ... I rewrite ... I do a lot of research. I read, read, read for my preliminary work. I've been spending as much as six hours a day in the library on background material..." Perhaps Yerby's attention to detail added to his wide readership, yet despite all that research, "his work is rarely anthologized and almost never taught" (Brown 68–69). Perhaps his calculated approach to his readers left little room for contemporary analysis, or perhaps Yerby's philosophy on writing kept critics from digging deeper. In the same interview with Breity, Yerby said, "I write exactly what I feel and think I want to do, but within the framework I try to give pleasure to the reading public ... the novelist hasn't any right to inflict on the public his private ideas on politics, religion or race. If he wants to preach he should go to the pulpit. I mean this from a professional, artistic point of view." Being an unobtrusive author could be attributed to his popularity as a serial Book of the Month club romance choice for several years. It seems that both the club and Yerby shared a similar philosophy. Writing about the Book of the Month Club, Janice Radway claims "what they [the book of the month club readership] were after, the editors made clear, were books written by writers who had designed those books for readers, not for other writers" (117). During the height of Yerby's career as a novelist, there had not been a recorded demographic of Yerby's readers. However, the fact that he was one of only a few writers of color whose work was chosen for the book club suggests that he had a broad reader appeal. Radway has pointed out that "there is some evidence that the [book club] judges ruled out of consideration (especially as main selections) books and literatures that detailed the experiences of people thought to be too different from the white middle class that seemed to stand at the center of middlebrow culture" (285). Radway explains that Richard Wright also understood how the game was played. In order to have *Native Son*, the first book by a black author included in the book of the month club in 1940, Wright had to make a considerable number of changes to his story. Several themes of racial conflict were dampened in the narrative about Bigger Thomas and his killing a white woman in 1920s Chicago. Wright made these changes to appease the judges. Unlike contemporary Langston Hughes, who was determined to overtly address the issues of black people, Wright negotiated some of the language in his work for this particular audience. Seeing that the book club "could clearly ensure him a much larger audience for his book" (287), the changes that Wright made appeared small because the book "sold 215,000 copies within three weeks" (287). The success of *Native Son* led to the club's 1945 selection of his memoir, *Black Boy*. Both Yerby and Wright portrayed racial conflict in their texts. Still, they created wider audiences than their peers through their ability to understand the people who would distribute their books, thus giving them a diverse spectrum of readers. However, while Wright and Hughes still appear in anthologies and classrooms long after their deaths, Yerby's novels have faded to the point where it's necessary to hunt many of them down in second-hand book stores. One wonders with such a large reading audience why Yerby's novels have fallen out of print. Was it because he was successful in ways most of his peer weren't?

Writer, poet, and playwright Langston Hughes, born in 1902, took a different approach to his own work. As stated before, he had fully "committed himself . . . to writing mainly about African Americans" (Rampersad 207). Hughes and several authors like him, for most of their careers, had a side hustle. His career began similar to Yerby's, in that he was first recognized in black-owned newspapers. However, unlike Yerby, Hughes purposely used the black struggle as a primary theme in all his work. Where Yerby distanced himself from defining his voice by his cultural background, Hughes felt that it was a vital component to his work. According to Arnold Rampersad, "Hughes always remained loyal to the principles he had laid down for the younger black writers in 1926. His art was firmly rooted in race pride and race feeling" (Rampersad 208). Hughes "could sometimes be bitter, but his art is generally suffused by a keen sense of the ideal and by a profound love of humanity, especially black Americans" (208). On the other hand, Yerby's allegiance was to whomever chose to pick up his work. His readers, he believed, deserved a good story, not an author's agenda. Yerby despised "above all things the heavy hand of the author off-stage creaking the on-stage machinery. The novelist must try to write with a universality of appeal so that it hits all segments of the people. To do that, a novel must have characters that are alive and a story that is interesting" (Breity). Throughout his interview in the *New York Times*, Yerby's blackness, though not addressed, becomes apparent in his responses, particularly when discussing the responsibility of the writer to his readers. Breity appears to be asking why Yerby hadn't written books specifically for black readers. Yerby, instead, doesn't talk about race but addresses anyone who would pick up his books by saying, "I write because I have to. What I get out of it financially doesn't come under consideration at all. I write exactly what I feel and think I want to do, but within this framework I try to give pleasure to the reading public." Here Yerby iterates that his books are mostly for entertainment, not for instruction or for illuminating the problems of black Americans. Furthermore, Yerby's choice of genre did not diminish or negate what he believed was his personal responsibility as an author. Later in the interview, Yerby states,

> I think the novelist, has a professional obligation to please his reading public. . . . Because a writer has a duty to his reader, it doesn't mean in any way that he has the right to write down to his reader. All the brows, high, middle and low, should be able to read his book, but for different reasons. The novelist has no right whatsoever to insult his public. (Breity)

Yerby instructs his readership by creating a set of rules for himself that he dared not deviate from. He discusses them in a personal essay, "How and Why I Write the Costume Novel." For Yerby "[t]he protagonist must be picaresque . . . a charming scoundrel, preferably with a dark secret in his past and . . . [t]he heroine must have an aura of sex about her" (146–47). Yerby was warned early on in his career that altering his concept of historical romance would alienate his fan base (147). However, this set of rules seems to be at the heart of the criticism of most of Yerby's novels.

Stephanie Brown's analysis of Yerby's unpublished manuscript "Ignoble Victory" discusses how Yerby "deviates almost immediately from the plot of the standard romance . . . by refusing to focus on any particular couple for too many pages" (82).[1] Though he did not care for the final text, which underwent a series of rewrites, Yerby's sophomore effort still did well financially. The draft seemed to have cast the women in a nonconformist light. In "Ignoble Victory," Yerby's subversive effort to undermine traditional southern-themed historical romance reveals that black people had a significant role in Reconstruction; their lives were not simply decided for them. The timeline Yerby used suggests that, in the manuscript, the romance took a backseat to politics. The manuscript "sets up the historical context for the rest of the narrative . . . indicating that its scope will encompass . . . not only the beginning of the Reconstruction era but also its end following the compromise of 1877" (Brown 89). As a result, the oppression of black people in a different form of slavery comes full force by passage of the Jim Crow laws.

While Yerby claimed that "Ignoble Victory" was the best novel he had ever written, he admitted that he could not reread *The Vixens*; perhaps because "Ignoble Victory" initially intended to focus on blacks actively acclimating to a possible new reality through Reconstruction, but the published version focuses on whites such as Laird Fournois and Denis Lascals (Yerby 147). In his essay "How and Why I Write the Costume Novel" Yerby notes that he would receive "pithy memos [from publishers], 'More sex, Frank!' . . . So I went overboard. "Ignoble Victory" was downgraded into *The Vixens*, a book I have never since been able to read . . . It should have been banned or burned" (147). Still, a considerable amount of research is detailed in the manuscript. More importantly, "Ignoble Victory" "emphasizes the horror of [the Reconstruction period and its] tragic effects but also foregrounds black agency and perspective. In a series of scenes cut from the published version of the novel, Inch explains not only the realities of black life during Reconstruction but also the intricacies of Louisiana politics" (Brown 91). Moreover, *The Vixens* is still, in its own way, subversive. Even if Yerby cloaked the events of Reconstruction and used it as a subplot, the final version still has elements of politics and black nationalism. For example, Inch becomes lieutenant governor, takes Stephen Fox's former mistress Desiree as his own, and in turn "introduces his son who looks eerily like Stephen. The insinuation is that Desiree had a son by Stephen, who is now being raised by Inch" (Jerng 1198). By holding a political post in Louisiana, Inch gains a level of status nearly equal to that of his former master.

Considering the discussion of race in *The Foxes of Harrow* and politics in *The Vixens* and the large readership of both, is it possible that Yerby is not read now because of the lack of a specifically black readership? As a rich writer, Yerby did not have to seek an audience. On the other hand, author Terry McMillan, from early in her career (late 1980s) went on a campaign specifically to court black audiences. Before the availability of social media, McMillan went to black-owned bookstores and anywhere black people customarily gathered. As a result, her books sold consistently well and ended up on the *New York Times*' bestseller list. In order to be successful, McMillan, unlike Yerby, actively sought an audience that publishers still tend to put on the back burner. Her strategy is not new. Rather, as McHenry points out, McMillan was following a long line of other black authors and booksellers such as Kathryn Johnson who hustled to achieve success by actively cultivating a black readership. Bookseller Kathryn Johnson, in the 1920s, fully "understood the importance of as well as the obstacles to getting books into the hands of black readers. . . . Johnson located and served a black readership overlooked . . . but eager to own books and to read them" (McHenry 300). By addressing an audience where their voices were not heard, McMillan gained financial success similar to Yerby's; yet, from the onset she kept herself rooted within the black community. Much as Langston Hughes and other writers of color knew and understood, there was a sense that black audiences had always been there. Yerby's frustrations with his fellow writers, coupled with the rejection of his first manuscript, made him a wealthy author whose fan base had no particular loyalty.

As McHenry details when discussing African American book clubs, black readers have always been a voracious and willing audience. Still, it seems that Yerby abandoned black readers by not aggressively pursuing them. Did he have to specifically write protest novels? No, as Yerby said in interviews, his main concern was his current readers: "I cannot repeat often enough that the novelist's concern is not what interests himself, but what interests his readers" ("How and Why" 149). He did not appear to have thought about maintaining some sort of legacy. Even though Yerby published over thirty novels and made millions of dollars, he did not ultimately cultivate an audience that would preserve his name and reputation. Yerby excelled at writing historical romances by deploying the formulaic pattern that makes the genre successful. Each novel focuses on the hero, contains a subplot, is populated with endearing characters, and culminates in a satisfying ending. More specifically, the better historical romances, or what Yerby would have called "costume novels," are well researched. Yerby's books contain all of these elements. Yet, in his pursuit to be a success, early in his career Yerby left black readers behind. He may have believed that in order to continue being published he would have to continue writing books that did not directly deal with racism.

Yerby did tackle racism and bigotry head on in *Speak Now* (1969), his first novel with a black protagonist, Harry Forbes. Set in 1968 Paris, the novel focuses on the relationship between Harry, a black ex-patriot jazz musician, and Kathy Nichols, a young, white southern woman who is pregnant with another man's child. Yerby tells readers from the beginning that the thesis of this novel concerns miscegenation. Then he tells the reader about all he struggled through to get the words on the page. Here is where I believe he does a disservice to his potential readers. *Speak Now* deals with politics as well as the systemic racism that occurs within the US and other countries. For Harry "marriage is *not* a private matter when your hides don't match. . . . There isn't anywhere in the U.S.A., from Augusta, Maine, to Miami, Florida, from Montauk Light to 'Frisco Bay, a black boy can live. Nowhere at all"

(80). There are also references to racism within the black community. Harry tells Kathy how his parents were educated and about his upbringing as an Episcopalian. He also refers to his first girlfriend as being "from the wrong side of the tracks . . . where 'the lowdown niggers' lived" (109-10). More importantly, the book deals with the racist attitudes Americans tended to bring with them wherever they went. While in an airport Harry and Kathy are engaged in a conversation where at one point they decide to push the boundaries of miscegenation. Kathy tells Harry, "'That man over there. He's a southerner. . . . Apart from the fact that he almost had a stroke when you put your hand over my mouth, it's written all over him.' . . . The man, about sixty, was beet red, and glowering" (177). After a long kiss the man leaves, but it adds to the point Yerby makes throughout his narrative—racism comes in different forms. The white man who glares at Harry and Kathy confronts her later because he feels as if it's his right to police white, southern womanhood wherever he happens to be at the time. These prejudices even come from Kathy; early on in the first chapter Kathy believes that Harry is some sort of pimp. When he offers to pay her rent after hearing about her pregnant state and financial situation, the racist attitudes Kathy brought with her from North Carolina display themselves in full effect when she states, "'Oh!' and looked at him. He could see fear tightening her mouth, draining the color out from behind her faint dusting of freckles" (12). Of course, Harry immediately becomes sarcastic, using his wit as a defense mechanism. This diffuses the situation, as does Harry's ability to speak French like a native to Kathy's landlord. More importantly, these, along with several other instances, show how black people have learned to deal with stereotypes, not just with their skin color, but also with their countries of origin. Harry is disparaged by the landlady because he dresses like an American, yet when he opens his mouth, she nearly treats him like a long-lost relative. Harry also states to Kathy, "You're at rock bottom, and I'd have to climb up through twenty tons of shit'n gravel to even get to where you are now" (31). Still, Harry never draws away from confrontation, particularly when it involves racism.

Several parts of this novel reveal the "struggle" of articulating a complex black protagonist that Yerby alludes to in his "Note to the Reader." Yerby's extensive research is apparent: there are references to Vietnam (Harry received an injury during the war and met his first wife, Fleur, in Vietnam); poetry in the original French and translated into English; the nonchalant way that Harry weaves in and out of French and English; and the southern drawl Harry uses to antagonize Kathy. Yerby seems to speak directly to his readers in the fifth chapter where Harry has a spirited debate with his host,

Ahmad, regarding the atrocities humans have committed against each other. Yerby includes references from the Vietnam War to the Tonton Macoutes in Haiti. However, the heart of his argument is when Harry points a finger at his native country:

> In America we are guilty of an even more unpardonable crime—being there at all. If our ancestors had had either brains or balls, they'd have died first. For a man who accepts slavery is like a woman who assists at her own violation by removing her panties. And what is even more unpardonable, we made *good* slaves. In three hundred years of North American slavery, there were only one hundred and twenty-five trifling, half-hearted revolts, every one of them—except Nat Turner's—betrayed by a black man to his master for a pair of cast-off boots, or a worn and faded coat. And now our younger idiots are on record as demanding their own version of the segregation we were fighting against in the first place. . . . I am not proud of being black. (100)

Harry saves the last point of his argument for the end by saying, "You whites have your private hell inside you. And the name of it is guilt. Or, the consciousness of guilt" (101). He punctuates this point by stating that his only belief is in evil: "That it persists. That it endures" (101). This chapter includes a dialogue which covers the recent history of how people in power oppress others. The overall theme of *Speak Now* seems to be what Darwin T. Turner in his 1968 essay "Frank Yerby as Debunker" has referred to as the "theme of the outcast who, as in existentialist literature, pits his will against a hostile universe. By intelligence and courage, he proves himself superior to a society which rejects him" (570). By his twenty-third novel Yerby creates a black protagonist who is unapologetic in his beliefs. Yerby's novel includes a "somber hint that man's life is a joke played by a merciless and senile deity" (Turner 571).

The Dahomean, published in 1971, was another financially successful and well-researched work of fiction. Although Yerby made his protagonist superhuman and irresistible to women, he made his hero plausible by grounding him in an actual place in West Africa. The novel centers on Hwesu and his story of being born into a wealthy African family and sold into slavery. Darwin T. Turner points out in "Black Fiction: History and Myth" that "unlike many of Yerby's American [white] protagonists who are scoundrels, though charming, Hwesu—no less bold, intelligent and manly—is a thoroughly decent man" (124). Yerby's novels featuring black leads reflected not only his range as a writer but also his ability to use different types of fiction to tell a story. In *The Foxes of Harrow* Yerby uses historical romance, while in *The Dahomean* Yerby "discovered . . . the varied ways the historical novel can be used" (Turner "Black Fiction" 125). Turner emphasizes this idea when he mentions that "sales figures proved that more readers bought [Yerby's] books than bought those of William Faulkner" ("Frank Yerby" 569). Moreover, as of 1968, "a novelist who has produced twenty books, most of them bestsellers, in twenty years deserves at least cursory examination, if for no reason but that he is the first to prove that a Negro American can write fiction which consistently sells well" (570). Including his modern-day novels such as *Speak Now*, Yerby conveyed more than what his critics minimized or saw lacking in his work.

In order to understand Yerby's near-extinct reading base, I tend to think of Oprah Winfrey when she had her talk show and invited to her book club several authors who had inspired her in her childhood and as an adult. When Winfrey chose a novel for her book club sales of that novel increased exponentially. The book would become popular and make an unknown author a considerable amount of money. More importantly, books that were close to going out of print would be reissued. Winfrey said her book club's chief purpose was "creating and spreading positive images of black people" (McHenry 307). When people read the same book on a massive scale, they are able to talk about it because it creates a shared experience. People may no longer feel alienated or alone. One wonders if Yerby had not chosen a limited, possibly fickle reading base, he might have book clubs or literature champions to save his vanishing legacy.

Gene Andrew Jarrett claims that critics cast aside Yerby's novels because there has been a "longstanding aesthetic devaluation of popular fiction in academic literary studies" (23). He notes that essayist, teacher, political analyst, historian, and novelist C. L. R. James made a compelling argument for why Yerby's novels should be studied on a scholarly level: "James attributes the success of Yerby's novels to their accomplished depiction of free individualism and their commercial appeal to a large and diverse American readership. Their particular representations of individualism reflect certain ideological trends" (162). Jarrett goes on to say that "James argues, Yerby's novels undermine the notion that literature cannot achieve the instantaneous aesthetic effect of film" (162). Still, James's commentary in his posthumous work *American Civilization* best puts Yerby's novels into a literary perspective. James writes that "Yerby's books are a primitive elemental response to some of the deepest needs of the American people in their reaction to society" (129). James distinguishes his personal taste in what may be considered highbrow literary work from literature that can still be profitably examined. Essentially, James believed that although Yerby's first few novels were poorly written, they should nevertheless be studied. Gene Andrew Jarrett in his essay, "'For Endless Generations': Myth, Dynasty, and Frank Yerby's *The Foxes of Harrow*," agrees with James's assessment of Yerby's critical importance in the African American literary community:

> Granted, Yerby's novels consistently suffered unfavorable reviews, but such harsh criticism—which contemporary literary scholars might be more than willing to reiterate—should not discourage us from speculating on how and why such constrictive aesthetic judgment has persisted around popular fiction and Yerby's novels. (54)

James and Jarrett suggest that Yerby's novels contain many resources appropriate for academic study. Their conclusions bring me back to the theories behind Yerby's disappearing readership and to the lack of a clear explanation of why his novels are not studied much in academia. His chosen genre, whether it be historical romance or western, should not preclude scholarly discussion.

A reason why Yerby's novels are no longer printed, but are still collected, may be because he followed a philosophy Emily Bernard articulates: "African-American authorship begins with a disallowing and then disbelieving white readership. It is this audience whose sympathies the black writer must solicit in order to have public existence" (90). Yerby himself admitted that he got stuck in that pattern of writing. In his desire not to be pigeonholed as a black writer, he failed in what W. E. B. Du Bois believed "black literature to be[,] an essential tool in the race uplift project.... If African American writing was to transform the social and political positions of African Americans, then it had to present black people in a manner that made obvious their respectability according to the norm of the day" (Bernard 91). This explanation as to why his initial protest novel or the revisions did not work seems more plausible than Yerby not being black enough. Rather, black readers may not have been able to identify with his mostly white protagonists. It may also be why his fame, though monetarily successful, did not place him in the same literary space as his contemporaries. It is a precarious situation to be in.

NOTES

1. "Ignoble Victory" would become Yerby's second novel, *The Vixens*. According to Stephanie Brown the original intent of "Ignoble Victory" was to deeply examine racism and politics during Reconstruction. Brown mentions that scholars had not studied the original manuscript and as a result the novel that was published had been seen as a work solely building on the "costume novel" genre. Yerby himself has said of "Ignoble Victory" that it was "far better written . . . than anything [he] had ever done before or since."

BIBLIOGRAPHY

Bernard, Emily. "'Raceless' Writing and Difference: Ann Petry's *Country Place* and the African American Literary Canon." *Studies in American Fiction*, vol. 33, no. 1, 2005, pp. 87–117.

Breity, Harvey. "Talk with Frank Yerby." *New York Times*, 13 May 1951, p. BR11.

Brown, Stephanie. "Frank Yerby and the 'Costume Drama' of Southern Historiography." *The Postwar African American Novel: Protest and Discontent 1945-1950*. UP of Mississippi, 2011, pp. 67–98.

Charles, John C. *Abandoning the Black Hero: Sympathy and Privacy in the Postwar African American White-Life Novel*. Rutgers UP, 2012.

Fast, Howard. *Freedom Road*. Routledge, 2015.

Folkart, Burt A. "Frank Yerby; Novelist Felt Rejected by His Native South." *Los Angeles Times*, 9 Jan 1992, p. 22.

Ford, Nick Aaron. "Four Popular Negro Novelists." *Phylon*, vol. 15, no 1, 1954, pp. 29–39.

Glasrud, Bruce A. and Laurie Champion. "'The Fishes and the Poet's Hands': Frank Yerby, A Black Author in White America." *Journal of American and Comparative Cultures*, vol. 23, no. 4, 2000, pp. 15–21.

Hughes, Langston. "Introduction." *The Best Short Stories by Black Writers: 1899-1967*. Little, Brown, 1967, pp. ix–xiii.

Hulett, Skip. "Celebrating The Georgia Writer's Hall of Fame." *The Georgia Review*, vol. 66, no. 3, Fall 2012, pp. 422–31.

Jackson, Blyden. "Silver Foxes." *Journal of Negro Education*, vol. 15, no. 4, 1946, pp. 649–52.

James, C. L. R. *American Civilization*. Edited by Anna Grimshaw and Keith Hart, Blackwell, 1993.

Jarrett, Gene Andrew. *Deans and Truants: Race and Realism in African American Literature*, U of Pennsylvania P, 2006.

Jarrett, Gene Andrew. "'For Endless Generations': Myth, Dynasty, and Frank Yerby's *The Foxes of Harrow*." *Southern Literary Journal*, vol. 39, no. 1, 2006, pp. 54–70.

Jerng, Mark C. "Reconstructions of Racial Perception." *New Approaches to "Gone with the Wind,"* edited by James A. Crank, Louisiana State UP, 2015, pp. 38–65.

Locke, Alain. "Review and Race: A Review of the Literature of the Negro for 1946." *Phylon*, vol. 8, no. 1, 1947, pp. 17–27.

Lyon, Bill. "Expatriate Writer Frank Yerby Is Grousing Even Though His 30th Bestseller Is Coming Up." *People Magazine*, 30 March 1981, p. 99.
Match, Richard. "The Vulpine Master of Harrow." *New York Times*, 10 Feb. 1946, p. 118.
McHenry, Elizabeth. *Forgotten Readers: Recovering the Lost History of African American Literary Societies*, Duke UP, 2002.
Radway, Janice. *A Feeling For Books: The Book-of-the-Month Club, Literary Taste, and Middle-Class Desire*, U of North Carolina P, 1997.
Rampersad, Arnold. "Langston Hughes." *The Concise Oxford Companion to African American Literature*, edited by William L. Andrews, et al., Oxford UP, 2001, pp. 207–8.
Turner, Darwin T. "Black Fiction History and Myth." *Studies in American Fiction*, vol. 1, no. 5, 1977, pp. 109–26.
Turner, Darwin T. "Frank Yerby as Debunker." *Massachusetts Review*, vol. 9, no. 3, 1968, pp. 569–77.
Webster, Harvey Curtis. "Six New Novels." *New Republic*. 21 Feb. 1955, pp. 24–26.
Yerby, Frank. *Benton's Row*. Dial Press, 1954.
Yerby, Frank. *The Foxes of Harrow*. Dial Press, 1946.
Yerby, Frank. "How and Why I Write the Costume Novel." *Harper's Magazine*, Oct. 1959, pp. 145–50.
Yerby, Frank. *Speak Now*. Dial Press, 1969.

"I AIN'T NO MAN!"

Blackness, Wartime Masculinity, and the Protest Tradition in Frank Yerby's Short Fiction

VERONICA T. WATSON

BORN ON SEPTEMBER 4, 1916, IN AUGUSTA, GEORGIA, FRANK YERBY WAS primed to write protest literature. As an African American man in Augusta, a town deeply rooted in the racist ideologies and practices of the segregated South, he certainly had had enough experiences with Jim Crow living, discrimination, and racial terrorism to fuel his writing for a lifetime.[1] According to James Carter, a local historian of black history in Augusta who knew the Yerby family personally, Frank Yerby "detested segregation." An experience that impacted him significantly happened in the 1930s when, as a young man, Yerby was harassed by an Augusta officer for "walking with a White girl" ("Author" 13). That young woman was his fair-skinned sister Eleanor, but the incident did not end before the outraged officer threatened to arrest Yerby for his perceived transgression (Giddens 8). Carter recalls that Yerby was beaten and needed medical attention after the encounter. Although Augusta of the early twentieth century had a thriving African American middle class comprised of entrepreneurs in the fields of education, the medical professions, insurance, and banking, these types of abuses were always a possibility in the segregated town. Yerby came from a hard-working family "whose list of ancestors read like a mini-United Nations," and lived in a Georgia community that was home to black leaders who would make their mark nationally despite the racism of their homeland (Folkart 22). But the family and community could, at any moment, face the routine atrocities and violence of segregation and white supremacy.

Mallory Millender, Augusta native, former faculty member and university historian at Paine College (Yerby's alma mater), believes that this personal history helps to explain Yerby's intellectual and artistic pursuits as well as his personal temperament. Millender, during an interview in 2015, shared that Yerby had a "mission to interpret the world, particularly the world as it affected black people." Despite becoming best known, perhaps, for his prolific authorship of novels that focused primarily on white lives and characters, Millender's assessment is one the author, himself, would seem to support. Yerby commented in an interview with Maryemma Graham, "In every novel I have written about the American South, I have subtly infused a very strong defense of Black history and Black people" (70). Rhetorical defenses in novels that are largely not about black lives are certainly worth noting; however, here I argue that the exploration of the world as it impacted black people was a more consistent interest for Yerby than many—including, perhaps, Yerby himself—recognized. He wrote a number of short stories that specifically focused on the impacts of racism and subjugation on the black psyche and identity, the intimate relationships between men and women of African descent, and the understandings and performances of black masculinity.

While a notable number of Yerby's short stories focus on these issues, the feedback he received from potential publishers suggested to him that the public did not share his interests and concerns. In "How and Why I Write the Costume Novel," Yerby notes that when he wrote socially and racially conscious fiction, he collected a "houseful of rejection slips," leading him to conclude, "the reader cares not a snap about such questions" (146). A man who understood the centrality of writing to his identity, Yerby turned his attention and talents to the genre of romantic historical fiction, what he termed "costume fiction," to pursue the one path he believed he could not help but to pursue—writing. The decision led him to commercial success and financial stability, but it also led him to produce a string of novels that did not feature black characters in significant or expected ways, leading to his reputation as a socially disengaged writer. Claiming that "dealing with racial issues" was an "artistic dead end" for writers, in fact he did not publish a novel that featured a black protagonist until the 1969 publication of *Speak Now* (Yon 99). Two years later, *The Dahomean* (1971) became his first published novel that focused exclusively on a black cast of characters.[2] By the late sixties and early seventies, however, as Yerby commented on and lamented, he was well outside of the interest or regard of most scholars.[3]

Not much is known about Frank Yerby's short fiction. The unpublished stories that are held at the Howard Gotlieb Archival Research Center of Boston University could very well have been part of the "series of short stories" that were in progress in 1955 when *Ebony Magazine* did a feature on Yerby entitled, "Mystery Man of Letters." Because he began his long and prolific career as a novelist when he signed with Helen Strauss in 1944, publishing a novel every twelve to eighteen months for the remainder of his career, it is simply not clear when Yerby wrote most of his short fiction or why he did not pursue publishing more of it throughout his lifetime. When asked by James Hill if he writes short stories "now" (1977), Yerby simply says, "I don't have time.... There is nothing more difficult than condensation, and since any story is at least five hundred pages long, to reduce ... [it] to two and a half or three is major labor.... A short story is much more difficult than a novel" (239). Yet, the fact that so many of Yerby's stories remain unpublished—or that they only appeared in small journals and magazines without wide circulation—clearly contributed to scholars' sense that he was a writer disengaged from issues and debates of his day about racism and discrimination, and the impact of both on black Americans. However, as a young writer beginning to explore his craft, Yerby set off on a path that would have aligned him with many of his more famous contemporaries, including Richard Wright, Zora Neale Hurston, Langston Hughes, and James Baldwin. And though he ultimately chose a different direction for his work because he felt that "Jimmy [Baldwin] and other black novelists of his group and of his school ... were preaching to the converted, that they had no possible way of reaching the people whom they needed to reach," Yerby's short fiction suggests an intellectual who remained interested in the very questions he was condemned for failing to engage (Hill 211).

This chapter will examine several of Yerby's short stories for the ways they explore the intersections of race and masculinity in wartime and postwar America. It is a topic worth consideration because it runs so strongly counter to the established narrative about this author, and because questions of manhood and masculinity run throughout Yerby's work. Echoing contemporary masculinity scholars like Riché Richardson, Maurice O. Wallace, and Arthur Flannigan Saint-Aubin, from his first short story and novel to his last, Yerby considers the social codes that govern the conduct of men and exposes how those codes shape their often-unexamined interior lives. He also explores the differing regional performances of masculinity and dives deeply into the impacts that race and class have on men's understandings of masculine identities. Focusing on two previously published stories, "Health Card" and "The Homecoming," as well as two unpublished pieces preserved in the Yerby collection at Boston University— "The Schoolhouse of Compere Antoine" and "Supper for Louie"—I argue that Yerby thought deeply about the cost of racism on the interior lives of black

Americans, especially men. While these black male characters act within racist systems that circumscribe their rights and deny them full recognition, Yerby chooses to break with the politics of representation exemplified in the literary practices of racial realism and protest literature to foreground the fullness of black male self-conceptions and resistant masculine identities. It is this latter concern, combined with a reconsideration of Yerby as an intellectual and writer, with which this chapter is most interested.

Historically there has been a connection between citizenship and one's commitment to defending the nation. According to Neil Wynn, "[i]n 1863 during the Civil War, US officials stipulated that any alien who had formally declared his intention of becoming a citizen and had exercised political rights under state law was subject to conscription" (2). Being a citizen carried with it the duty of protecting the state, at least for those who were petitioning for citizenship at certain historical moments. Perhaps it was based on this understanding as much as anything else that so many black men, and eventually women, volunteered to fight in wars and pressed for the right to serve in all sectors of the military establishment. Yet, as Wynn notes, "while it follows that members of a minority group called to serve their country in times of war can ask to be recognized as first-class citizens, it also follows that the state's refusal to permit armed service, or restrictions upon such service, can provide a rationale for denying equal rights" (3). Thus, military service was a battleground filled with meaning and signification. Black men fought on behalf of the state, at least in part, to demonstrate their loyalty to the nation and to assert a moral claim for the rights that they were often denied. The federal government, on the other hand, generally sought to limit and circumscribe the participation of Black men in order to disrupt their assertions of citizenship and claims for full rights. These ideological and rhetorical battles, of course, also involved divergent assertions about black *manhood*, as African American men were the ones enlisting and fighting for inclusion while women were still barred from most military service.

In *A Freedom Bought with Blood*, Jennifer James chronicles the ways that black writers and intellectuals have reflected on and theorized the meaning of wartime service for African American men and women. Building on long-standing analyses that suggested that "war was a means for blacks to demonstrate national loyalty, and that the narration of war was a means of writing blacks into the national 'historical destiny,'" James expands those critiques by examining the body of fictional war narratives penned by African American writers from the mid-1800s through the 1950s (6). She finds in these novels and poems a series of "overlapping and interrelated strategies" for abstractly representing the experience of war. Of import for my work is her finding that the wartime narratives of black writers inevitably, invariably, ask a central question, "*What*, exactly, are *we* fighting for?" (33). It is a question that is central to the short fiction I examine in this chapter and an intriguing question indeed, given that Yerby was traveling extensively and living abroad by the time the stories were likely written. His sense of belonging was clearly not anchored to the soil of the United States, and one might argue that as a "citizen of the world," his investment in the destinies of an oppressed people that he only partially claimed as his own was perhaps understandably weak (Millender). However, the topics of race, masculinity, and resistant black identities that make themselves most keenly felt around times of national armed conflict clearly intrigued Yerby. In stories such as "Salute to the Flag," "The Helicopter," as well as the ones discussed in this chapter, Yerby features black men, often veterans, struggling to actualize their senses of self in a world that is, or recently has been, fractured and disrupted by war. They also make appearances in several of his novels, though not always the central characters of those stories.[4] So how did an expatriate who never served in the military and who had escaped many of the pressures of the US racial caste system by leaving the country answer the question, "*What*, exactly, are *we* fighting for?" especially when he did not necessarily consider himself part of the "we" about whom he was writing?

"Health Card" is one of the few short stories by Frank Yerby that has been anthologized and consistently available to readers. It won the O. Henry Memorial Short Story prize, widely regarded as the most prestigious award for short fiction, in 1944, and was included in Langston Hughes's collection, *The Best Stories by Negro Writers: An Anthology from 1899 to the Present* (1967).[5] Yerby's efforts to get the short story published played a role in how he came to the attention of his longtime literary agent, Helen Strauss. As Strauss retells it in her autobiography, *A Talent for Luck*, Yerby submitted the story to *Redbook* magazine, where it came to the attention of Strauss's good friend, editor Muriel Fuller. Fuller did not think the story a good fit for her magazine, but she was impressed enough that she shared the story and all of Yerby's biographical details with Strauss. She also sent "Health Card" to *Harper's Magazine*, where it was published. After receiving the O. Henry award, Fuller subsequently arranged a meeting between Strauss and the struggling young writer, Yerby, beginning a collaboration and friendship between the two that lasted for over twenty years.

"Health Card" tells the story of Johnny, an enlisted soldier who is looking forward to reuniting with his wife, Lily, when she comes to visit him in the town where he is stationed. When we first meet him, he is at the home of the pastor of the Baptist Church, seeking a respectable place, not "one o' these heah ho'houses they calls hotels," where he and his wife can stay together (193). As he leaves the pastor's house, he comes upon a scene that seems familiar to him, black GIs leaving bars and hotels with "girls clinging onto their arms," wearing "dresses that stopped halfway between the pelvis and the knee and hugged the backside so that every muscle showed" (194). White military police (MP) would routinely intervene in these scenes, demanding health cards from the women and arresting those who could not produce them.[6] This night, when one woman refuses to comply with their request, the MPs respond violently. Before Johnny quietly leaves the scene to avoid becoming embroiled, he witnesses "squads of white MPs hurling around the corner and going to work on the Negroes with their clubs" (195). Just as the bus pulls away, he hears gunfire.

Johnny returns to base with one thing on his mind, requesting leave so that he can stay with his wife in town during her visit. As a black man in "a white man's army," however, gaining access to the commanding officer to make such a request is potentially as perilous as the scene he sees unfolding as he escapes on the bus (James 13). Yet, he daringly and courageously navigates, and at times subverts, military bureaucracy to make his petition to the colonel. Johnny's efforts are rewarded when the colonel approves his request. He meets Lily at the train station at the appointed time, but as they begin to walk toward the place where they will stay, they literally bump into two MPs. It is an encounter that Johnny clearly dreads; no longer appearing to be the confident, masterful man who secured the leave, Johnny "jerk[s] his head around and look[s] nervously" toward the MPs as the couple initially passes the police; he begins to "push Lily along faster" to avoid any further interaction with them (199). But the MPs catch up to them and brusquely demand that Lily produce her health card. When she responds, "I ain't got no card, mister. I dunno whut you talkin' about," one of the MPs notices her suitcase, and though they do not arrest her because they recognize that she has just come into town, they give her twenty-four hours to get a health card (200). Johnny is outraged at the implication that Lily is a prostitute and responds, "This girl my wife! She ain't no ho'!" (200). One of the MPs replies by spitting tobacco juice that splashes onto Lily, which goads Johnny to fight. Only Lily's pleading and physical intervention keeps him from an altercation that might have ended in his death. Lily restrains Johnny by "fastening" her two arms around his neck and "doubling her knees so that all her weight was hanging from his neck" (200). The "two of them went down in the dirt" as the offending MPs "turned the corner out of sight," leaving Johnny unable to do anything other than sit "in the dust staring at her" until he hides his face "down in her lap and crie[s]" (201). She is fearful for his safety, but the story makes it clear that there are greater concerns than physical security in a man's life.

In this story we see one of Yerby's recurring concerns, the racial and social prohibitions that deny black men the right to behave according to the norms of masculinity of their time. Johnny understands that one of his duties, as a man, is to protect his wife from harm and affront. When the MPs ask her for a health card, they are explicitly associating her with prostitution. Though Johnny reveres her as a queen, reflecting on her "velvety nightshade skin . . . glossy black lacquered curls . . . [and] clean legs"—legs that are symbolically dirtied by the MP who spits tobacco juice at her—the white MPs assume her to be promiscuous, and they refuse to distinguish between her and the other women who they harass at the start of the story (199). Even her marital status and failure to understand what is being asked of her do not deter the MPs from demanding that she get a health card, effectively denying her the respectability that was supposed to be ensured through marriage.[7] Johnny's response, which is the central focus of the story, is to feel diminished by his failure to defend his wife's honor. At a time when the expectation would have been that a man fight for his wife no matter the personal cost, Johnny is devastated at his lack of response, repeating, "I ain't no man," before they continue their trek to the preacher's house (201). Her actions, grounded in a desire to preserve his life, undermine Johnny's sense of himself as a man and potentially weaken the bonds between them in a society where their ability to trust and rely on each other is an important bulwark protecting their emotional and psychological health.

A similar set of issues is explored in "The Homecoming," a story that appeared in a 1946 issue of *Common Ground*. It was subsequently reprinted in John Henrik Clarke's 1966 collection, *American Negro Short Stories*. In the story, Sergeant Willie Jackson returns to his childhood home in the South after serving in World War II and losing a leg in the conflict. The heat of the early scenes is unrelenting, an ominous foreshadowing of the blistering events that will follow. As the train he is on chugs its way toward the town, Sergeant Jackson notes the fields are "parched" and the heat "blast[s] in the window in solid waves, bringing the dust with it, and the cinders" (148). Perhaps for this reason, Willie smiles when he sees the town water tower and recalls "play[ing] under that tower as a boy" (148). The heat, for a moment, seems to give way to his memory of childhood joy and contentment. He becomes lost in these memories as the train draws near the town, where a "few dozen buildings" sit "clustered around the Confederate Monument" (148). But by the time he disembarks from the train, the heat is back, "pushing down" on the town square "like a gigantic hand, flattening it against the rust-brown earth" (148). Barely a page later, Willie confronts something else that flattens the town: the unrelenting reality of racism. Upon disembarking, he immediately comes under the surveillance of a group of white men sitting nearby. It quickly becomes clear that they are not interested in simply monitoring his presence.[8]

Sergeant Jackson, who is in his uniform which is decorated with "little strips of colored ribbon"—the Purple Heart, the Good Conduct Medal, and one to mark his service in the Pacific Theater of War—stops to read the inscription carved in stone in front of the monument: "No nation rose so white and pure; none fell so free of stain" (148, 149). He stands erect before the monument, "letting the words sink into his brain," and when his harassers ask, "What do it say, boy?" he at first refuses to answer, and then replies simply, "You talking to me?" (149). His refusal to answer to the common southern address of "boy," which was used to denigrate black men of all ages, reflects his quiet confidence and dignity and serves as a form of resistance to the position assigned him because of his race. His initial response is followed by a barrage of pointed questions from the crowd of white men, all of whom back up their inquires with unspoken threats while they constantly address Sergeant Jackson by the racial slur "nigger."

Importantly, the harassment Sergeant Jackson experiences in this moment echoes the very real violence black veterans faced when they returned to the United States from theaters of war, including the well-known 1946 case of Sergeant Isaac Woodward who boarded a bus in uniform in Atlanta, Georgia, to return home after being discharged from the Army. When confronted by a sheriff at a rest station in North Carolina, Woodward was beaten and arrested for a trumped-up offense. While in jail, he was attacked and struck in the eyes by assailants so violently that he was permanently blinded and suffered partial amnesia (Edgerton 161–62). This incident, just one of many acts of violence directed at African American veterans and service members in uniform, highlights the continuing racial animosity and danger faced by black men who had served their country. Willie's reaction to the white mob is all the more noteworthy because black veterans recognized the possibility that they might be violently attacked despite their wartime sacrifices. Through his responses it becomes clear to the white men that Sergeant Jackson knows the racial codes and Jim Crow laws that are supposed to govern his speech and behavior in the South and that he is choosing to challenge their socially ascribed authority. To the final question, "Nigger, do you know where you're at?" Willie responds, "Yes, I knows. And I knows you can have me killed. But I don't care about that. Long time now I don't care. So please don't come no closer, white man. I'm asking you kindly" (149–50). In these few lines Willie demonstrates not only his refusal to acquiesce to racial performances that reinforce a sense of his inferiority to all involved, but he also subtly signals his willingness to defend himself. Both of these positions cause his interlocutors to hesitate. When he begins walking toward them, "They stood aside and let him pass" (150). His masculinity asserted and dignity defended, Willie continues his journey with a stop in the local store.

In the store he has yet another encounter with Jim Crow social codes and scripts. Here, he interacts with two white women, one a customer and the other the salesperson working in the store. As the saleswoman approaches him to take his money for a purchase, "a white woman came toward the counter, so the girl went on past Willie" (150). Refusing to remain silent in the face of this assertion of his invisibility and the assignment of white superiority that is signaled in the act of serving the white customer first, Willie directly responds to the affront: "'Look a here, girl,' Willie said sharply. 'I was here first'" (150). When they "turned toward him, their mouths dropping open," Willie continues, "My money the same color as hers" (150). He concludes the encounter by tossing his payment on the counter, refusing to wait for the sales clerk to total his purchase or take his money. By the time he leaves the store, a larger group of white men has gathered at the Confederate Monument. Though they do not immediately engage him, the crowd reminds readers of the real, bodily danger Sergeant Jackson faces because of his actions and words. He continues his journey toward home but looks back several times to see if anyone is following him.

These first two encounters evince a rebellious masculine performance that has grown more fearless in its public display. While certainly African Americans had long been dissatisfied with the social position enforced upon them by white supremacy, terrorism, and violence, resistance to that enforced marginalization was often surreptitious, small, and private. Public displays that did not align with white expectations for black behavior carried the risk of economic retaliation, the endangering of home and family, and physical violence. Willie Jackson's willingness to face such threats and perils seems to be directly connected to his service, which was an awakening that was best exemplified by the "Double V" (double victory) campaign launched on the pages of the *Pittsburgh Courier* in 1942. W. E. B. Du Bois had laid the groundwork for a coordinated and sustained Black resistance effort at the end of World War I when he wrote, "By the God of heaven we are cowards and jackasses if now that the war is over we do not marshal every ounce of our brain and brawn to fight a sterner, longer, more unbending battle against the forces of hell in our land" (qtd. in Astor, 126). The rhetoric of the "Double V" campaign was an answer to his call, designed to encourage African American men to enlist in the military in World War II to support US efforts overseas, *and* to underscore the need for them to actively oppose repressive and discriminatory customs, practices and policies that violated the rights of black Americans at home. Willie exemplifies the emerging, courageous performances of a larger segment of black men who were no longer willing to quietly acquiesce or dissemble in order to survive.

Willie Jackson's final stop is his former home, an old plantation where he is met by "The Colonel," the white homeowner and local man of influence who greets him with "his hand outstretched" and the words, "You little black scoundrel! . . . You aren't little any more, are you?" (151). As Willie catches him up on his life and military service, Colonel Bob offers him his old job. Willie replies, "I ain't suited for here no more," and goes on to explain his plans for heading to the North (152). The Colonel tries to dissuade him by arguing, "those dang-blasted Yankees would let you starve to death. Down here a good boy like you always got a white man to look after him" (152). But these are the very conditions that Sergeant Jackson opposes. He wants the freedom to stand erect, speak what is on his mind, and to live or die by his own effort. Not surprisingly, Colonel Bob misses the point; he retorts, "Somebody's been talking to you . . . teaching you the wrong things" (152). He cannot fathom a world in which a black man would want freedom from white control and patronage, a world in which a black man would risk death to secure those very rights. When Colonel Bob receives a call informing him that "there's trouble up in town," perhaps enlisting him to join the mob who will confront the "colored soldier" who passed through town earlier that day, he immediately understands that the person they are looking for is Willie. He asks, "Did you tell two white men you'd kill them if they came nigh you? . . . And did you have some kind of argument with a white *woman*?" (153). When Willie confirms the reports, the Colonel falls back on the racial schema that structure his thinking and actions: he offers to get Willie out of town after nightfall.

To the man who has tried to explain that he "done forgot too many things . . . done forgot how to scratch my head and shuffle my feet and grin when I don't feel like grinning," slinking away from the mob would be the equivalent of denying the man he has claimed and created himself to be (152). It would be a capitulation to white dominance, even if that dominance occurs through violence, and it would be as if he were confirming white society's vision of his diminished capacity as a man and as a human being. Thus, it is with some irony that the Colonel determines the way to save Willie's life is to claim that he is insane.[9] He reports Sergeant Willie Jackson to the military psychiatric unit, citing his behavior in the town as evidence of his mental instability. When the ambulance arrives to carry Willie away, the officer confirms, "This man is a combat fatigue case—not responsible for his actions" (155). This explanation, of course, is the very assertion about his racial identity and humanity against which Willie is fighting. He is completely responsible and has chosen his actions in town knowing fully what the repercussions might be. As he is dragged away, Willie weeps the words, "Let me go!" (156). However, the white patriarchal structure—represented first by the men in the town square, then by the Colonel, and finally by the white military officer who commits him—refuses to honor this simple yet profound demand, especially when it has been preceded by the actions of a free man. Their "care" for him in the last scene is simply another form of bondage and control.

"Supper for Louie," another story set after World War II, presents a more hopeful picture about the ability of black men to perform mid-twentieth-century masculinity. It is one of the stories preserved at the Gotlieb Center without a date of composition. The story centers on Annie May, a dark-skinned African American woman who learned to despise her appearance as a child and to pity herself as a "little old black girl" (1). As an adult, she does not think herself attractive and concludes a few discouraging things about men: "The better looking ones had the idea that Annie May should give them all the money that she had worked so hard for . . . The uglier ones were willing to pool their resources with hers, but she soon discovered that this pooling included moving into her apartment without benefit of clergy" (2). As a result of her experiences with men and her reading "that a woman should be loved for herself alone," Annie May spends most of her time alone, longing for a relationship that she does not feel she will ever have (2). When she meets Louie, an immigrant from the West Indian island of Antiqua, at a ballroom she went to for an evening of dancing and socializing, she thinks he is the "handsomest" man she had ever known, but immediately becomes sad because she does not believe he could ever be, or remain, interested in her.

Focalized through Annie May, "Supper for Louie" takes readers on an emotional ride of doubt and fear. Annie May never feels secure in Louie's attention or affection and as a result, neither does the reader. We trust Annie May's analysis of men, that they would use her for financial gain and that they have no interest in marriage, and we fear that she is so vulnerable and lonely that she might settle for less than she deserves. So when Louie acts like a gentleman and refuses to come to her room when invited, readers feel suspicious of him; when he tells her a parable about "an old African man in Antiqua who carves statues out of wood," we become anxious that he sees her as a lump of clay to be manipulated instead of the beautiful woman she is (7). When she buys him a new chair and footstool and says she will provide for them when Louie loses his job, we fear she has become the person she never wanted to be, a woman who tries to buy the love of a man.

Louie, however, has already signaled that he is not the typical "American boy"; his diasporic blackness sets him apart and renders him a "man" where others are considered only "boys" (4). Much like Annie May, he has drawn some unflattering conclusions about women in his adopted country: "American girl like a man, she want to give him stuff. Suits, money, buy his wine. Well, I ain't for sale" (5). This strength and independence are quite different from what Annie May has come to expect. Louie not only has a job, he also suggests that accepting gifts from a woman cheapens him as a man. He says African American men are "forever and ever fool" for not recognizing Annie May's beauty (4). He does not subscribe to the standards of American beauty that judge darker-skinned women as less desirable or beautiful than African American women who are "dusk rose," "copper complexion[ed]," or "whose skin was the color of the keys of a piano that has been used for several years," as are the women in Annie May's family (1). He lavishes attention on her, eventually announcing, "I'm going down and get us a license tomorrow. Then we go and get us a blood test. That way we can be married on Friday by the judge" (9). Shortly after this announcement, however, Louie is released from his job, and when he returns to tell Annie May that they must postpone their wedding, we see how serious he is about what he has previously said. His "jaw was iron" when Annie May offers to provide for them financially so that they can continue with their plans to be married; only her offer to "lend" him money and "keep account of every penny" persuades him not to delay their nuptials (9).

Whatever doubts Annie May and readers may have harbored about Louie are resolved, albeit uneasily, at the end of the story. The two of them do, indeed, marry, and live a frugal life on Annie May's income. When he tells her one evening after she comes home from work that they are going out for dinner, Annie May protests that they cannot afford the outing. He insists and takes her to a local diner before eventually informing her that he bought the restaurant. Like Tea Cake from Zora Neale Hurston's *Their Eyes*

Were Watching God, Louie has used money earned by his wife without being honest about his own resources. Yet, all seems forgiven when he announces that he has invested in their future by buying a business to support them, proving that he is both capable of providing for them as well as seeking a level of security that they could not have as long as they were employed by other people. When Annie May points out, "People gotta eat. And eating here won't cost much, so we'll always have business, no matter how hard times get!" she perhaps overestimates the restaurant's ability to weather "hard times" and not to be a drain on their resources (12). But most importantly for the story, she expresses her confidence in the choice Louie has made for them as head of their household. Yerby, who made no secret of his preference for traditional performances of masculinity and patriarchal family arrangements, rejects the racial fatalism/realism that characterized so much protest literature and crafts a black male character who successfully transcends the obstacles that would deny him access to the American dream.[10] Thus, Louie emerges as a strong black man worthy of Annie May's love. By seeing her beauty, Louie has proven himself to be the man that she deserves.

As several scholars have noted, Yerby conducted meticulous research for his novels, which he often used to challenge official histories of American exceptionalism and white moral superiority. This penchant prompted James Hill to assert that Yerby was "one of America's greatest debunkers of historical myths" (206). When talking about his writing process, Yerby admitted that he researched exhaustively and "repeatedly loaded . . . [his novels] with history" ("How and Why" 145). It is hard to know whether he was happy about the fact that "ninety-nine and ninety-nine one-hundredths of said history land[s] on the Dial Press cutting-room floor," but in the unpublished story, "The Schoolhouse of Compere Antoine," much of the historical detail remained intact, giving the reader the feeling of being transported back to a different time as the events of history unfold ("How and Why" 145). Set during and in the years following the Civil War, the story uses the Reconstruction period in Louisiana as its context and backdrop; it is dotted with references to W. B. Mumford removing the Federal flag from the mint, General Benjamin Butler's occupation of New Orleans, and the exemplary service of African American political officials Oscar J. Dunn and Antoine Dubuclet, all men who were young enough to believe they could preserve/change the world in which they lived. However, the story is actually centered on Compere Antoine, a man who, according to the narrator, "was already an old man" at the time the story begins (1). Thus, "The Schoolhouse" marks a divergence from the formula that Yerby once described he used for his work:

The protagonist must be picaresque. In other words, he must be a charming scoundrel, preferably with a dark secret in his past.... He must be a doer, never resignedly submitting to the blows of fate; but initiating the action of the plot himself ... he must be a dominant male ... Physically, he can be of almost any type except short, bald, and bearded.... And ... in his emotional relationships he should not be too bright. ("How and Why" 146–7)

In exploring a character who is not young, not dashing, and not able to steer the plot by force of will, Yerby recognizes that questions of masculinity and manhood are not limited to people under a certain age. In later stages of life, perhaps the avenues for masculine performativity become more fraught as opportunities for expressing one's manhood become unmoored from traditional enterprises like military service, physical confrontation, romantic attachment, and sexual expression.

Compere is a mixed-race New Orleans Creole, a business owner, and father to five sons; he had always been free but lived within the racist social and political systems of his time. Described as "a simple man," he is at first unconcerned with the Union Army's entry into New Orleans; he spent the five days of the siege "trying vainly to keep up with his boys" (2). Only slowly does he come to realize that he is in the middle of history, and "something of the excitement of the day ... gradually work[ed] within him" (2). He manages to keep up with the celebrating crowd, but there is little that Compere can do but "limp along ... over the entire parade route" (2). Following the end of the war, he watches the politics of Reconstruction unfold in his lifelong home. One of his sons even becomes politically active but is corrupted after being elected to the legislature. After losing that son in a riot that erupted during a parade, Compere takes his remaining four sons and relocates, but leaving New Orleans does not provide him with the quiet existence he hoped for. As the narrator explains, "Even here there was no chance for a quiet life. Every time there was an election people got killed. Since nobody paid dollars and cents for Negroes any more, the native whites declared open season upon them the whole year round" (3–4).

Though he continues to try to vote despite obstacles placed before him, it is not until Compere witnesses a group of white men harassing a young white woman, Miss Varick, because she has come to town to teach freedmen, that he becomes more politically active himself. Initially a bystander, he is brought into the ruckus by the hecklers; they tease the woman, "So you come down here to teach niggers. Well, here's yore chance. You kin start wit

Uncle here!" (5). They clearly do not see Compere as anyone who might take exception to their behavior or who might dare to intervene in any way. They also clearly do not believe he would have any interest in education, or that Miss Varick would have any interest in teaching someone of his age. When she walks toward his wagon, Compere "smiled timidly" at her approach; he sits perfectly still as she begins to climb into the seat beside him, but eventually he "put[s] out a trembling hand" and draws her into the wagon (5). As they ride away, Compere says, "Maybe you come down to our parish an teach us. We ain't got not school, us; but we build you one. And we build you nice house where you kin stay" (6). With this offer, Compere becomes more visible, and communal, in his efforts to improve the lives of black people. His initiative and commitment lead to "a widening island of black folks who could write their own names and read their Bibles and count money" (7). The acquisition of these basic literacy skills so moves Compere that when he finds out the school would no longer receive funding from the Freedman's Bureau or state taxes, he begins a petition asking "the Yankee General to please collect the tax and offering to pay extra so that the schools could go in in Louisiana for the black children and the white children too" (8). We are reminded that Compere Antoine took these bold steps "during the time when for a black man to stay alive at all was a victory" (9).

Having lived through the Civil War and the promise of a reconstructed nation where more people would have basic rights, Compere saw that dream flourish and wilt again. He could have remained uninvolved, seeking only to protect his own family, but instead practiced an activism that was practical, expansive and fearless. It was not until the "White Leaguers . . . [set] his schoolhouse afire . . . and chased . . . the Yankee schoolmarm away, and whipped Compere Antoine" that anything other than the "earnest sweetness of his nature" came forth (9). But instead of defeat, we are told "bitterness entered his soul like iron and acid" (9). The comparison is not, perhaps, what one would have anticipated for him. He does not appear broken or defeated as much as boiling over with rage. He becomes harder, like iron, and has an anger that threatens to scorch and burn. Yet, despite all he has seen and lived through, and perhaps even *because* of all he has seen and lived through, Compere weeps at the end. The times may be dark for the nation that chooses to close rather than open doors for more of its citizens, but Compere has fought a fight that enabled more people to participate in social and political change. His tears are ineffectual, but perhaps his attempts at reform have not been.

During a 1983 interview with Emilio Garcia Gomez, Yerby stressed, "the American definition of race is the most ridiculous thing... the concept of race leaves me indifferent" (9). But the short fiction of Frank Yerby indicates anything but a man who is indifferent to race. The four short stories covered here—"Health Card," "The Homecoming," "Supper for Louie," and "The Schoolhouse of Compere Antoine"—all evince a man who, though expatriated and removed from the context of American racism, remained deeply interested in exploring the intersections of race and masculinity for black men. It seems to me no accident that these stories feature black men negotiating their performances of masculinity during times of postwar change. Historically, as social historian Arthur Marwick has established, war can precipitate social change because, in part, it "necessitates *participation* of underprivileged groups, and is a colossal *psychological* experience" (qtd. in Wynn, 1). Making a similar point more recently, James notes that war has had a tremendous destabilizing effect that leads to new identities:

> allegiances are made and broken, geographical boundaries crossed, countries renamed, and territories redistributed; ... women become the heads of households and neighbors become adversaries; ... the oppressed may rise up against domination only to become oppressors.... The use of war as a narrative context allows black writers to seize these moments of historical rupture to assert newly formed notions of a black "self..." (10)

These are the times when the possibilities for envisioning and/or claiming new meanings of manhood seem most open. That Yerby's characters most often sought traditional enactments of masculinity is perhaps understandable, given the ways that those possibilities were so often denied to them socially. The right to defend and protect a spouse, to be respected as an equal in the world, to fulfill the American dream of financial security and prosperity, to receive education, and to have a political voice: these are the rights and behaviors that seem quintessentially American and fundamentally human in Yerby's short fiction. It is also true that in all but one story these attempts at self-actualization are thwarted. But this was the southern world that Yerby knew, and little in his lifetime suggested that his analyses were inaccurate or exaggerated.

I return now to the question with which I opened this chapter: "How did an expatriate who never served in the military answer the questions, 'What are *we* fighting for?' especially when he did not necessarily consider himself part of the 'we' about whom he was writing?" In many ways, these are deeply existential questions. They are centrally about what type of person you create yourself to be in a hostile world. Will you be broken, tamed, and made meek in the face of an adversary with more power and strength? Or will you stand in the face of these overwhelming odds and *create* yourself, will yourself into being? For Yerby, these were also questions that transcended race. Every man had to find the front upon which to make himself. For Yerby, an intellectual, the field of play was writing. As he told Maryemma Graham in 1975, "I decided early that I would get out there and compete; that I was not going to shelter myself in a tight little world. I was going to get out there and present what I did in the world-literature markets with everybody else" (88–89). As a writer he believed "any time you present a person who is crushed, distorted, and annihilated by overwhelming forces which he cannot possibly combat, you have automatically reduced a man out of his humanity into a thing," and he resisted the mandate for black writers to produce racial realism to show how hopeless black lives are because they are ensnared in the American racial capitalist patriarchal system (Hill 213). Instead, Yerby created a set of stories with characters who are heroic in their resistance, who are *made* (rather than unmade) by their efforts to define themselves and to live out their lives based on those self-conceptions. In short, it is *the fight* that marks these characters as men. Despite the propaganda and uses of force that threaten to turn them into beasts, as Yerby saw it, "a hero is a man who is scared shitless and who then goes on in spite of his fear. That's the correct definition of a hero, a man who really conquers himself, who conquers his weaknesses and insists on overriding them" (Hill 218). It is perhaps understandable, then, that Yerby would posit that times of war, during which men have defined themselves *as men* for centuries, should be the location for his characters to discover, once again, the men they were meant to be.

NOTES

1. Yerby would assert when interviewed that he should be considered multiracial. When the question of his racial identity was raised, he often pointed out that he was "85% Seminole Indian," while in an interview with James Hill he also claimed Irish, Scottish, Haitian, French, and Black ancestry (Author 13). Yerby's mother, Wilhelmina Ethel Smythe Yerby, was of Scots-Irish ancestry while his father, Rufus Garvin Yerby, had both African American and Seminole ancestry.

2. The distinction of "published" is important here. According to Bruce Glasrud and Laurie Champion, authors of "'The Fishes and the Poet's Hands': Frank Yerby, A Black

Author in White America," Yerby completed a manuscript that was never published, a "race-based novel" centered on a "black man who is a steel worker as well as successful boxer, and exposes the problems of being an independent black man in racially-biased white America" (16). Yerby scholar, James Hill, writes in his dissertation that after failing to find a publisher for the book, Yerby eventually destroyed the manuscript.

3. While Yerby may have begun his career with little regard for how critics regarded his work, his desire to be considered a serious American author rather than exclusively a writer of popular fiction asserted itself more strongly later in his life. By the early to mid 1960s, letters between Yerby and his agent indicate Yerby was dissatisfied with the insistence of Dial Press (his longtime publisher) that he keep writing the formulaic fiction that had gained him both audience and commercial success. Yerby felt they had encouraged, and at times pressured, him into conforming to a particular style of writing to increase sales. By the 1960s, however, he was quite tired of the limitations being placed on his creativity and was pushing hard to write the great novel of which he felt himself capable. He commented to his agent, Helen Strauss, "I should like to be allowed to make up for my literary sins by writing some good books before I die" (April 16, 1964, letter from Yerby to Strauss). To help Yerby achieve his goal, Strauss courted Random House to take him on, but that publisher also signaled that they were most interested in his popular fiction, and Yerby was wary of switching to them (November 11, 1964, letter from Yerby to Strauss). In the end, he stayed with Dial Press for the remainder of his career. It is not clear that he felt he ever published the "great novel" that would have garnered him the attention and regard of literary critics and scholars.

4. Yerby's first published novel, *The Foxes of Harrow*, showcases the character of Inch, who is born into slavery, escapes from bondage (and the narrative), only to reenter the the last pages of the novel as a decorated veteran and commissioner of police for New Orleans. In *Speak Now*, the main character, Harry Forbes, is a wounded Vietnam war veteran.

5. Yerby was only the second black writer to be awarded an O. Henry Prize. Richard Wright won the accolade for "Fire and Cloud," published in *Story Magazine* in 1938. He won it a second time in 1940 for "Almos' a Man," published in *Harper's Bazaar*.

6. Health cards, also known as health certificates, were a form of medical documentation that certified a person was free from infectious venereal diseases, especially syphilis and gonorrhea. The cards were widely used as part of a national, multipronged approach during World Wars I and II to decrease the rates of venereal disease among enlisted servicemen and the broader civilian population.

The rates of infection for syphilis and gonorrhea were alarming to government officials in the 1930s and 1940s when, according to one official, in a single year "more than five times as many new cases of syphilis were reported to health departments as were new cases of tuberculosis"; both diseases, when left untreated, could result in serious mental and physical debilitation (Ness 89). Sex workers were a particular target for state interventions as it was believed that most venereal diseases were spread by women in this profession. Cast as an issue of national defense, the 1937 Venereal Disease Control Act established "military policing of danger areas at times of particular hazard," which authorized military police to check that sex workers were in possession of health cards and arrest those found without the certification. Those arrested could be sent to treatment or rehabilitation facilities. The use of health cards was often expanded to professions that were held largely by people of color, such as domestic workers and food service employees, either by local law or custom, especially in the South.

7. As established by Patricia Hill Collins, Carolyn West, and Ella Bell, black women have historically been portrayed in popular culture as being sexually promiscuous and insatiable. These stereotypes led to the common view during and after the period of slavery that black women could not be raped, and that they always solicited or initiated any sexual contact that might occur. Black women, according to these popular misconceptions, were never worthy of social protections or to be regarded as "respectable women," regardless of marriage, education, or professional accomplishment.

8. The racism and discrimination faced by black veterans when they returned from deployment is a theme Yerby explores in several of his works, including *Speak Now* (1969) and the short story, "The Helicopter."

9. The Colonel's decision to have Sergeant Johnson removed from town because he was suffering from combat fatigue recalls a nineteenth century disorder that was attributed to enslaved Blacks, drapetomania. It was believed that this was a mental disease that caused slaves to run away. Mental illness was the only explanation that whites in American society would accept for why enslaved Africans, whom they believed should be content with their bondage, would seek their freedom. The obvious answer that blacks did not want to be enslaved was apparently too disruptive to fantasies of white moral superiority and goodness to be contemplated.

10. Yerby was clearly a man of a certain generation and corresponding ideology. He writes in "How and Why I Write the Costume Novel" that one element of his formula for writing included creating a male protagonist who was "a dominant male." The reasoning he offers is revealing: "For, after having had their mothers and grandmothers convert the United States into a matriarchy with their ardent feminism, and reduce the bearded patriarch…into the pink and paunchy Caspar Milquetoast of today, the average American female reader subconsciously enjoys reading about a male who can get up on his hind legs and roar" (147). In a 1977 interview with James Hill, he speaks of men being "unmanned" and "deballed," two terms that signal a belief in the biology of men as the justification for their familial roles as heads of household and source of their socially ascribed power (220). His son, Jacques Yerby, also claims that his father "admired" Hemingway, a writer whose machismo and misogyny are legendary. Both statements, as well as other evidence, suggest that Yerby (like Hemingway, perhaps) believed deeply in the value of a masculine performance/identity rooted in strength and patriarchal dominance.

BIBLIOGRAPHY

Astor, Gerald. *The Right to Fight: A History of African Americans in the Military*. Presidio Press, 1998.

"Author Frank Yerby, 76, Dies; Buried in Spain." *Jet*, vol. 81, no. 14, 27 Jan 1992, pp. 12–13.

Bell, Ella. "Myths, Stereotypes, and Realities of Black Women: A Personal Reflection." *The Journal of Applied Behavioral Science*, vol. 28, no. 3, January 1992, pp. 363-76. Sage Journals.

Carter, James. Personal interview. 4 August 2015.

Collins, Patricia Hill. *Black Feminist Thought: Knowledge, Consciousness, and the Politics of Empowerment*. Routledge, 1999.

Edgerton, Robert B. *Hidden Heroism: Black Soldiers in America's Wars*. Westview Press, 2002.

Folkart, Burt A. "Frank Yerby; Novelist Felt Rejected by His Native South." *Los Angeles Times*, 9 Jan. 1992. p. 22. ProQuest Newsstand.

Giddens, Tharon. "Novelist Soured on His Home, Stung by Racism, Black Native of Augusta Left America for Europe to Write Popular Historical Romances." *The Augusta Chronicle*, 4 February 1999, p. 8.

Glasrud, Bruce A., and Laurie Champion. "'The Fishes and the Poet's Hands': Frank Yerby, A Black Author in White America." *Journal of American and Comparative Cultures*, vol. 23, no. 4, Winter 2000, pp. 15–22. EBSCOhost Online.

Gomez, Emilio Garcia. "Interview with Frank Yerby." *El Pais Semanal*, translated by Veronica Watson, August 12, 1984, pp. 8-12.

Graham, Maryemma. "Frank Yerby, King of the Costume Novel." *Essence*, vol. 6, October 1975, pp. 70–71, 88–92.

Hill, James. L. "An Interview with Frank Garvin Yerby." *Resources for American Literary Study*, vol. 21, no. 2, 1995, pp. 206–39.

James, Jennifer C. *A Freedom Bought with Blood: African American War Literature from the Civil War to World War II*. U of North Carolina P, 2007.

Lyon, Bill. "Expatriate Writer, Frank Yerby, is Grousing Even Though His 30th Bestseller Is Coming Up." *People*, 30 March 1981, p. 99.

Millender, Mallory. Personal interview. 5 August 2015.

"Mystery Man of Letters." *Ebony*, vol. 10, February 1955, pp. 31–32, 35–38.

Ness, Eliot. "Venereal Disease Control in Defense." *The Annals of the American Academy of Political and Social Science*, vol. 220, March 1942, pp. 89–93. JSTOR.

Strauss, Helen M. *A Talent for Luck: An Autobiography*. Random House, 1979.

West, Carolyn. "Mammy, Jezebel, Sapphire, and Their Homegirls: Developing an 'Oppositional Gaze' Toward the Images of Black Women." *Lectures on the Psychology of Women*, edited by J. Chrisler, et al. McGraw Hill, 2008, pp. 286–99.

Wynn, Neil A. *The Afro-American and the Second World War*. Holmes & Meier Publishers, 1975.

Yerby, Frank. "Health Card." 1944. *The Best Short Stories by Negro Writers: An Anthology from 1899 to the Present*, edited by Langston Hughes. Little, Brown, 1967, pp. 192–201.

Yerby, Frank. "The Homecoming." 1946. *American Negro Short Stories*, edited by John Henrik Clarke. Hill and Wang, 1966, pp. 147–56.

Yerby, Frank. "How and Why I Write the Costume Novel." *Harper's Magazine*, Oct. 1959, pp. 145–50.

Yerby, Frank. Letter to Helen Strauss. April 16, 1964. Frank Yerby Papers, Howard Gotlieb Archival Research Center, Boston. Box 53, Folder B53 F7.

Yerby, Frank. Letter to Helen Strauss. November 16, 1964. Frank Yerby Papers, Howard Gotlieb Archival Research Center, Boston. Box 53, Fold B53 F7.

Yerby, Frank. "The Schoolhouse of Compere Antoine." N.d. Howard Gotlieb Archival Research Center, Boston University. Box 23.

Yerby, Frank. "Supper for Louie." N.d. Howard Gotlieb Archival Research Center, Boston University. Box 23.

Yerby, Jacques. "Re: Legal Questions and Medical Problems." Message to the author. 7 July 2014. Email.

OVERSTUFFED AND UNDERCOOKED

The Film Adaptation of Frank Yerby's The Foxes of Harrow

MATTHEW TEUTSCH

INFAMOUSLY, ROBERT BONE, IN HIS 1958 *THE NEGRO NOVEL IN AMERICA*, called Frank Yerby the "prince of pulpsters" because he chose to write popular fiction rather than social protest fiction in the manner of Richard Wright (176).[1] Bone was far from a lone voice criticizing the Augusta-born Yerby for failing to overtly address racial discrimination and oppression. By 1958, Yerby had published thirteen novels, essentially one a year, and the majority were what he termed "costume novels": novels laced with conventions of the historical romance that appealed to a mass audience. Yerby's first novel, *The Foxes of Harrow* (1946), epitomizes this formula with its focus on the meteoric rise of Irish immigrant Stephen Fox amongst the Creole community in New Orleans. Opening in 1825, the novel traces Stephen's rise, his romantic relationships, and his ultimate downfall during the Civil War. On the other hand, the film version ends around the panic of 1837, thus eliminating the crucial story of Little Inch, who is enslaved by Stephen and rises to a position of power at the conclusion of the Civil War. While on the surface the novel appears to hold up the Old South as a romantic, bygone era, as does Margaret Mitchell's *Gone with the Wind* (1936), the novel, and all of Yerby's oeuvre, work to destabilize the myths of the Old South that Mitchell and others constructed. As James L. Hill notes, "Yerby reveals gross historical inaccuracies, corrects common misconceptions, reaffirms historical truths, and comments on human nature" throughout his work (405). However, the film version of Yerby's debut novel obscures his critique of the "moonlight and magnolia" depictions of the Old South.

Bosley Crowther, in his *New York Times* review of the 1947 film adaptation of Frank Yerby's *The Foxes of Harrow*, calls the celluloid version an "orotund picture" that "manifests over-stuffing with the fattiest romantic clichés" (35). One year earlier, in his review of Yerby's debut novel, Richard Match proclaimed, "Here is a good, old-fashioned, obese historical novel of the Old South that seems, more than once, haunted by the affluent ghost of Scarlett O'Hara" (118). Both critics see Yerby's novel and the film adaptation as overstuffed with filler and no true meat; however, Match notes that while Yerby's novel does not have the "ideological intensity" associated with Richard Wright, there "are some sympathetic evidences of the Negro's deep resentment against slavery" (118). Match rightly observes that Yerby's novel contains these instances of resentment, yet the film version tosses discussions of race to the side, choosing to focus on the "fattiest romantic clichés" that encompass Stephen and Odalie's relationship. Ultimately, the movie falls short of serving as a major touchstone in cinematic history on the representation of African Americans on screen. Instead, it perpetuates, while also challenging in some ways, the continued view of African Americans in roles subservient to white masters.

Published in 1946, *The Foxes of Harrow* sold over 500,000 copies within its first two months; the novel's sales numbers led to a film adaptation by 20th Century Fox the following year. Directed by John M. Stahl with a screenplay by Wanda Tuchock, the film eliminates most of the novel's subversive elements that counter the glorification of a mythologized Old South. The removal of these aspects perpetuates the image of a glorified, idyllic, and nostalgic South that the adaptation of *Gone with the Wind* (1939) epitomizes on screen. Crowther even asks, "Do you mind if we call its effort 'The O'Hara of Twentieth Century-Fox?'" (35)[2] Ultimately, though, as Barbara Tepa Lupack notes, the film version "made appreciable gains over other more regressive Southern sagas in depicting some of the harshness of plantation life, [yet] it nonetheless deemphasized the unique strengths of black women [and men] that Yerby had highlighted" in the novel (216). Some reviewers noted these gains as well; a southern reviewer wrote about the importance of the film adaptation, commenting that the "revealed operations of slavery . . . should convince even the United Daughters of the Confederacy that it was wrong" (qtd. in Campbell 163).

Reviewing Yerby's debut in 1946, Blyden Jackson argues that *The Foxes of Harrow* will not rank in the pantheon of great literature, although it achieved market success. Jackson laments that Yerby's narrative exists more as entertainment than a polemic on race in America during the mid-twentieth century because of its focus on Stephen Fox's rise to prominence, and in part, Jackson states that Yerby may well have said to himself when composing the novel, "It is possible as never before, to get rich quick with one novel. No Negro has ever turned the trick, and nobody really believes that any of us are quite ready or lucky to bring it off. But I understand the winning formula, and I can work it—now" (650). Yerby masterfully worked "the winning formula" that structured plantation romances and myths of the Old South; he applied that formula so well that many of his readers failed to see the subversive manipulation that Yerby undertook to dismantle the false narrative of the South as a pristine, chivalric, and genteel region of the country, ravaged by the Civil War and Reconstruction.

Most notably, Jackson compares Yerby's bestseller to a series of "scenes which you would have seen done over and over so much in movies that they have become stock shots" (650). This observation points to the cultural milieu within which Yerby wrote *The Foxes of Harrow*, almost a decade after the debut of Margaret Mitchell's novel and seven years after the cultural phenomenon of David O. Selznick's *Gone with the Wind* film adaptation in 1939. Commenting on Mitchell's Pulitzer Prize-winning novel in 1937, George Schuyler proclaimed, "It is just another Rebel propaganda tract to the colored citizen who knows our national history and knows the South" (205). When the NAACP heard about the plans to adapt *Gone with the Wind* for the big screen, they paid close attention to the film's production and the NAACP's Walter White contacted Selznick expressing concerns and even suggesting that the film hire an African American in an advisory capacity (Woodley 134). The NAACP recognized the ways that the medium of film could affect audiences by presenting real-life representations on screen that did not require the audience to imagine the scene based solely from the words on the page. Writing to Selznick in 1938, White informed the producer that the "motion picture, appealing as it does to both the visual and the auditory senses, reaches so many Americans, particularly of the middle classes, that infinite harm could be done in a critical period like this one when racial hatred and prejudices are so alive" (qtd. in Woodley 133). The ways that cinema can affect an audience's perceptions and thoughts is understandable. What sticks out in White's letter is his comment about the way the film may affect "the middle classes." Yerby, in his writing, goes after this same audience, and his approach should be seen as a rebuttal to the formulaic and stereotypical *Gone with the Wind*.

When he read the book, Darryl Zanuck, studio head at 20th Century Fox, "saw [*Foxes*] for its black angle embedded in conventional plantation legend stuff" (Cripps 209). Noticing Yerby's reworking of the idyllic South, Zanuck brought "race-conscious people" like Tuchock and Stahl on board.

Tuchock wrote *Hallelujah!* (1929), and Stahl directed *Imitation of Life* (1934). This combination, along with the later addition of film arbiter Joseph Breen, created the recipe for the production of "a real black film"; however, those hopes soon faded when "Zanuck began to chip away at its substance" (209). Early in the process, Zanuck centered the theme on Stephen's rise to prominence, a theme that would go over well with an audience in postwar America. This shift removed the undercurrents of "the black story" in Yerby's novel, pushing his black characters, including those with significant roles in the novel—Tante Caleen, Achille, La Belle Sauvage, Inch, Desiree, Aupre— either to the margins or off screen entirely (209).[3] The most notable change involves Little Inch, Achille and La Belle Sauvage's son, who in the novel rebels against the slave system and ultimately ends up in a position of power in post–Civil War New Orleans. In the film, however, Inch remains a child and a servant to the Fox family.

Both the novel and the film appeared at the end of World War II, during a time when soldiers returning to the United States experienced changes regarding "the position of women in American society as it did on the positions of African Americans" (Charles 147). In "How and Why I Write the Costume Novel," Yerby argues that one of the key ingredients of a successful "picaresque protagonist" in a "costume novel" is that it must be a "dominant male," because he

> appeals most of all to American women readers [who] after having had their mothers and grandmothers convert the United States into a matriarchy with their ardent feminism, and reduce the bearded patriarchy that grandfather was into the pink and paunchy Caspar Milquetoast of today, the average American female reader subconsciously enjoys reading about a male who can get up on his hind legs and roar. (147)

John C. Charles argues that with Stephen Fox's plantation, Yerby created a domestic space that appealed to his audience of primarily white, middle-class women because it represented a temporally remote space that had a sense of social stability, unlike post-war America, when the country "was busy putting its house back in order, settling in after years of straitened depression and wartime disruption" (147).

Tuchock's screenplay uses Stephen's family history to highlight some of these tensions of social stability. It differs from Yerby's novel because, rather than making Stephen's lineage ambiguous and thus questioning his ancestry, the film positions Stephen as the descendant of a noble Irish family. The opening scene takes place at the House of Harrow in Ireland in 1795. Even though his mother is a noblewoman, we learn that Stephen is illegitimate, and the family patriarch seeks to maintain his respectability by giving Stephen away to Sean Fox and his wife. Sean tells the Master of Harrow that he will make sure Stephen never knows "of the blood that flows through his veins." Stephen's identity is thereby altered and erased at birth, causing a disruption, one that the baby does not register. However, by having Stephen lose his stable, aristocratic standing, only to regain it by the end of the film, the film plays upon the anxiety, identified by Charles, of white males feeling displaced in the workforce and American society.

Along with the displacement of male centrality, the scene also works, as Phyllis R. Klotman contends, to reinstate the myth of southern aristocracy. Darwin Turner points out that Yerby's chief contribution to American literature comes from his attacks on America and the American South in his writing. Writing in 1968, Turner argues, "Until recent years [the South] has received literary glorification as a region of culture and gentility. The males reputedly were aristocratic, cultured, brave, and honorable. The females were gentle and chaste. Savagely, Yerby has ridiculed these myths" (572–73). Yerby does challenge these myths in *The Foxes of Harrow*, especially through the construction of Stephen's background and through the passionate Cecile Cloutier.[4] Neither of these deconstructions, however, appear in the film. Rather, on screen, Stephen hails from an aristocratic family, a class that, according to Yerby, had "nothing to gain by emigration" so they stayed in Europe (Turner 573). Instead, "the South, [Yerby] has pointed out, was founded by adventurers, outcasts, and failures who migrated to America because they had nothing to lose" (Turner 573). Stephen fits this description because, as a man with an ambiguous background, he comes to New Orleans in search of an opportunity to make a name for himself and become the richest landowner in the region.

The film's opening runs directly counter to the novel not just through Stephen's ancestry but also by beginning with a shot of the opulent House of Harrow. The novel begins by asking the reader to examine the remains of Stephen's Harrow in Louisiana from a present-day perspective. Yerby depicts Harrow as a shell of its former self with walls where "the white paint has peeled off," pathways with weeds, a "mud-filled birdbath and the broken crystal ball on the column of the smokehouse and the kitchen house and the sugar mill and the slave quarters" (vii). As the reader wanders the grounds in the daytime, the decay becomes evident, but Yerby notes that Harrow's splendor reemerges a bit at night because "the moonlight is kinder" (vii). At the most basic level, though, Harrow exists as a repository for "ghosts ... and figments of the imagination" rather than for living beings with connections to reality (viii).

The opening pages call upon the reader to ignore the big house, claiming that we will "resist the impulse to whirl suddenly in [our] tracks and look back at Harrow"; rather, the wanderings take the reader on a tour of "the brick kitchen house" where Tante Caleen would prepare meals for Stephen, his family, and his guests (vii–viii). Importantly, the novel turns its focus onto spaces where enslaved individuals lived and worked to make Harrow a magnificent house and the envy of the Creoles around New Orleans. Caleen is the only character mentioned in the first pages as she works "to bake her master's bread" (viii). Stephen's name does not even appear; instead, he simply becomes the "master." The novel, before Stephen even arrives on the scene, foregrounds those that he enslaves and the effects of that action on his own legacy. Yerby concludes the opening by telling readers, "And you don't look back" as you speed down the river in your boat (viii). This imperative situates his novel as a contradiction to the mythologized South; however, the film reestablishes the image of an aristocratic upper class through its opening at the House of Harrow in Ireland.

Immediately following their respective beginnings, the novel and film both show Stephen disembarking from a riverboat in the middle of the Mississippi River because he was cheating at cards and got caught. Standing on a sandbar, Stephen thinks to himself about his past and his current situation, even questioning whether his life will end there, in the middle of the Mighty Mississippi. Stephen declares that he will give up a life on the river as a gambler and look to the land, a thought that amuses him to no end because, as he says, "A Dublin guttersnipe don't become one of the landed gentry—not even in this mad new land" (4). From the outset of the novel, Yerby positions Stephen not as an aristocrat but as a "Dublin guttersnipe" who has survived through his wits and cunning. Stephen is one of the "adventurers, outcasts, and failures" who ultimately succeeds. He marries into Creole society, builds Harrow on the backs of fifteen hundred enslaved individuals, rises to be the wealthiest landowner in the New Orleans region, and becomes respected among Creoles and Americans alike. Yerby constructs "Creole" in relation to American society, but as Gene Andrew Jarrett notes, "he leaves Creole identity vague enough to invite racial distinction," thus calling into question perceived racial differences among individuals (153).[5]

Telling his Creole friend Andre LeBlanc about his history, Stephen simply says, "I'm a bastard" (51). Rather than looking down on Stephen for having been born out of wedlock, Andre responds by telling the newly arrived adventurer that even Pierre Arceneaux "swears" that nearly every family of substance in the state "descended from a band of female petty thieves and prostitutes who were brought from La Salpêtrière" (51). Stephen then questions Andre's story because he had heard that the women who came over did not have any children. In response, Andre asks, "Who wrote the histories, my friend?" (51). Through Andre's brief description of the origins of the Arceneaux, the LeBlancs, and other wealthy Creole families, Yerby subtly deconstructs the myth that the South has always been "a region of culture and gentility." By tracing the wealthy family's origins backs to "a band of female petty thieves and prostitutes," Yerby upends not only the perception of the South as a whole but also the idea of "gentle and chaste" white, southern womanhood.

None of this upheaval appears in the film. Instead, the film links Stephen's success to his ancestry, and in the process, "reinstate[s] the myth" that the South originated from aristocratic families (Klotman 213). Stahl and Tuchock's adaptation also fails to display the complexities of race in antebellum New Orleans, offering instead a binary construction of black (enslaved) and white (master). One such instance occurs with their treatment of Desiree, Stephen's mulatto mistress. While she does appear on screen, she does not speak until the end of the film, and Patricia Medina, a white actress, portrays her. As Stephanie Brown points out, the novel "overturns this convention in its opening pages, introducing light-skinned blacks as a central feature not only of plantation life but also of social life in sophisticated New Orleans, where they are not slaves but rather free blacks who may be tradesmen . . . or the paid mistresses of well-off white men" (76). Yerby displays the complex social structure of antebellum New Orleans when Andre takes Stephen around the town the morning after he arrives. Walking through the Vieux Carré to catch a glimpse of the Marquis de Lafayette, Andre gives Stephen an education in the rules, customs, and racial stratification of New Orleans, a stratification that does not fall easily into the dichotomy of black and white. After Andre stops to buy some pieces of cake, *estomac mulâtre* (mulatto belly), from a vendor, he gives Stephen four of the cakes and asks, "Our mulattoes have delicious bellies, do they not?" (26). Labeling the "gingercakes" *estomac mulâtre* draws attention to the ways that, as Mark C. Jerng notes, "racially othered bodies are consumed and cannibalized" in the novel (54). While the cakes are a symbolic cannibalization, Stephen, his son Etienne, and Mike Farrell, among others, prey upon the "racially othered bodies" around them—when Stephen buys and sells individuals, when Etienne orders the mulatto Aupre beaten up, when Mike attempts to rape Suzette, when Stephen has an affair with Desiree, and when Etienne rapes Desiree. The film removes most of these scenes from the screen. Etienne dies as a young boy. Aupre never enters the narrative. Mike never encounters Suzette. The absence of these scenes eliminates the horrors of slavery that Yerby places within the novel. Instead of seeing Stephen, Mike, and Etienne "cannibalize" others, we see Stephen as a man struggling to maintain his marriage, Mike as a loyal friend, and Etienne as merely a child, sans the violent, racist tendencies he embodies from an early age in the novel. The film version thus mostly eschews issues of race and the psychological effects of slavery and subjugation.

After eating the *estomac mulâtre*, Stephen espies "a group of young girls, afoot, and dressed in bright colors" who wore "the bright tignons of slaves" and not the bonnets that Creole ladies wore (26). Stephen looks on and proclaims, "They're dressed like blacks" (26). The girls' phenotype disorients Stephen, and Andre explains to him that the girls he sees are "quadroons" and free. While Stephen espouses his repulsion at the idea of sleeping with "a black," Lafayette arrives and the Arceneaux sisters cross Stephen and Andre's path. Stephen sees Odalie and proclaims she will one day be his. After Lafayette's speech, Stephen and Andre walk "through the multicolored throngs, whites and octoroons, quadroons and mulattoes, raged blacks, and sober merchants, and the sombre-gowned priests and nuns moving quietly off like dark strands in the patterns of bright colors" (29). Stephen's first sight of Odalie, situated alongside images of New Orleans as a multicultural city, places her amongst the "multicolored throngs." If, as Odalie's father Pierre Arceneaux claims, his family wealth originated with "petty thieves and prostitutes," then the only thing that separates Odalie from the people around her is the money that her family has amassed. She is no different than Desiree, who amasses her money through the *plaçage* system, even posing nude for Paul Dumaine in order to increase her income. The only difference is that the Arceneaux have built their wealth over generations and seek to maintain that wealth partly through the social construction of race that limits Desiree's options for ascending the social ladder.

The film does portray Andre and Stephen buying *estomac mulâtre* from a "Negro woman" in the market; however, this is all that happens before they walk into the La Bourse de Maspero. In the film, Stephen does not see the "quadroons" walking by, and he does not see Odalie. Instead of seeing her in the market, Stephen sees her at the beginning of the movie as the riverboat captain expels Stephen from the vessel. He sees her again while dining at Andre's. By removing Odalie from the market amidst the "multicolored throngs," she becomes set off and separate because of her color and her class, thus muting the racial complexities of antebellum New Orleans and maintaining a binary view of race while ignoring the social constructions that allowed Odalie's ancestors to rise within New Orleans society to their current stature.

Even though the film alters this aspect of the narrative, it draws attention to the ways in which postwar America was coming to terms with women in the workforce. At the party where Stephen displays Harrow to those around him, he and Odalie step outside. Trying to figure out why she fights his romantic advances, Stephen asks, "Why do you resist me so, Lily?" Unsure, Odalie answers, "Perhaps it's the great violence I find in you. The way you look at me, as if I'm a slave, as if you own me." Odalie's response mirrors the way she responds to Stephen in the novel as well. When Stephen tells Odalie about the sleepless nights he has endured because of her, she tells him she is glad because she initially thought she meant just as much to him as a horse. Continuing, she tells him, "I was unaccustomed to being looked at appraisingly like a slave girl" (115). Both the film and novel draw connections between Odalie and the enslaved individuals at Harrow, even though they do not play as significant a role in the film as they do in the novel. The film highlights the construction of these linkages through the framing and positioning of characters on screen, most notably with Odalie and Little Inch.

With La Belle Sauvage, both the film and the novel counter the mythological image of southern white womanhood that Odalie represents. Stephen purchases La Belle Sauvage specifically to be a wife for Achille. In both versions, the union between La Belle Sauvage and Achille coincides with the marriage between Stephen and Odalie. This pairing, especially in the film, subtly underscores differences between the two unions. La Belle Sauvage, in the novel, refuses Achille's initial advances because, as she says, he is not a man; instead, she refers to him as a "Slave Nigra!" (127) Achille points out that she is enslaved as well, but Sauvage denies that label because she is "still princess," and if anyone ever enslaves her, she will commit suicide (127). Sauvage's challenging of the slave system causes Achille to feel inferior, and as a result he "sweep[s] her up light as a leaf into his arms" as she kicks and screams (128). He carries her into the cabin and kicks the door shut. While Achille "lightly" takes Sauvage into his arms, he forces her to have sex with him, thus ultimately raping her.

The film shows a different image of how Achille and Sauvage begin their relationship and juxtaposes it with Stephen and Odalie's wedding. On the night of Stephen and Odalie's nuptials, Mike Farrell and his crew arrive at Harrow to celebrate the event. Stephen goes into the cellar and drinks with the men, causing Odalie to lie awake in bed hoping that they will soon leave, while in the novel she does not want Stephen to touch her. When Stephen finally comes up to join her, he finds the doors to their bedroom locked, is infuriated, and breaks the door down, essentially severing any semblance of union between the newly married couple. The scene ends with Stephen walking through the broken door as ominous music swells. Presumably, Stephen takes Odalie, as Achille does Sauvage in the novel, by force, raping her. The next morning Stephen tries to apologize by giving Odalie a necklace; she accepts it and tells him, "I suppose this sets everything right? I'll wear your jewels; I'll reside at your table." Through the gift, Stephen acts as if he can purchase Odalie's affection in the same manner that he purchases and sells enslaved individuals such as Achille and Sauvage. In the novel, Stephen does not drink with Mike on his wedding night, and he does not break down the door; he does, though, take Odalie by force because she does not want him to touch her.

On screen, as Stephen returns to Harrow one night after a night of drinking and gambling in New Orleans, he comes upon those he has enslaved dancing around a fire in a voodoo ritual. The scene shows Tante Caleen presiding over the festivities and Achille and Sauvage dancing together. As they dance, Achille takes Sauvage up in his arms and runs off. Instead of having Sauvage push back against the slavocracy, the scene comes off as a sort of wedding ceremony for the couple. Achille does not violently force himself upon Sauvage as he does in the novel. Rather, Achille acts in almost direct opposition to Stephen. He does take Sauvage up in his arms, but the framing makes it appear as if the act is consensual, not predatory. With this contrast, Stephen becomes the predatory, hypersexualized character who does not maintain the chivalric codes of the South, while Achille comes across as loving partner to Sauvage instead of as the stereotypical brute Negro.

The novel and the film also connect the births of Etienne, the son of Stephen and Odalie, and Little Inch, the son of Achille and Sauvage, born at the same time. Tante Caleen and Doctor Terrebonne assist Odalie, but Sauvage births Little Inch on her own. This difference positions Sauvage as a stronger woman, both physically and mentally. When Stephen enters Achille and Sauvage's cabin, he takes a look at the baby and states, "I want him trained as a manservant for my Etienne" (156). At Stephen's pronouncement, Sauvage sits up in bed, proclaiming, "My child no slave! . . . Him prince—warrior prince! Him killer of lions and master of men! Him nobody servant, nobody slave!" (156). Achille tries to calm his wife, but she refuses. Sauvage takes up Little Inch and runs out of the cabin towards the levee overlooking the Mississippi River. Achille and Stephen reach her, taking the baby from her arms. At that, Sauvage jumps into the river and kills herself, making good on the promise she espoused earlier. Even though her body lived in bondage; her mind did not. Holding the baby, Caleen names him Little Inch after her husband and Achille's father who died in a slave revolt, and she muses to herself, "His body will they enslave, yes, but never his mind and his heart" (157).

The film maintains the gravitas of this scene, but it alters it in a couple of significant ways. For one, Pierre—not Caleen—goes with Stephen to see the baby. Caleen's absence means the absence of her prophetic pronouncement that Little Inch may be enslaved in body but never in mind. While we do not hear this line, we do receive something similar. Achille dives into the water after Sauvage, and when he climbs back up on the levee, he takes Little Inch in his arms. Holding his baby, Achille kneels and cries, "She free, her. Yes, she free now." Here, Achille points out the psychological effects of a system of bondage on the minds of enslaved individuals. In the novel and in the film, he does not challenge the system; in fact, Stephen notices "no trace of rebelliousness in Achille" (110). Caleen even tells Little Inch that she hopes he will become "never such a one like Achille, but a man" (157). Achille comes across as a submissive servant willing to do anything to make Stephen happy. He does not push back at any point, yet as he holds Little Inch in his arms and laments Sauvage's suicide, he expresses the problem inherent within the slave system and upends the "moonlight and magnolia" image of the ideal South. Achille points out that he, Sauvage, Little Inch, Caleen, and the other enslaved individuals do not maintain a free and happy existence. Instead, they exist as Stephen's property.

In the novel, Stephen does broach the topic of Achille as property. Immediately after Sauvage jumps into the river, Stephen tells him, "Trouble yourself not about her. . . . She was never the one for ye. I will get you another—gentle and comely, better for ye and the baby" (157). Achille does not answer Stephen's flippant response; he walks away crying. Stephen's comment positions Sauvage not as a human but as a commodity that he purchased to breed with Achille and to work the fields, and we need to consider Stephen's remark in relation to Odalie's comments about Stephen treating her as property as well. Achille's reaction undercuts this positioning by highlighting the emotional intimacy and bond that he and Sauvage created. He leaves heartbroken, and he only appears sporadically throughout the rest of the novel, without any dialogue. Achille goes into mourning, and Stephen sees him "hunched over on his mule, his face half covered by the big straw hat," looking at the empty levee while Stephen thinks about the future "unborn ghosts" and the past occupants of Harrow who rest in the ground (207). Odalie's sister Aurora asks what ails Achille and Stephen responds, "[H]e is dying of heartbreak" (204). Juxtaposed with Odalie and Stephen's frigid relationship, Achille's character, both in the film and the novel, presents an image of complexity and interiority that counters stereotypical images of African Americans by showing his heartbreak and depression.

In the film, Caleen brings Etienne into Odalie's bedroom following Sauvage's suicide. Caleen walks to the bed smiling—the image of a happy, submissive servant—hands Etienne to his mother, and Odalie fawns over her newborn son. The camera focuses on Odalie as she kisses Etienne and proclaims, "His little hands are perfect." The camera then changes perspective to show that Caleen's countenance transforms to one of sadness as she leaves the room. Within this brief shot, the psychological weight of the disparities between Etienne and Little Inch, between Odalie and Sauvage, and between Stephen and Achille manifest themselves in Caleen's face. When she leaves, Odalie asks the doctor and Stephen, "Is anything wrong?" Rather than acknowledging Sauvage's suicide, the doctor simply tells Odalie that Etienne has a slight turning in of the right foot, and Stephen walks over to Odalie, telling her that they will make him perfect. While Odalie recognizes the sadness in Caleen, the men fail to even register Caleen as present. To them she exists only in the background, and their response leaves Caleen's brief two-second expression hanging in the air. It would be easy to miss Odalie and Caleen's exchange, considering the drama that surrounds it. This subtle moment, however, links Odalie to those she enslaves, mirroring white women activists such as Angelina and Sarah Grimké, Lydia Maria Child, Margaret Fuller, and others who associated their fight for equality with the emancipation of enslaved individuals and to their opposition to Native American Removal during the abolitionist period. During a sequence in which Stephen teaches Etienne fencing, cards, and horseback riding, Odalie stands at a distance, sometimes on the gallery, sometimes at a window, looking on with trepidation. In one scene, Odalie and Little Inch look out a window while waiting for Etienne and Stephen to return from a horseback ride. Rain cascades outside the window as they see Etienne and Stephen approaching Harrow, jumping a hedge in the process. The initial outside shot shows Odalie and Little Inch looking out of the window and toward the riders. The framing within the window causes us to associate Odalie and Little Inch; they stand together within a confined space looking outwards. We understand that both are limited: Odalie because of her gender and Little Inch because of his enslavement.

At the end of the film and after Etienne dies from injuries he sustains from falling down the stairs, the correlations between Little Inch and Odalie crumble. The scene takes place in Etienne's bedroom, from which Odalie hears crying. Hoping it is Etienne, she walks over to the window seat and finds Little Inch. Little Inch expresses his sorrow at the death of Etienne, and Odalie begins to talk about her memories of her son. She concludes by looking at Little Inch, placing her hand on his face, and saying, "From now on, Little Inch, I want you to attend to me personally ... the way Etienne used to do." Odalie does not present this request in the manner of a master ordering an enslaved individual to perform a task; rather, she gives Little Inch a choice to help her "be less lonely." Little Inch responds, "Yes maitrese." Odalie seeks a replacement for Etienne, and Little Inch provides that psychological comfort. While this aspect is obvious, the film does not address the underlying, unstated dimensions of Odalie's request. Would a contemporary audience think about Little Inch as property or as an individual who can choose whether or not to attend to Odalie? The dialogue pushes the issue of slavery and subjugation to the background, foregrounding the mourning process of Odalie and Little Inch. Altering Yerby's novel, the film's depiction of Little Inch's sorrow over Etienne's death subsumes the racist education that Etienne learns and exhibits in the novel towards Little Inch and others. The film shows no indication of Etienne's cruelty. Instead of seeing Etienne attack Little Inch during a game of cards, the film shows Pierre teaching his grandson to play *vingt et un*. Instead of seeing Etienne whip his pony during his birthday party as he would an enslaved man or woman, the film shows the family, Little Inch standing and Etienne in Stephen's lap, watching fireworks. On screen, Little Inch sleeps at the edge of Etienne's bed, awakening at the slightest sound of fear in his master's voice. Slavery's harshness and brutality, which Etienne embodies in the novel, becomes supplanted by an image of Little Inch as a filial servant who mourns the loss of his young, innocent master.

The final image of Little Inch on screen occurs when he brings Odalie a glass of water before she leaves Harrow, stripped of its opulence due to the panic of 1837, to confront Stephen at Desiree's house on Rampart Street. In the novel, Little Inch grows up, learns to read (even though Stephen provides the books), and runs away from Harrow to the North, only to be returned as a result of the Fugitive Slave Law. Upon his escape, Inch leaves a letter for

Etienne, and in it, he describes the dehumanizing effects of slavery on himself, his mother, and others: "I don't want to be treated kindly like a valuable animal: I want to be treated like a man" (308). Inch continues by stating his humanity through his God-given "Freedom of Will," even pointing out that Etienne, who has "wealth and power," is only "a mere man." He concludes by invoking the memory of his mother "who died rather than submit to servitude" and his grandmother Caleen, who longed for freedom her entire life (309). Inch's letter gets erased in the film when he does not grow up and challenge the institution that keeps him in subjugation. Through the elimination of such plot points, the film adaptation maintains the stereotypes and images that Yerby sought to subvert with the novel.

On screen, Etienne serves as a means of reconciliation between Odalie and Stephen. As the couple argue, Etienne overhears them and falls down the stairs, eventually dying from his injuries. Etienne's death corresponds with the panic of 1837. Etienne's death, coupled with the panic, causes Odalie to sell off everything at Harrow in order to survive, while Stephen stays with his mistress Desiree in the Vieux Carré. The film culminates in Odalie's return to Harrow in an impending storm, quite possibly a hurricane. She encounters Achille and asks him about the drums she hears, and Achille tells her that the people are saying that Stephen is ruined, so they will not work. Odalie attempts to assert control and avoid financial ruin by forcing the enslaved workers to cut the cane, but she does not succeed. Despondent, Odalie walks towards the house, and as she reaches the door, she turns around to see Stephen arrive and take control, ordering the cane to be cut and the house to be looked after.

This scene initially places Odalie as the master of the house, mirroring in some ways the role of women in the workforce during World War II that Charles mentions in relation to the novel. However, the workers only obey Stephen. This initial positioning and then removal of that position work to create an image of stability after the war and the Great Depression by representing social relations as they were before the war. The film placates the men returning from the war, who perceived that their societal position was threatened by the women and African Americans who entered the workforce in large numbers during the war.

More importantly, the culminating scene in the cane field completely eliminates the ultimate agency of Achille, Caleen, and the other enslaved individuals. While they do refuse to obey Odalie, they obey and work for Stephen. This is not the key point, though. The key is that the film places the hurricane at the end, as a disaster that can destroy an already successful

Harrow. In the novel, the hurricane occurs during Harrow's infancy, as Stephen tries to build up the land and his wealth so that he can marry Odalie. Here, Caleen warns Stephen of an impending storm. The exchange between them becomes important. Caleen approaches Stephen and tells him that he should not be riding through the brush because he could injure himself. Stephen then snaps at her, commenting, "Ye're a bossy old devil, Caleen. I sometimes wonder if I own ye, or ye own me" (81). Caleen calmly responds, "We own each other" (81). Caleen equates herself to Stephen. According to Caleen, there is a mutual relationship, both individuals owning one another. Legally, Caleen is Stephen's physical property, but Caleen owns Stephen because she, essentially, leads to the success of Harrow.

Caleen's premonitions about the hurricane lead Stephen to make arrangements, harvesting the sugarcane early in preparation for the impending storm. Because of these actions, Stephen's crop is the only one that ultimately survives the devastation: "Many planters were completely ruined. But when Stephen Fox walked out of the offices of the factors of New Orleans his eyes were dancing in a face deliberately kept grave and still" (82). Stephen sold his crop for close to one hundred thousand dollars. Caleen's prediction allowed Stephen to cut the cane early and sell it for a profit while other planters suffered. This aspect gets lost in the film because the individuals that Stephen enslaves do cut the cane, but they only do so after Stephen commands them to do so and without any premonition from Caleen.

Yerby, from the outset of the novel, draws attention to the role that enslaved blacks played in constructing and sustaining Harrow, a representation of the genteel, idyllic Old South. Stephen works in the fields alongside those he owns to build Harrow, and when Caleen dies during a yellow fever epidemic in 1853, he states, "She will lie in state at Harrow—not in the slave cabin. God knows 'twas much her home as mine. She did as much and more to make it what it was" (277). The film presents the rise of Harrow occurring through Stephen's luck and work; however, the novel presents a different image. While the film does show moments of "the Negro's deep resentment against slavery," it does not portray the work of the enslaved in the building of Harrow. Rather, it focuses on Stephen and Odalie's tumultuous marriage and their apparent reconciliation at the end. The film could have done more; it could have served as a touchstone at the beginning of a cinematic period that strove to move away from mythological representations of the South and toward greater realism. At points, the movie attempts this greater meaning; however, by maintaining the "fattiest of romantic clichés" and trimming the meat of Yerby's text, the film maintains the mythological more than it presents the realistic.

NOTES

1. Yerby began his career by writing protest fiction in the form of short stories and poems. His story "Health Card" (1944) won the O. Henry Memorial Award for the best short story that year. However, he was unable to get a publisher to take his protest novel. Publishers' lack of interest led him to shift focus to the "costume novel" and eventually led to the publication of *The Foxes of Harrow*.

2. Along with *Gone with the Wind*, we must also consider Yerby's novel in relation to William Faulkner's *Absalom, Absalom!* (1936). Gene Andrew Jarrett writes about this connection in *Deans and Truants: Race and Realism in African American Literature* (2007).

3. Throughout, I switch between Little Inch and Inch when referring to Le Belle Sauvage and Achille's son because Yerby does this in the novel. When Inch grows up and runs away, Yerby refers to him as "Inch" from that point forward.

4. Cecile Cloutier does not appear in the film version because the movie focuses only on the first generation. In the novel she marries Etienne Fox.

5. Throughout, *Creole* refers to individuals of French or Spanish descent in Louisiana. Over time, the definition came to include any mixed-race individual of French, Spanish, Native American, or African descent. Jarrett discusses the fluidity of *Creole* in Yerby's novel, even noting the darkness of Andre's and Etienne's skin.

BIBLIOGRAPHY

Bone, Robert. *The Negro Novel in America*. Yale UP, 1958.

Brown, Stephanie. *The Postwar African American Novel: Protest and Discontent, 1945–1950*. UP of Mississippi, 2011.

Campbell, Edward D. C. Jr. *The Celluoid South: Hollywood and the Southern Myth*. U of Tennessee P, 1981.

Charles, John C. *Abandoning the Black Hero: Sympathy and Privacy in the Postwar African American White-Life Novel*. Rutgers UP, 2013.

Cripps, Thomas. *Making Movies Black: The Hollywood Message Movie from World War II to the Civil Rights Era*. Oxford UP, 1993.

Crowther, Bosley. "'Foxes of Harrow,' Fox Film, Starring Rex Harrison and Maureen O'Hara, Bill at Roxy—'Desert Fury' at Paramount." *New York Times*, 25 Sept. 1947, p. 35.

The Foxes of Harrow. Directed by John Stahl, screenplay by Wanda Tuchock, performances by Rex Harrison and Maureen O'Hara, 20th Century Fox, 1947.

Hill, James L. "Frank Garvin Yerby." *Writers of the Black Chicago Renaissance*, edited by Steven C. Tracy. U of Illinois P, 2011, pp. 386–412.

Jackson, Blyden. "Silver Foxes." *The Journal of Negro Education*, vol. 15, no. 4, Autumn 1946, pp. 649–52.

Jarrett, Gene Andrew. *Deans and Truants: Race and Realism in African American Literature*. U of Pennsylvania P, 2007.

Jerng, Mark A. "Reconstruction of Racial Perception: Margaret Mitchell's and Frank Yerby's Plantation Romances." *New Approaches to Gone with the Wind*, edited by James A. Crank, Louisiana State UP, 2015, pp. 38–65.

Klotman, Phyllis R. "A Harrowing Experience: Frank Yerby's First Novel to Film." *CLA Journal*, vol. 31, no. 2, December 1987, pp. 210–22.

Lipack, Barbara Tepa. *Literary Adaptations in Black American Cinema: From Micheaux to Morrison*. U of Rochester P, 2002.

Match, Richard. "The Vulpine Master of Harrow." *New York Times*, 10 Feb. 1946, p. 118.

Schuyler, George. "Not Gone with the Wind." *Crisis*, vol. 44, no. 7, July 1937, pp. 205–6.

Turner, Darwin T. "Frank Yerby as Debunker." *Massachusetts Review*, vol. 9, no. 3, 1968, pp. 569–77.

Woodley, Jenny. *Art for Equality: The NAACP's Cultural Campaign for Civil Rights*. UP of Kentucky, 2014.

Yerby, Frank. *The Foxes of Harrow*. Dial Press, 1946.

Yerby, Frank. "How and Why I Write the Costume Novel." *Harper's* October 1959, pp. 145–50.

PIRATES OF THE CARIBBEAN IN FRANK YERBY'S THE GOLDEN HAWK

JOHN WHARTON LOWE

FRANK YERBY (1916–1991) IS STILL THE BEST-SELLING AFRICAN AMERICAN writer in literary history—over sixty million copies of his thirty-three novels have been purchased in over twenty countries. Today, however, his once wildly popular works have largely been forgotten, and even those who continue to read them usually don't know he was a black man. Yerby's first stories did center on racial issues; indeed, his early tale "Health Card" (1944) about the prejudice a black soldier and his wife experience, won the O. Henry Short Story Award. He had little luck, however, placing his novel manuscript, "This Is My Own," about racial uplift, so he shifted to historical novels. The sensational success of his first, *The Foxes of Harrow* (1946), set him on a populist path. Only late in his career would he return to black protagonists, in *Speak Now* (1969), and, most memorably, *The Dahomean* (1971), and *A Darkness at Ingraham's Crest* (1979).

Yerby instinctively understood the appeal of exotic settings, and he clearly felt the Louisiana plantation setting for *The Foxes of Harrow*—which takes place before, during, and after the Civil War—would have the same magnetic appeal Margaret Mitchell, Stark Young, and many other southern writers had instilled in their plantation tales, especially Mitchell's *Gone With the Wind*. This genre had even more power after the success of the movie of *Gone With the Wind* after its premiere in 1939. *Foxes* features a riverboat gambler turned Louisiana planter and the black and white women who love him. The novel was adapted into a 1947 Hollywood movie starring Rex Harrison and Maureen O'Hara, and had many affinities, no doubt intentional, with both Mitchell's melodrama and Faulkner's *Absalom, Absalom!* (both published in 1936). *Foxes* also concerned Stephen Fox's black slaves, many of them imported from Haiti, and there are multiple references to the Caribbean cultures that helped form Louisiana's.

Flush with the success of his first novel, Yerby churned out a sequel, *The Vixens*, the following year. According to him, the original draft was a superb novel, but his editors forced him to drastically simplify and, in the end, diminish it. Although it enjoyed robust sales, it lacked the sharp detail and complex plot of its predecessor and cannot be counted as one of Yerby's better works. Perhaps sensing that he needed a fresh start, and continuing to enjoy the income from his first two books, Yerby and his first wife Flora embarked on a Caribbean cruise, which was intended to provide research material for his next narrative, a pirate novel tentatively titled *The Seaflower's Spawn*. In an interview with Muriel Fuller, he excitedly described his research on the age of Henry Morgan, L'Onais, Bartholomew Portuguese, Brazil Davio, and Laurens De Graff. As he told Fuller "with gusto,"

> Those boys made the exploits of Edward Teach [Blackbeard] and Captain Kidd, who came along in the next century, look like a pink tea party. My hero is Kit Gerado, a Spaniard of unknown ancestry, who takes to sea in his ship, the Seaflower, to seek revenge for his mother's death at the hands of the Inquisition. There are two major girls in the book, one English, the other Spanish. One of them is a woman pirate, in the tradition of those women pirates who came along a little later. (qtd. in Fuller, n. p.)

The Golden Hawk, ostensibly a lurid pirate tale, offers a fascinating early example of the transnational novel. Its rapidly shifting narrative cuts across artificial geographical borders, which in the late seventeenth century were fluctuating regularly with every new battle and conquest. This essay will therefore position Yerby as a writer well ahead of his time, who used racial masquerade to become rich, but also to provide strategic insights into colonial history, racial oppression, and class and gender relations.

Why was Yerby drawn to the Caribbean and this point—1697—in its history? He had certainly absorbed much pirate lore during his forays into New Orleans, where Pirates Alley was only one remnant of the city's extensive record of dealings with freebooters, smugglers, and (during Prohibition), rum runners from the islands. The legends of the pirate Jean Lafitte and his days in New Orleans were replete with fanciful addendums and romantic elements. It is likely that Yerby also became excited about a pirate novel once he began his extensive research and learned that 1697 was a turbulent year, when France, England, and Spain were engaged in fierce combat over New World possessions, native peoples, African slaves, and the slave trade. It was a time of shifting alliances, when the Spanish empire was declining, leading to new incursions by France and England. Moreover, there were natural disasters during the period, such as the earthquake that destroyed Port Royal, Jamaica, on June 7, 1692, which Yerby features in his pirate tale.[1] As Mark G. Hanna has demonstrated, piracy had expanded dramatically in the 1680s, and 1696 "marked the culmination of a number of significant movements, involving trade, warfare, colonial administration, economic policies, and information exchange, that all had an impact on the colonial support of illicit sea marauding" (223). A translation of Alexander Esquemeling's *Bucaniers* [sic] *of America, or a True Account of the Most Remarkable Assaults Committed of Late Years Upon the Coasts of the West Indies by the Bucaniers of Jamaica and Tortuga*, was published in both English and French in 1684; it dramatized the author's twelve years as a pirate, some of them served under the notorious Henry Morgan, and demonstrated the ways in which privateers contributed to the Empire. The British government encouraged privateering, partly because these ships were seen as a line of defense against competing colonial powers.

Yerby had heard exciting stories about the Caribbean from his supervisor on the Chicago Federal Writers Project, Katherine Dunham, whose pioneering research in the Caribbean Basin would lead to several important books and to her crucial contributions to choreography. He had also benefitted from working with the important writer Nelson Algren, whose penchant for the picaresque novel (such as *Somebody in Boots*, 1935) likely influenced Yerby's use of that mode in *The Golden Hawk*, a novel featuring constant motion, as Kit Gerado and his crew crisscross seas and islands. The hectic movements of the Caribbean's pirates in the seventeenth century met one of Yerby's qualifications for what he called the "costume novel":

> The protagonist must be picaresque. In other words, he must be a charming scoundrel, preferably with a dark secret in his past. His anti-social tendencies must be motivated by specific reasons—an unfortunate childhood, injustices heaped upon himself or upon his loved ones, physical and moral sufferings which incline the reader to sympathize with his delinquency . . . he must be a dominant male. I think this quality appeals most of all to American women readers [who enjoy] reading about a male who can get up on his hind legs and roar. ("How and Why" 146–47)

The novel also included several scenes on Caribbean plantations. Yerby knew such places in the US South firsthand and noted the similarities between slave-driven crop production in Louisiana and in the islands. During the years he taught at Tallahassee's Florida A&M and Southern University in Baton Rouge, he studied and researched plantation histories, diasporan cultures, and slave narratives, and it was only logical that his focus would eventually expand into the Caribbean. Although his historical novels were dominated by white characters, almost all of these works featured African, African descended, and/or ethnic characters, whose stories form an important backdrop to the central narratives. Weaving history and costumed drama tightly, Yerby came to understand the deep, persistent, and pervasive interplay between the US South and the Caribbean. Indeed, *The Foxes of Harrow* and *The Vixens* incorporated many elements and characters from the inland sea, including Haitian voodoo. Setting *The Golden Hawk* in the 1690s also enabled him to employ some of the most dramatic events of Circum-Caribbean history; Marcus Rediker has identified the years from 1650 to 1730 as the "golden age of piracy" (8), a subset of history full of potential for literary mining.

The Golden Hawk begins when Kit Gerado and his faithful companion, Bernardo, take over and command a pirate ship after the death of the British captain, a leper, whose abandonment by the horrified crew sets up the major theme of the outcast, a role that extends to all the piratical figures. All pirates lead nomadic lives and cross cultural and societal lines repeatedly. Here, Kit and Bernardo do so with even more aplomb, and for good reason; while both speak English, they are actually Spanish (Kit is from Cadiz), although the latter's mother, whose death was caused by Kit's father, was French. Thus Kit is also Christophe Giradaux and Cristóbal Gerado, and can easily code-switch between his linguistic and cultural heritages. He is bent on avenging his mother's death by killing the Spanish grandee, Don Luis Del Toro, unaware that the grandee is his father.

Early in the narrative, Kit's ship, *The Seaflower*, encounters a Spanish man o' war, *The Garza*. On its deck, a lovely redhead is fighting the man who has raped her (Del Toro), and who has just caused the suicide of her sister. We learn this woman (who is actually a British noblewoman, Lady Jane Golphin) is a female pirate who goes by the name of Rouge. Rescued by Kit, she resists his advances and in fact wounds him before escaping. Subsequently, *The Seaflower* plunders a Spanish ship, which is bearing Del Toro's fiancée Bianca to the New World. Kit takes her as hostage and demands a ransom from Del Toro. The long wait in Haiti's vermin-infested Cul-de-Sac results in Bianca falling in love with Kit, who is tempted, but remains true to Rouge, setting up dual heroines—one bright, one dark—in the method favored by Scott in novels such as *Ivanhoe*. Rouge founds a plantation in Jamaica; meanwhile, Kit has become the protégé of the governor of Saint-Domingue, Jean-Baptiste Ducasse, who presents him with a plantation, and then asks that he join him in a raid on—you guessed it—Jamaica. There Kit witnesses Rouge's former fiancé, Reginald Marsh, brutally beating his slaves, causing one to lose his arm in a sugar cane extractor. Moving on to another plantation (which turns out to be Rouge's), Kit's crew burns the house and crops, causing another rupture with Rouge, who flees back to her pirate life. Many scenes in the book that document the abuses of slavery were likely drawn by Yerby from C. L. R. James's magnificent *The Black Jacobins* (1938), which documented the horrors both before, during, and after the Haitian Revolution (1791–1804).[2]

In the other strand of the plot, Del Toro and Bianca take the difficult land journey across the isthmus of Panama in order to sail to Lima, where his nephew Ricardo is receiving his degree. Enamored of Bianca, Ricardo makes Del Toro think Kit is nearby, freeing Bianca to attend a highly erotic ritual dance in a filthy tavern. There she encounters Caviedes, who actually was Peru's greatest poet at that time. Del Toro, infuriated, enters, accuses Bianca of infidelity, and then murders his nephew, just before Bianca informs him she is pregnant and that she knows Kit is his son. She and Del Toro are reconciled, however, after she nurses him back to health after his fight with Ricardo, and he stands by her sickbed as she recovers from plague but loses their baby.

Kit, determined to kill Del Toro, comes to Cartagena, a city whose "mighty walls had stopped Drake and Morgan and that had caused every other freebooter in the Caribbean to take a second thought before attempting the richest prize of them all" (225–26), another example of Yerby's accurate citation of the basin's history.[3] *The Seaflower* is captured and destroyed, and the surviving crew are cruelly tortured before Kit's eyes; he is captured and sentenced with Bernardo to six years hard labor building the fortress of San Lázaro. Yerby devotes long passages to its construction by slave labor, detailing the cruelty of the Spanish overseers, who eventually cause the death of the Chibcha Indians, replacing them with black slaves, facts drawn from actual history. After two years of hard labor, Kit and Bernardo escape and join the French in Saint-Domingue, who are preparing an invasion of Cartagena. Kit is reunited with Rouge but prevented from marrying her as he promised Bianca (when he thought Rouge was dead) that he would never marry another.

The novel concludes with a fictional replay of an actual event, the 1697 French storming of Cartagena. Yerby had obviously read the history of that event carefully,[4] and populates his version of it with the actual leader of the assault, De Pontis, who fights alongside Kit. The city falls, and Kit rushes to Del Toro's palace for a duel with his father that is interrupted, first by Rouge, and then Bianca, who meet for the first time. Bianca, deciding to die, ascends the stairs to the flaming upper floor, and is followed by Del Toro. Kit retrieves Bianca and rushes back to try to free Del Toro from the beam that has crushed him, to no avail. "'My son,' Don Luis whispered, 'my son, go with God!'" (344), uttering the words that the Haitian Charles Bon longs to hear but never does from his father Thomas Sutpen in Faulkner's similarly constructed *Absalom, Absalom!* (which also ends with the burning of the ancestral home). As Bianca enters a convent, Kit takes Rouge in his arms. Finis!

Although historical accuracy isn't Yerby's chief aim, he did careful research and built his main plot around actual events. His governor of Saint-Domingue, for instance, is based on the very real Sieur Ducasse, who did sack Cartagena. In 1697 French military figures in Saint-Domingue posted an invitation on the door of the church in Petit-Goave, inviting filibustiers, boucaniers, and all other residents of the coast of Saint-Domingue—including blacks—to join in an attack on the Spanish citadel. The brutal siege and pillage of that fortress enabled many of the attackers from Saint-Domingue to create large estates upon their return to Hispaniola. Further, the Spanish defeat led to Spain ceding rights for the western part of Saint-Domingue to France in the 1797 Treaty of Rhyswick. A cross taken from Cartagena was placed in the church of Petit-Goave and attracted hundreds of devotees (Dubois 17–18). Yerby adds to this history in his consideration of the natives of the islands, enslaved Africans, and the harsh conditions suffered by both groups on the lucrative plantations. Significantly, Yerby portrays the key role black troops played in the French assault, yet another element in his undergirding of his romantic adventure tale with racial truths.

These elements, however, though significant, are secondary to the creation of pleasure for the reader. Yerby, who by this time was determined to support himself and his growing family by his writing, was keenly conscious of the popularity of pirates in American popular culture and film; he saw commercial gold in the subject of pirates, and particularly relished the concept of Rouge commanding under the Jolly Roger. In any case, by attracting the ordinary reader's attention through the incredibly popular genre of the pirate tale (there were over thirty-eight pirate movies churned out by Hollywood during the forties and fifties,[5] featuring major stars, and including dramas, comedies, musicals, and cartoons), he had a surefire subject. Pirates had fascinated the general public for centuries. As

Rediker puts it, "They captured the good ship Popular Imagination and three hundred years later they show no sign of surrendering it" (175).[6] As the map that Yerby had placed just within the covers of the book reveals, Cartagena and Saint-Domingue are the twin poles of the narrative. If one draws lines tracing the trajectories of the book's myriad voyages—which include slavers from Africa—we would have a map of the black Atlantic. The fact that Yerby makes Haiti the center of all these routes places him in conversation with other great African American writers of his time, such as Zora Neale Hurston, Katherine Dunham, James Weldon Johnson, and Arna Bontemps, who all wrote about the island, as did their fellow white Southerner, William Faulkner. Yerby's interest, however, unlike theirs, was in the Haiti of the buccaneering era, when France was just beginning its century-long domination of the island, a period that stretched from 1697 to the outbreak of the Haitian Revolution in 1791.[7] Perhaps he saw this earlier period as an essential backdrop for understanding the subsequent history of the Haitian Revolution, which he rightly saw as one of the triumphant moments in Caribbean and racial history. Undoubtedly, however, Yerby also seized an opportunity to dramatize in some detail part of the major, criollo cultural history of the time through the "costume drama." Yerby shrewdly placed his narrative at the crossroads of the adventure novel (traditionally aimed at a male audience) and the romance (a genre calculated to attract women readers). What better place to situate such a blending than the Caribbean, which had re-emerged after World War II as a magnetic tourist Mecca, but had always resounded within the South as an exotic realm with a fabled history of vanished Native Americans, plantations, smuggling, political turmoil, and piracy? Then too, the Native and African religious traditions were foreign, mysterious, and intriguing to his mostly white readers, and he took full advantage of it in all of his Caribbean works.

Let me first consider the adventure novel, a genre that had always included tales of piracy. Martin Green has identified seven types of this form: 1) the Robinson Crusoe story; 2) the Three Musketeers Story; 3) the Frontiersman story; 4) the Avenger story; 5) the wanderer story; 6) the Sagaman story; and 7) the Hunted Man story. *The Golden Hawk* contains elements of most of these types, but is pre-eminently a revenge narrative, and an Oedipal one as well, as Kit seeks the death of the man he does not know is his father. Further, as an outlaw of the seas, Kit and his movements are those of a hunted man and his crew. In light of the ending of the novel, where we find Kit planning a plantation, we would be justified in claiming the tale, ultimately, as an example of the Robinson Crusoe story, which of course is the model for colonialism and slavery. As Green also notes, many traditional adventure novels focus on outlaws: "smugglers, gypsies, pirates, and highwaymen" (29). All of these figures, save gypsies, were quite common in the seventeenth-century Caribbean. The Hunted Man variant overlaps with the avenger story here, and both Kit and Del Toro are hunted: by each other.

Conversely, Yerby was supremely aware of the fact that the majority of his readers were women, and all of his novels can also be classified as romances. According to Jan Radway, there are some key components of this genre: 1) the heroine's social identity is destroyed; 2) the heroine reacts antagonistically to an aristocratic male; 3) the aristocratic male responds ambiguously to the heroine; 4) the heroine responds to the hero's behavior with anger or coldness; 5) the hero retaliates by punishing the heroine; 6) the heroine and hero are physically and/or emotionally separated; 7) the hero treats the heroine tenderly; 8) the heroine responds warmly to the hero's acts of tenderness; 9) the heroine reinterprets the hero's previous behavior as the product of previous hurt; 10) the hero proposes/openly declares his love for/demonstrates his unwavering commitment to the heroine with a supreme act of tenderness; 11) the heroine responds sexually and emotionally; and 12) the heroine's identity is restored (Radway 187). *The Golden Hawk* meets virtually all of these components, beginning with Rouge's shipboard rape and the destruction of her identity; as she is "ruined" she deems herself unfit for her fiancé, and she then spurns Kit's well-meaning advances. Eventually, but without meaning to, he destroys her plantation and her crops. The two are separated for some years but reunited just before the invasion of Cartagena. Even before this, however, Rouge builds a new plantation, "treats her slaves well," and enjoys financial success as an independent woman. Another criterion the tale meets is that she and Kit make love twice during the rocky path of their relationship.

In contrast to the romance elements, we note that the adventure tale predominates; Rouge, in fact, disappears from the narrative for long stretches of time. We need to also note that both she and Kit—who end up in "respectable" roles and lord and lady of a prosperous plantation—are predatory people who are determined to get what they want and have few scruples about how to accomplish their aims. Both kill and rob, and they end up employing slave labor to complete their designs.[8] While throughout the novel we associate Kit with the golden hawk on the flag his ship bears, at the end of the narrative Rouge cries out "I am still more sea hawk than woman. Take me in your arms, and teach me to be gentle" (323), causing the reader to see that the title applies to Kit, his ship, and to Rouge as well. We might also adopt this fabled bird as a metaphor for Yerby as well, as his narrative swoops above the inland sea, yielding a detailed and sweeping view of the islanded sea.

Throughout the narrative, since the French and the British either practiced or condoned piracy of Spanish vessels, they too are "sea hawks"; Yerby stresses the theme—which is more narrowly focused on Kit, Rouge, and their crews—that piracy can lead to power. Kit preys on Spanish vessels because he intends to settle in France or its colonies, and English ships he spares because of Rouge. But the Spanish galleons also contain gold. The various ships fight under the owner's banner—Del Toro's *The Black Heron*, Kit's *The Golden Hawk*. Both, however, are birds of prey.

Moreover, Kit's lack of national allegiance abets his mobility and choices. On the other hand, Yerby seems to follow Fredric Jameson's dictum, "Always historicize! Is the one absolute and 'transhistorical' imperative of all dialectical thought" (9), an endorsement of the union of historicization and narrativization. Yerby, bitter about his racial position in the United States, readily embraced characters such as Kit, who owed no allegiance to national mythologies. Indeed, Yerby would eventually migrate, first to France, and then to Madrid, where he spent the last years of his life.

Although Yerby takes us to many ports and islands, the real arena, always, is the sea itself. The characters' ships move magically and rapidly across the basin, an often-necessary tactic since a safe port one day can become a trap the next. Fernand Braudel's advice to pay attention to details of trade when rewriting history finds application here as Yerby lists cargoes, from tallow and hides to human beings. Moreover, it is on the sea itself, rather than the separate island sequences or those in Cartagena, where Yerby chooses to probe the crosscurrents of colonial history and complex identities.

Although the other characters have mainly Spanish backgrounds, Yerby complicates identity for almost all of them. Bernardo, Kit's lieutenant, is part Spanish but also is a recently converted Jew, and had once been a slave. Don Luis, the Spanish grandee who serves as the novel's chief villain and Kit's main enemy, has an almost "Moorish" swarthiness. Slavery, prevalent all over the Atlantic world at this juncture, is a given for all the characters; for instance, Kit's benefactor Sieur Ducasse was once a slave trader. Hemispheric Indians appear as slaves as well, most memorably in the person of Bianca's servant Quita, whose mystic religion crosses a cultural line to sustain her mistress.

While none of the main characters are African American, conversations in the narrative frequently discuss the impressive qualities of some African peoples, while also casting aspersions on others. On the other hand, many of the crew are African, and as Rediker notes, pirate ships could be considered multiracial maroon communities "in which rebels used the high seas as others used the mountains and the jungles" (56). Clearly, Kit and Bernardo have studied Africans carefully; they discuss a kind of racial hierarchy more than once, always with the Dahomeans on top as the fiercest warriors who have the most sophisticated culture.[9]

One could argue that Kit/Cristoforo/Christophe represents the mingled races and nations of the Caribbean. An outsider, a bastard, yet a child of European nobility and a gentleman, he is led into a lucrative but lawless life on the high seas. We should not forget, however, that the source of his income is the freight of Spanish galleons, riding heavy in the waves with cargoes of gold and silver wrested painfully from Spanish mines by Native peoples of Peru and Mexico. The power and resilience of the South American Indians—whom Yerby relates to those being exterminated in the Caribbean—is testified to many times during the novel, particularly through the agency of Bianca's Indian servant and in the powerfully erotic scene where Del Toro's godson Ricardo, seeking to inflame her desire, introduces Bianca to an occult ritual in Lima, where a nude Indian dancer incarnates ancient sexual knowledge.

Kit's glamour as a leader among men masks his deep sense of bitterness and exclusion. A bastard whose lawlessness and mixed origins deny him a firm position in any group, he is a perfect example of the critic Darwin Turner's observation: "Significantly, Frank Yerby, a Georgia-born Negro exile from America, has concentrated on the theme of the outcast who, as in existentialist literature, pits his will against a hostile universe. By intelligence and courage, he proves himself superior to a society which rejects him because he is of alien, inferior, or illegitimate birth" (570). As Yerby perhaps knew, orphans, bastards, and outcasts often occupied central roles in sea narratives. Once conjoined with a pirate crew, however, the outlier's break with familial structures lead to affiliation. This pattern brings Yerby's Kit into configuration with postcolonial writing; as John Thieme puts it, "problematic parentage becomes a major trope in postcolonial con-texts, where the genealogical bloodlines of transmission are frequently delegitimised by multiple ancestral legacies [. . .] Orphans and bastards abound in postcolonial texts and the engagement with issues of parentage is often . . . intense" (8); similarly, in Yerby, the failed filial relations lead to affiliation.

As the map that Yerby placed inside both the front and back covers of *The Golden Hawk* reveals, the great force dominating this lively history is the sea itself. Elizabeth DeLoughrey has commented that "Geologically speaking, the global south is a space constituted by far more water than land and thus an apt place to consider the ways in which maritime histories and the transoceanic imaginary have been constituted in relation to landfall and settlement" (xi). Yerby, by choosing the late 1600s for his saga, purposely locates us in the bewildering flux of the European sea quests for dominance in the New World.

Like Kit's and Rouge's emotions, Yerby's tropics are violent. As we have seen, the novel opens with an attempted mutiny aboard Kit's ship, an earthquake and tidal wave that destroys much of Jamaica, and the appearance of Don Luis's ship; on its deck the female pirate Rouge is being raped after her besieged sister commits suicide. Indeed, the novel, full of chase, capture, and escape scenes, strings virtually all events along the trajectory of revenge. This motif, of course, became the commanding call of the Haitian Revolution, alongside the clarion appeal of liberation.

Some may object to Yerby's creation of a female pirate, but as Marcus Rediker demonstrates, there were more than a few female buccaneers. Anne Bonny and Mary Read were fearsome women with troubled backgrounds, who learned to kill and pillage. Wearing men's clothes, they were adept at cursing and swearing. Bonny was likely inspired to lead this life by the legendary career of Grace O'Malley, a pirate queen who terrorized Ireland's western coast in the late sixteenth century. As Rediker notes, there were many other female pirates who were celebrated in legend and song (103–26).

Despite his upbringing in Cadiz, and partly because of his determination to wreck revenge on Del Toro, Kit wages pirate war on Spain, capturing and sinking many vessels, which are abundant in the waters off Haiti—as Yerby remarks, "The booty [taken from Mexico and Peru] was excessive" for "the insatiable maws of the homeland would brook no waiting. Spain was too near disaster to wait long for the treasure that she was tearing from her colonies" (51). By chance, he captures a ship from Spain bringing Don Luis's fair betrothed, Bianca del Valdiva. Kit takes her to Cul-de-Sac, a miserable hole that will later become Port-au-Prince. Most of the inhabitants are black, and we learn how they construct huts and what they eat: boiled palm cabbage, plantains, and cakes of cassava or manioc, washed down with Veycou, made from fermented cassava meal, details Yerby had taken from various histories of Haiti.

Yerby utilizes even local vermin to aid his ongoing symbolism; at Cul-de-Sac, stinging insects called *bête rouge* lay eggs under the skin, leading to infection, just as Rouge has infected Kit's heart. Yerby has been called the "king of debunkers" (Turner, passim) and he takes care to dismiss the concept of Haiti as paradise:

> This, the chief island of the Antilles . . . was far from the jeweled isle of romance that the tellers of tales have made of the green chain that dots the Caribbean Sea. In addition to the five thousand varieties of insects, all of which stung or bit, there were the wild hogs that came rooting . . . the wild dogs that howled all night, the hideous-voiced parrots and crows. . . . In the swamps the frogs boomed . . . alligators bellowed . . . blue herons . . . with their ugly asslike braying. (65)

The beckoning sea can't cool one's heat because of the teeming Tiger sharks, and Bianca is almost eaten by an alligator while swimming in a jungle pool.

Elsewhere, however, Yerby reverses course: when Kit's ship is trapped in a harbor one night by Del Toro's fleet, a moon reveals a "night soft and slumberous with spring, the breeze perfume-laden with all the flowers of Hispaniola" (77). Later he waxes even more romantic with geography: Kit's ship glides through the sea,

> past islands strung like emeralds on a string looping in a great curve toward South America. To Kit's ears, even their names were like jewels: Hispaniola, Puerto Rico, Guadeloupe, Martinique, Granada, Santa Lucia, Trinidad. . . . And the sea that they encircled—cupped by them between the green poignard that is Florida and the long, rugged arm of the Isthmus, the blue crescent of the Gulf of Mexico and the towering peaks and mighty rivers of the mainland—was like sapphire, topaz, lapis lazuli. (91)

This method of alternate modes of description in fact allies Yerby with a subsequent writer, the historian C. L. R. James. In *The Black Jacobins*, the author's study of the Haitian revolution, James takes an identical tack. He can be lyrical:

> Field upon field, the light green sugar-cane, low and continually rippled in the breeze; above . . . the branches of the palm . . . gave forth, like huge feathers, a continuous soothing murmur. . . . [M]ango and orange trees . . . were a mass of green leaves and red or gold fruit. Thousands of small, scrupulously tidy coffee-trees arose on the slopes of the hills. . . . [M]ountain-sides were covered to the summits with

the luxuriant tropical undergrowth and precious hardwood forests.
... The traveller from Europe was enchanted at his first glimpse of this paradise. (28)

And yet there was monotony, disease, and the inevitable brutality occasioned by human slavery, all of this detailed in contrasting, starkly realistic language by James. His detailed description of the filthy streets of Le Cap comes from the historian Moreau de Sainte-Méry, who seems to have been Yerby's source as well, for the descriptions of open sewage, wandering animals, and garbage dumps are very similar to those of James.

As part of his correction of flawed histories, Yerby often focuses on native Central American culture. Bianca's maid, the Chibha mestiza Quita, gives her a magic gold necklace, a pendant with a small statue of a nude woman, which is to help her find her lost love. In a powerful scene, Bianca stares at the "grossly sexual almost to the point of obscenity" object, then moves to reject it after comparing it to her placid statue of the Virgin. But she stops, after sensing something

> fresh and free ... of open fields and blue skies and mountains veiled in rainbow mists ... suddenly Bianca understood that whatever evil there was in the little goddess she herself had read into it with her European-trained mind, with its habitual deification of the asceticism it finds so hard to practice. The little Indian figurine would henceforth represent to her the fertility of the earth, the fruitfulness of fields, and a clean and joyous love, free of shame and dark doubts and questionings, wholly good. (114)

The scene has an equivalent in Yerby's earlier *The Foxes of Harrow*, when the old, black character Caleen works the Haitian magic of an herbal bath and magic potion to awaken the desire of Odalie, who wants to win her husband back from his black mistress. The potent beauty of black women finds another echo in *The Golden Hawk* when Yerby draws, as he so often does, on conventions of the slave narrative. The slave market of Porto Bello on the isthmus of Panama is seen through Bianca's horrified eyes, as the nude, slim women of Dahomey are ogled by lecherous white bidders. The sensational aspects of this sexual material may have been commodification on Yerby's part, but they also open readers' eyes to the powerful lure of sexual power in slave societies, and to the outrages that resulted.

Many of these considerations of female slaves are set in Haiti. Kit's friendship with the French governor of the island, Sieur Jean-Baptiste Ducasse, offers Yerby an opportunity to employ a real historical figure whose earlier career as a slave trader and pirate ideally equipped him for the intrigues of Haiti. But better, his knowledge of the tribes of Africa lead to a formulation that Yerby finds intriguing: as Bernardo narrates, Ducasse saw that

> to continue to bring in Coromantes, Fantis, Ashantis, and Dahomeans was not only foolhardy but suicidal. Those tribes of blacks fear neither a white skin, God, nor the devil, and wait only for the first dark night to begin cutting their masters' throats. He came back loaded with Whydahs, Nagoes, Pawpaws, Congoes, and Angolans—all diligent, tractable slaves. And to prove that the man can think, he brought no one Ebo, the easiest of all blacks to obtain, and the stupidest. (125)

One wonders where Yerby got this formulation; in actuality, as Michel-Rolph Trouillot attests, Congolese slaves played key roles in the Haitian Revolution, as they had practiced guerilla warfare during Civil Wars in their homeland; particularly notable was Colonel Jean-Baptiste Sans Souci, who was a key rebel as early as 1791 (Trouillot 40).

Yerby attributes Haiti's rise as the richest French colony to Ducasse and to his drive to expand the production of sugar. Bernardo counsels Kit to wrest a Haitian plantation from Ducasse, for "the white crystals of the sugar mills and the great hogsheads of rum will make all the gold of El Dorado paltry by comparison" (126), which of course did happen. After Ducasse learns Kit's mother was French and that her son speaks perfect French, he "adopts" Kit, who then considers permanent residence in Haiti. As Bernardo states: "you have no country. By birth you are a Spaniard, but Spain's star is setting ... you are not French, for men reckon descent after the father [Kit doesn't know who his father is]. As a planter of Saint-Domingue, who knows what greatness you might attain?" (130). What Kit seems to have is the option of ethnicity by consent, rather than determined descent, an option that of course concerned Yerby personally, in terms of his racial masquerade and self-chosen exile.

As is his habit, Yerby has two women in love with his hero, and he uses one of them, Bianca, to create an alternate narrative. She travels with her husband across the isthmus of Panama, boards another ship, and then sails to Peru, where Del Toro's godson Ricardo is to receive his doctorate. The Peruvian cities of Callao and Lima are depicted as almost entirely Indian, although there are many black slaves as well. Yerby delights in presenting local details, such as the herds of llamas and alpacas, the adobe huts of the Indians, the local guano works, the storied cathedral of Lima and its cabildo. The filth of the streets, the myriad animals, and the naked children are vividly rendered, as are the streets of the goldsmiths, the Portuguese Jews, and the numerous nuns and friars; these depictions create a vivid portrait of Spanish Colonial life, one in sharp contrast to the just-beginning-to-prosper Haiti.

The novel is rife with Freudian, Oedipal themes. The most overwhelming aspect of this lies in the book's not-so-hidden secret, namely, that Del Toro is actually Kit's father, which explains why he doesn't kill Kit when he gets the chance. Since Del Toro has raped Rouge, Kit's love, and Kit is suspected by his father of deflowering Bianca, we have overlapping sexual triangles, both of them Oedipal. Further, Bianca is coveted by Del Toro's godson, Ricardo, and she is attracted to him because of his resemblance to Kit. Perhaps most interestingly, Bianca admits to herself, finally, that her husband's lovemaking has become more acceptable to her, because he has "something of another"—which we ultimately learn is Kit, his son. Indeed, this realization comes to Bianca suddenly as she muses on her husband's face, so it is through her that we learn the "secret" of the book on page 187, roughly in the middle of it. Bianca, who is pregnant, bitterly reflects that her child will be the sibling of her beloved! Yerby here rehearses the old script of passing novels and other racial melodramas, where brothers and sisters, separated from birth, fall in love, as in Faulkner's *Absalom!* Here, the other side of the Oedipal configuration is stressed. This theme of fathers and sons is complicated by Bernardo's insistence that Kit is like his son, and that he wants him to marry and set up a plantation in Haiti for his grandchildren. Bernardo favors Haiti as the tolerance of the island means that people can overlook his Jewish heritage, unlike the in Spanish colonies, which are still controlled by the Inquisition. Ducasse, too, "adopts" Kit and bestows a patrimony on him, so there are two surrogate fathers here, and one actual but concealed one.

At this point in the novel, Kit believes Rouge is dead, and he thinks of bringing Bianca here as his wife after killing Del Toro; if this had happened, he would thereby become like Oedipus, who similarly did not know he was marrying his father's wife. Bianca's situation becomes quite comparable to that of Queen Elizabeth of Spain in Schiller's *Don Carlo*, where the queen, once betrothed to the prince, was eventually married to his father, King Philip. A devout woman, she agonizes over her doomed love for Carlo, a plot further immortalized in Giuseppe Verdi's grandest opera, *Don Carlo* (1867). Yerby likely knew this opera, for he has Bianca pose her own problem almost identically:

> After having been married to the father, after having more than a little loved the father, could she then turn to the son without having a secret feeling of guilt in the whole matter—as though the new relationship were a little beyond the pale? And it would be even worse if Kit killed Luis [and Don Carlo draws a sword on his father in Verdi's opera], for in that she, being the cause, would be bloodguilty also— and with the blood of parricide. (294)[10]

The highly Oedipal plot, it should be said, is also an example, as was the Oedipal saga, of what Freud termed "the return of the repressed." In Freud's formulation, this is a psychological situation in which previously repressed memories emerge again; however, in literature, repressed memories and actions often become embodied, as they are here. Yerby may well be once again mimicking William Faulkner's *Absalom, Absalom!* where the Mississippi planter Sutpen is confronted with a son he abandoned many years ago in Haiti, a son who has African ancestry through his mother, and thus may not be acknowledged by the father. But Caribbean literature has situations like this too, and Yerby may also have known Victor Séjour's classic "Le Mulâtre" ("The Mulatto" in English translation), in which a rejected black son reappears in his white father's life as an enemy and a sexual rival. First published in 1837 (the first printed African American short story), it is narrated by an old black man who tells of a beautiful African girl, Laïssa, who is sold to the planter Alfred, who rapes her. He then abandons her and their son, Georges, who grows up not knowing his patrimony. As an adult, married to Zelia, he saves Alfred's life, but the latter then tries to rape Zelia, who he then has executed. Georges flees with his son to a Maroon colony. Years pass; Alfred, now married with a child, loses his wife when Georges poisons her and wounds Alfred; the latter's dying words reveal he is his murderer's father, causing Georges to commit suicide.

Oedipus was abandoned in the wilderness; Charles Bon in Haiti; and Georges finds refuge in the Maroon settlement in the swamps of Haiti. All three of these "repressed" characters surge back and confront their fathers. In *The Golden Hawk* Kit may be said to have vanished into the watery waste of the sea; pirate culture could also be seen as similar that of the Maroons, as apart from the rule of law. Additionally, Maroons, especially in Haiti, were skilled at theft from the plantations, and played a central role in the revolution that raged from 1781 to 1804.

Haiti is pictured as a base of operations for the continuing war between France, on one side, and the unholy alliance of England and Spain, on the other. Toward the end of the book, the French force Ducasse to join them in an expedition designed to capture Cartagena. The governor prefers to drive the Spanish from the eastern side of Hispaniola: "Wealth, true wealth, consisted of trade and produce, not this delirium of gold fever in the blood" (312), for clearly the French force is sent to steal the gold the Spanish have wrested from enslaved Inca and Aztec peoples. Rouge volunteers to lead her pirates as part of the force, vowing to Ducasse that she will become a citizen of Saint-Domingue if Kit is alive. He is, of course, and he and Bernardo, escaped from long bondage in the prisons of Cartagena, know the terrain and the layout of the battlements. Ducasse then sends Kit off to a reunion with Rouge at the formerly deserted De Ville plantation, which Rouge has already begun to restore. Their reunion is bittersweet, however, for Kit is still bound by his promise to Bianca to never wed any other woman. As discussed previously, Rouge sees herself as a sea hawk, and because Kit is the Golden Hawk, this metaphor unites them, but so does Haiti, with its Edenic elements and its potential for riches. Yerby paints a tropically sublime landscape ideal for this final submission of Rouge to love: "The air was heavy with the perfume of tropical flowers, barbaric scents, rich with an opium-drugged compulsion" (323).

This romantic extravaganza, however, is juxtaposed with brutal facts, since the siege of Cartagena in 1697 under the command of Ducasse, aided by Baron Jean Bernard Desjeans and by French pirates is reprised here, with Kit and Bernardo playing crucial roles. Cartagena at that time was part of Peru and was the chief Spanish city on the northern shore of the Caribbean. It was named after the Spanish city, which earlier took the name of fabled Carthage in Africa, site of trade routes and a center for slavery, characteristics of the South American metropolis as well. Cartagena was the port that funneled all the cargoes ferried across the isthmus from the Pacific into boats bound for Spain. Also, as Yerby knew, the King of Spain had granted Cartagena a monopoly on the slave trade; Veracruz was the only other Spanish slaving center. A stone-built, fabulously wealthy city, Cartagena preceded the great wealth of Haiti, and as such, attracted the steady interest of other colonial powers and pirates. Yerby may have also known the book Jean Bernard Desjeans wrote about the 1697 siege, as like that author, he lists all the great ships that took part in the attack, but includes Kit's fictional vessel,

The Providence, in the fleet as well. Kit functions as one of the key heroes of the successful siege, claiming that he and the real figure of De Pointis's son "fought side by side, for during the battle they had become as brothers" (335); young De Pointis, however, is shot just as victory is won, and dies in Kit's arms. Significantly, Yerby also has a company of Saint Domingue blacks win the day under the command of Pally, informing readers of the courage and key role blacks played in the wars of conquest.

Yerby was only one of many US writers who set narratives in the Caribbean in the mid-twentieth century, when war-weary readers were seeking pleasure and escape. He stood out, however, by inserting valuable history lessons in his costume novels, especially when he treated the abuses of colonialism, slavery, and sexual oppression. *The Golden Hawk* also represents an ingenious amalgam of the adventure and romance genres, both enriched and enhanced with telling portrayals of the colonial Caribbean, a realm that had been regularly colonized in later centuries by the United States, and one where, in the 1940s when Yerby was writing, more and more citizens were gravitating as tourism began its exponential boom after the introduction of air travel. As Gordon Hutner has observed, "if we are interested in the relation between the Caribbean islands and North America, it would be a shame to lose sight of the several dozen novels laudable American writers have devoted to the subject, just as it would be lamentable to lose sight of the American writing staged throughout the world, especially as we move toward a critical value for globalization" (331).

Some of our most distinguished critics have commented on the value of Yerby's oeuvre. C. L. R. James, no fan of Yerby's writing style, nevertheless declared that "it is in the serious study of . . . genuinely popular novels like those of Frank Yerby . . . that you find the clearest ideological expression of the sentiments and deepest feelings of the American people and a great window into the future of America and the modern world" (119). Further, he writes, "Yerby's books are a primitive elemental response to some of the deepest needs of the American people in their reaction against society" (129). He continues, "The popular writer who in his books has most expressed the modern American feeling for violent, uninhibited direct action and individualistic self-expression is Frank Yerby, a Negro writer" (211).

Years later Yerby would return to the Caribbean as the setting for *The Old Gods Laugh* (1964) and its sequel, *Hail the Conquering Hero* (1978). These tales take place in a mythical Latin American country going through guerilla rebellions in the wake of Castro's insurrection in Cuba; the dictators in these novels strongly resemble the Dominican Republic's brutal Rafael Trujillo.

Both novels employ picaresque white heroes from the United States, but again, include many indigenous/African descended characters, and build on Yerby's command of both colonial history and the Spanish language, which he mastered after moving permanently to Madrid, where he spent the last forty years of his life. Ensconced in his palatial Madrid residence, and attended by his doting second wife, Yerby produced even more books, most of them "costume dramas" calculated for popular consumption. Of his thirty-three novels, fifteen are set in the US South. By contrast, two take place in the North, three in the West, and seven in Europe (most of these written after his removal to that continent in 1953); *Judas, My Brother* (1969) treats biblical times.

Despite the presence of his picture on some dust jackets, few readers ever realized they were reading novels written by an African American. Indeed, his books sold especially well in the segregated South, partly because many of them were set there; probably too, they were regarded as escapist fiction. Nevertheless, the best of his narratives contains astute readings of the history they portray and sometimes provides subversive commentary on the Cold War, a segregated United States, and the increasingly existential nature of Western life after the decline of religion, community, and democratic institutions.

Yerby's transnational, cosmopolitan, and diasporic vision in the late novels had roots in his early efforts to shed the bonds of narrow nationalism and expectations for black writers. Even as early as *The Golden Hawk*, however, Yerby displayed a skillful blend of US southern and Caribbean history, culture, and politics, demonstrating his impressive research, his creative flair, and his keen understanding of the Circum-Caribbean, whose northern rim he understood to be the coastal US South. While Yerby chose to perhaps unwisely term his works "costume novels," virtually all of them can be seen as historical novels which Yerby researched diligently. He always sought to achieve what Georg Lukács has noted is the purpose of the historical novel: "to awaken distant, vanished ages and enable us to live through them again ... to depict this concrete interaction between man and his social environment in the broadest sense" (40) and to "demonstrate by artistic means that historical circumstances and characters existed in precisely such and such a way" (43). Yerby's "artistic means" were far more elaborate than the methods Lukács delineated, for he strung his very often accurate historical laundry on a fanciful line of adventure and romance, elements that could find a new appeal among today's audiences, who might find much pleasure—but also wisdom—in this neglected writer, whose works often have great relevance to the issues we face in today's troubled transnational arena.

NOTES

1. Port Royal was at one time the largest city in the Caribbean. The 1692 earthquake killed over two thousand people, many of whom died in the subsequent tsunami.

2. In some ways, Kit seems, as an outcast, to be similar to the black children abandoned by white fathers. Further, some of the most indelible images of slave abuse came in photos of the backs of blacks who had "trees" of scars from whippings. Late in the novel, Kit strips off his shirt to show a similar "tree" he incurred during his two enslaved years building the fortress of San Lázaro.

3. Cartagena was founded in 1533 by Pedro de Heredia, and became noted for both its beauty and its commercial success as a market place for Spanish goods, and as a terminal for the Spanish Caribbean fleet. It also became a principal citadel for the Catholic faith. The sacking of the city Yerby presents here was preceded by Francis Drake's capture of the city in 1586, which caused Philip II to commission Bautista Antonelli to revamp and strengthen the city's fortifications (Dorta, *passim*).

4. For a detailed presentation of this event, see Lynn (1999), *passim*.

5. Some of the escapist fare of the forties included *The Sea Hawk* (1940), starring Erroll Flynn, which was set in the Caribbean; *Reap the Wild Wind* (1942); *Captain Kidd* (1945); and *The Spanish Main* (1945). *The Golden Hawk* was transformed into a film in 1952 starring Sterling Hayden and Rhonda Fleming.

6. We should also note the resurgence of the popularity of pirate lore in the incredibly popular Disney movie sequence that began with *Pirates of the Caribbean: The Curse of the Black Pearl* (2003), leading to many sequels and a popular ride at Disney theme parks. It seems no accident that the pirates of the title are linked to the Caribbean—the tropical and nautical allure of the setting seems as important as the characters.

7. As Yerby knew, the Haitian Revolution had a reverberating effect in Caribbean culture; as I have recently documented, this seismic event found many renditions in Circum-Caribbean literature, including that of the US South—even though white Southerners tried to impose a silence on reports, fearing similar revolts among their enslaved (Lowe 93–144).

8. In these ways, Rouge resembles Mitchell's Scarlett O'Hara (another murderess) whose name is a variant of hers. She proves to be a ruthless entrepreneur, but also a determined lover. When she goes to Sieur Ducasse for news of Kit, she wears "a dress of green velvet, and a hat of the same material ornamented with peacock feathers" (265), a clear echo of the dress Scarlett has Mammy make from her mother's curtains.

9. Yerby's admiration for the Dahomeans would climax in what many feel is his most impressive novel, *The Dahomean*, which is almost entirely set in Africa (1971).

10. Indeed, Gene Jarrett has noted the parallels between Faulkner's novel and Yerby's first one, *The Foxes of Harrow*, where Stephen Fox must confront the child he sired with his black mistress (Jarrett 57–59).

BIBLIOGRAPHY

DeLoughrey, Elizabeth M. *Routes and Roots: Navigating Caribbean and Pacific Island Literatures*. U of Hawai'i P, 2007.

Dorta, Enrique Marco. *Cartagena de Indias, puerto y plaza fuerte*. Alfonso Amadó, 1960.
Dubois, Laurent. *Avengers of the New World: The Story of the Haitian Revolution*. Harvard UP, 2004.
Fuller, Muriel. "Frank Yerby Plans Novel About Caribbean Pirates." Muriel Fuller papers, Hunter College library.
Glasrud, Bruce A., and Laurie Champion. "'The Fishes and the Poet's Hands': Frank Yerby, a Black Author in White America." *Journal of American and Comparatives Cultures*, vol. 23, no. 4, 2000, pp. 15–21.
Hannah, Mark G. *Pirate Nests and the Rise of the British Empire, 1570–1740*. U of North Carolina P, 2015.
Hutner, Gordon. *What America Read: Taste, Class, and the Novel, 1920–1960*. U of North Carolina P, 2009.
James, C. L. R. *American Civilization*. Edited by Anna Grimshaw and Keith Hart, Blackwell, 1993.
James, C. L. R. *The Black Jacobins: Toussaint L'Ouverture and the San Domingo Revolution*, 2nd ed. Random House, 1989.
Jameson, Fredric. *The Political Unconscious*. Cornell UP, 1981.
Jarrett, Gene Andrew. "'For Endless Generations': Myth, Dynasty, and Frank Yerby's *The Foxes of Harrow*." *Southern Literary Journal*, vol. 39, no. 1, 2006, pp. 54–70.
Lowe, John Wharton. *Calypso Magnolia: The Crosscurrents of Caribbean and Southern Literature*. U of North Carolina P, 2016.
Lukács, Georg. *The Historical Novel*. 1936, translated by Hannah Mitchell and Stanley Mitchell, U of Nebraska P, 1962.
Lynn, John A. *The Wars of Louis XIV: 1667–1714*. Longman, 1999.
Radway, Janice. *Reading the Romance: Women, Patriarchy, and Popular Literature*. U of North Carolina P, 1984.
Rediker, Marcus. *Villains of All Nations: Atlantic Pirates in the Golden Age*. Beacon Press, 2004.
Thieme, John. *Postcolonial Con-texts: Writing Back to the Canon*. Continuum, 2001.
Trouillot, Michel-Rolph. *Silencing the Past: Power and the Production of History*. Beacon Press, 1995.
Turner, Darwin. "Frank Yerby as Debunker." *Massachusetts Review*, vol. 20, 1968, pp. 569–77.
Yerby, Frank. *The Foxes of Harrow*. Dial, 1946.
Yerby, Frank. *The Golden Hawk*. Dial, 1948.
Yerby, Frank. "How and Why I Write the Costume Novel." *Harper's*, vol. 219, October 1959, pp. 145–50.

VICTIM'S GUILT

Frank Yerby's Speak Now *and the "Politics" of Miscegenation*

GENE ANDREW JARRETT

THE WEDDING OF HARRISON FORBES (HARRY) AND KATHERINE NICHOLS (Kathy) represents a climactic moment in Frank Yerby's *Speak Now: A Modern Novel* (1969). For Harry, a black expatriate jazz musician, and Kathy, a white southerner who was once broke, homeless, and pregnant with her exboyfriend's child, the event signifies a remarkable stage in their bittersweet relationship. Byproducts of the American South, the two have overcome several things that could have torn them apart: their anxieties over her pregnancy; the taboo of miscegenation; the racial prejudice and stereotypes to which they cling and which continue to strain their bond even after their marriage. Yet the love they possess for one another proves resilient in the face of their personal and ideological differences.

Harry and Kathy's love also grows despite the student revolts, political upheaval, and social changes that boil around them and ravage Paris in 1968, the year they meet and the setting of *Speak Now*. Inevitably, the political storm outside La Mairie (City Hall), the site of the wedding, interrupts their exchange of vows. Presiding over the event, *monsieur le maire* (the mayor) delivers a soliloquy beseeching the couple to "love one another, honor and cherish the *amour* that today publicly [they] pledge" (151).[1] Then, after scanning the courtroom, he announces, "If there be any person present who knows of a valid reason why this man and this woman should not be joined in the bonds of Holy Wedlock, let him speak now, or forever henceforth hold his peace!" (151).

Right after the mayor invites the audience to "speak now," Raoul Levi, a college student in Paris and a leader of the 1968 anarchic rebellion against the French government, emerges from nowhere and objects. (Eventually, he allows the wedding to finish.) For him, the institution of marriage is reprehensible for privileging "contracts and empty legalisms" over true love (151). When the mayor calls for the police, Harry waves them off, explaining that the student suffers more from an anarchic mental "condition" than from a sincere objection to the wedding. He learned of Raoul's condition from a contentious conversation in which they disagreed over the meaning of the bourgeoisie, political activism, and victim's guilt—namely, the controversial idea that blacks are as guilty as whites for their status as victims of racial oppression. Taken together, the wedding of Harry and Kathy, Raoul's objection to it, and Harry's empathetic defense of Raoul afterward foreshadow the racial intersection of love and politics in *Speak Now*. This fateful intersection turns out to pose one of the greatest challenges to the couple's marriage.

Speak Now, Yerby's twenty-third novel, marks the first time he cast a black protagonist to discourse on racial politics—that is, on the race relations between blacks and whites, and/or on how these relations factor into political action. The novel's opening episode introduces Harry, who regularly plays at a jazz club called Le Blue Note, witnessing North African members of a "terrorist" group, El Fatah, attempt to assassinate Harry's best friend and the Arab owner of the club, Ahmad Zahibuine, because he refused to help the group purchase arms (6).[2] In his discussion with a French police officer, Harry opines that "the motive of this affair" was nothing less than politics (4). Planted in *Speak Now* even before we meet Kathy, this thematic seed of political rebellion and violence grows as the story progresses and entwines with the complex romance of a black man and white woman who try to come to grips with their pasts, their heritages, and their prejudices.

At the same time, the novel highlights the degree to which Yerby was sensitive to the legal and cultural controversies surrounding interracial marriage across the United States from his position in Europe. Two years prior to the release of *Speak Now*, the Supreme Court unanimously ruled in the case *Loving v. Virginia* that the Racial Integrity Act of 1924, a Virginia anti-miscegenation statute that prohibited the marriage between blacks and whites, was unconstitutional. "Even though the novel does not mention the *Loving* case explicitly," according to scholar Matthew Teutsch, "it does allude to it through the conversations that Harry Forbes and Kathy Nichols have about the institution of marriage, especially between individuals of different racial backgrounds in the United States" (341). Attending to both the national and international realities of societal and legal norms, *Speak Now* stands as a remarkably global analysis of the sexual politics of race relations.

Ultimately, *Speak Now* is an outstanding and complex novel about love, politics, and the social construction of human identity. Studying it affords us yet another opportunity to recover Yerby. Despite his literary ambition and commercial success, Yerby remains marginal in African American literary studies. From *The Foxes of Harrow* in 1946 to *McKenzie's Hundred* in 1986, he published thirty-three different novels. Three adaptations appeared on the big screen, and one appeared on television. Twelve were bestsellers, and almost all were selections of the Book of the Month Club. They have been translated into over thirty languages, and close to sixty million copies of them have been sold around the world.[3] Nonetheless, Yerby is often absent from anthologies of African American literature and from those of American literature generally. In addition, only a handful of scholarly studies of him exist, as Matthew Teutsch's introduction to this volume makes clear. For the most part, the academic stigma of Yerby's novels as lowbrow, pulp fiction, and hack writing—as subliterary, in short—has persisted ever since the mid-twentieth century, when Robert Bone disregarded him as the "prince of pulpsters," a disregard consistent with Bone's broader dismissal of "raceless" fiction by African American writers.

Just because Yerby did not cast black protagonists in his novels until 1969 does not mean that he avoided the theme of racial politics in the novels prior to that year. Rather, he resisted the racial realism that Richard Wright, the so-called Dean of the Chicago Renaissance, had advocated in the 1930s and 1940s. Thereafter, while Yerby's philosophical turn toward black characterization in *Speak Now* happened to be an anxious one—he feared that the novel might be too literary for commercial success—it still allowed him to probe the issues of class, race, and politics in ways he had never done before.

"THE RACE PROBLEM WAS *NOT* A THEME FOR ME"

Born in the same month but seven years apart, Frank Yerby and Richard Wright came from the American South—Yerby from Augusta, Georgia; Wright from Roxie, Mississippi.[4] During the Great Depression, poverty forced Yerby to drop out of a doctoral program in English at the University of Chicago, where Wright happened to read sociological literature during his formative stage as a writer. Toward the latter part of the 1930s, Yerby participated in a Chicago-based New Deal program where he probably rubbed elbows with other Chicago Renaissance authors such as Wright, Margaret Walker, William Attaway, and Arna Bontemps.[5] And like Wright, James Baldwin, Chester Himes, and William Gardner Smith, Yerby became an expatriate, moving in 1951 to Paris. Five years later, he relocated to Madrid, where he lived until his death on November 29, 1991.

Early in their respective literary careers, both authors won the prestigious O. Henry Award; Wright won in 1939 for "Fire and Cloud," and Yerby in 1945 for "Health Card." Yerby's story critiques the ideology and practices of racism in the United States in ways that Wright, a decade later, found provocative. For Wright, "Health Card" relates "a variation of the same theme, a man subjected to a sort of psychological castration, as it were, directly in front of his wife's eyes.... This Negro, being further from his roots, weeps tears of innocent rage" (qtd. in Fabre 177).[6] Despite the similarities between his early work and Wright's, beginning in the mid-1940s Yerby tried to rid himself of the expectations and responsibilities that came with writing both as an African American and in the wake of Wright's success.

In a 1963 letter written to Michel Fabre, who was working on a biography of Wright, Yerby clarifies his dissociation: "I knew Dick Wright none too well. I admired him immensely as a man. I visited him in Paris circa 1953 or 4, I don't remember which. I was not at all influenced by him as a writer, except perhaps negatively.... I liked, admired, enjoyed his earlier books; but if they influenced me at all, it was to confirm my growing suspicion that the race problem was *not* a theme for me."[7] Yerby is referring here to the "race problem" as constructed by a special brand of African American literature led by Wright. Specifically, literary naturalism, Marxism, and the Chicago school of urban sociology provided the conceptual frameworks that enabled Wright and fellow African American writers of his generation to elucidate the complex connection of race and class in the "Negro Problem." In adopting these perspectives, Wright also sought to distinguish his generation's mode of African American literature from what he believed were the romantic and ultimately self-defeating approaches of the New Negro Renaissance in Harlem. In the first sentence of "Blueprint for Negro Writing," for example, Wright lays down the gauntlet: "Generally speaking, Negro writing in the past has been confined to humble novels, poems, and plays, prim and decorous ambassadors who went a-begging to white America" (53). In contrast, Wright's embrace of the capacity of art to serve as a political tool symbolized the new focus of his generation.[8]

Yerby's aversion to Wright's brand of fiction, as suggested in his letter to Fabre, did not exist throughout his career. Nor was it the sole reason for his production of thirty novels between 1946 and 1986 that were characterized mostly by nonblack protagonists and eclectic historical settings, cultural geographies, and political themes. During the early 1930s, Yerby was a poet ambivalent both in his employment of outdated atavistic tropes attributable to the New Negro Renaissance and in his experimentation with classical Western verse forms and humanistic themes. In the latter part of the decade, he shifted to writing short stories such as "Health Card," capitalizing with great critical success on the prevailing interest in Wright's brand of fiction.

Around this time Yerby started to become increasingly aware of the racial politics and commercialism of the American literary industry. Yerby was learning that as an African American writer he had to deal with the market of racial stereotypes that appreciated Wright's Bigger Thomas at the expense of other kinds of characterizations, including uplifting black protagonists that roamed the novel he was trying to publish in the early 1940s, "This Is My Own." After several failed attempts to publish this book, Yerby decided that he would never kowtow to the demands of a literary market in which racial myths, stereotypes, and other related discourses so constrained his creative options. With this in mind, his first published novel, *The Foxes of Harrow* (1946), signified a philosophical turn toward a literary aesthetic that rejected the staple black protagonist of African American literature.[9]

Yerby was not the only African American writer who faced the daunting critical and commercial consequences of Wright's popularity. Complaints that Wright's school pigeonholed literary expression coincided with the prevailing insistence that, according to Sterling Brown, Arthur P. Davis, and Ulysses Lee, the "bonds of literary tradition," or how texts aesthetically or thematically speak to each other, "seem to be stronger than race" for African American writers (6–7). In reaction to Wright's celebrity, a critical camp formed with the hope of performing the kind of racial desegregation of American literature that Wright and his school allegedly hindered. Instead of appreciating Wrightean African American literature, which reflected such radical doctrines as proletarianism, Marxism, and Communism, some African American writers saw it as a professional handicap. They also believed that the racial desegregation of American literature required avoiding the dominant genre of African American literature at the time: racial realism.

Racial realism comprises black protagonists alongside certain historical themes, cultural geographies, political discourses, or perspectives defined by race. To some critics, this approach bespoke the immaturity of African American authors who could not think beyond the so-called Negro Problem. Purportedly characterized by propaganda and didacticism, and informed by racial hypersensitivity, it spawned, some argued, the shortsighted and dangerous expectation among American readers that black authors could not help but write about race and racism.[10]

Not all black writers were willing to avoid racial realism, however. In a 1961 interview published in *December*, Ralph Ellison was asked what seemed to be a straightforward question about the early part of his literary career: "Did you think you might write stories in which Negroes did not appear?" Ellison's elaborately autobiographical and theoretical answer reveals that the question actually was not so straightforward: "No, there was never a time when I thought of writing fiction in which only Negroes appeared, or in which only whites appeared. And yet from the very beginning I wanted to write about American Negro experience and I suspected that what was important, what made the difference, lay in the perspective from which it was viewed. When I learned more and started thinking about this consciously, I realized that it was a source of creative strength as well as a source of wonder" (16). The benefits of writing directly on the "American Negro experience," according to Ellison, outweighed those of eliminating this experience in order to demonstrate one's Americanness. Rather, Ellison contends, the literature should prove its Americanness *through* depictions of African American experiences.

Critic and novelist Lloyd L. Brown was even blunter than Ellison about the problems of avoiding racial realism. In "Which Way for the Negro Writer?" an essay serialized in the March and April 1951 issues of *Masses and Mainstream*, Brown argues that the abandonment of "racial material" for "universal perspectives" and "global points of view" only perpetuates the ideas and values of "the white ruling class," "American imperialism," and the "melting pot" paradigm by which "all so-called inferior cultures must be re-molded to conform to the Anglo-Saxon ideal" (60–61). The black avoidance of racial realism and gravitation toward a kind of aesthetic universalism reflected the self-destructive internalization of antiblack racism. Brown's complaint that African American literature "has not been Negro enough—that is, it has not fully reflected the real life and character of the people"—anticipates the Black Arts Movement of the 1960s and 1970s, with its call for black authors to remain dedicated to racial realism for the sake of black cultural nationalism and political action (54).

Nonetheless, if Wright was the first great Negro novelist, then another group had succeeded in coming of age by, in a sense, emancipating themselves from Wright's school. More than any other African American writer of the postwar 1940s, Yerby dedicated himself to this philosophy by playing truant from Wright's literary school when he published *The Foxes of Harrow*.[11] Despite the criticism of its poor literary quality, *The Foxes of Harrow* achieved remarkable commercial popularity and distinguished Yerby from his African American peers.[12] Beginning in 1946, he became a regular on the *New York Herald Tribune Weekly Book Review*'s survey "What America Is Reading." According to Louis Michaux, manager of the National Memorial Book Store—"the largest Negro book-selling establishment in the United States"—*The Foxes of Harrow* was among the top three books of 1946 sold in Harlem, listed alongside Ann Petry's *The Street* and Fannie Cook's *Mrs. Palmer's Honey*. The Frederick Douglass Center in Harlem also ranked Yerby's novel as a top-three book in 1946, alongside Petry's *The Street* and Oscar Micheaux's *The Case of Mrs. Wingate* (originally released in 1944).[13] Within three years, *The Foxes of Harrow* had sold over two million copies, marking the beginning of what would turn out to be the most commercially successful career of any African American writer in the twentieth century.

RACIAL CHARACTEROLOGY AND THE TABOO OF MISCEGENATION

In 1969, Yerby's literary philosophy changed. While penning *Speak Now*, he was beginning to produce "literature," as opposed to the bad writing that he admitted characterized his earlier novels and that reviewers criticized so harshly. Indeed, Yerby never denied that bad writing was an initial phase of his first novel, *The Foxes of Harrow*. In a 1982 interview, Yerby states that he "remembered that nobody ever went broke underestimating the taste of the American public, so I set out to write the worst possible novel it was humanly possible to write and still get published but it sort of got hold of me, and about half way through, I started revising and improving it" (qtd. in Parker 227). By contrast, when he was not creating the "worst possible" novels, such as when he wrote "seriously" in his nineteenth and twentieth novels, *The Old Gods Laugh* (1964) and *An Odor of Sanctity* (1965), he was scared that they would not sell well and would spur his decline. Yerby was half correct; while the novels failed to sell as much as his early ones, his career survived the philosophical turn.

Speak Now also signals Yerby's turn toward the racial casting and characterology of people of African descent in major roles. This does not mean that he avoided talking about the politics of race and racism in his novels prior to 1969. Quite the contrary. Both *The Foxes of Harrow* and its sequel, *The Vixens*, touch on the racial implications of the Civil War. He wrote his tenth novel, *Bride of Liberty* (1954), to educate young readers about the role of New World Africans in the American Revolution. His thirteenth novel, *Fairoaks* (1957), examines the brutality of the slave trade and its impact on the consciousness of white Americans. His next novel, *The Serpent and the Staff* (1958), traces the relationship between two doctors, one white and the other black, who were childhood friends and who reunite as adults. *Griffin's Way* (1962), Yerby's eighteenth novel, explores the violent conflicts between blacks and whites in Mississippi shortly after the Civil War. And the foregoing descriptions do not include the various instances within these novels where Yerby analyzes race apart from the African diaspora. Constructions of white, Creole, and Spanish identity—and the various ways that they factor into the historical stratification of society along lines of class, color, or caste—are recurring themes in the twenty-two novels Yerby wrote prior to *Speak Now*.

Despite the racial insight of these novels, the fact that they do not cast African-descended people in major roles has convinced many readers that Yerby does not deserve a place in the tradition, much less the canon, of African American literature. Yerby himself proposes a thesis that blurs the canonical and the popular, the classic and the modern in "How and Why I Write the Costume Novel." "The classics of today are very nearly always the best sellers of the past," Yerby writes. "Thackeray, Dickens, Defoe, Byron, Pope, Fielding—the list is endless—enjoyed fabulous popularity in their day. And, crossing the channel, what can one say of Balzac, Hugo, Maupassant, Dumas?" (145–46). The advocacy for racially authentic African American literature became especially prevalent with the rise of the Black Arts Movement, which valued black-authored literature that focused explicitly on the black experience. By this standard, the only "authentic" novels that qualify Yerby for canonical admission include *Speak Now* and his twenty-fourth and thirtieth novels—*The Dahomean: A Historical Novel* (1971) and its sequel *A Darkness at Ingraham's Crest: A Tale of the Slaveholding South* (1979).

More assertive in its study of black character than *The Dahomean* and *A Darkness at Ingraham's Crest*, *Speak Now* even overstates the blackness of its protagonist, seemingly trying to distinguish his racial identity as much as possible from those in Yerby's prior novels. When we meet Harry for the first time, we encounter several overdetermined signals of his African ancestry and his experience of racial difference and racism. In his conversation with the police officer about the murder of a waiter at Le Blue Note, Harry insists that he is not just an American but one whose "ancestors did not invite themselves aboard the vessels of the Slavers, nor choose the country to which they were sent. Given a choice, they would have stayed in Africa. My connection, then, with the Anglo-Saxon bloc is, one could say, involuntary" (2). By discussing the American slave trade, Harry is making clear to the agent—and to us, the readers—that he is aware of the tension between the races as well as the traditional Anglocentric definition of Americanness. Harry suggests that the term "American" does not yet apply to him. His racial identification with Africa trumps his national identification with the United States, and his misery growing up in Georgia justifies his expatriation to Paris.

Harry's social history, aesthetic preferences, and skin color also confirm his racial ancestry and politics. Early in *Speak Now*, while observing Kathy eating breakfast, he realizes the potential racial gulf that separates him from this attractive white woman: "He supposed that she was a very pretty girl; but all his concepts of beauty had been changed by Fleur so that this classic Nordic type seemed to him singularly uninteresting, even dull. He saw his hand, so black that it looked faintly bluish, lying on the table beside her pale, freckled one, and smiled" (8). Harry met a Vietnamese woman, Fleur Quang Dang Hoc, while serving in the military during the Vietnam War, where he tried to prove that he "still had the balls. That the life of a black man in white America hadn't robbed [him] of them" (96). Fleur sustains him during this introspective time; he comes to love her; and they marry once the army discharges him after a mortar shell severely injures his right calf. Eventually she becomes the highest paid model in Paris, but at the height of her career she contracts pneumonia and dies.

Admired by Harry and his friends for her magnificent appearance, Fleur has taught Harry to appreciate the racial and ethnic diversity of beauty, not merely the singularity of whiteness that had come to define Western aesthetics. At the same time, her statement to him, "You're more like us," signifies the analogy of their racial otherness in Western civilization. After her death, he realizes that he could never really connect with a white woman in the way he connected with Fleur (20).[14] In having such thoughts while looking at the "faintly bluish" color of his hand, he realizes the supposed purity of his racial blood and the problem of having sexual relations with a white woman at a time when miscegenation is still taboo.

Harry demonstrates a keen awareness of how such taboos and related racial stereotypes restrict social relations between blacks and whites, and thus stand in the way of his relationship with Kathy. In his conversations with her, his constant self-mockery is responsible for the novel's overstatement of his racial consciousness. In order to play to white impressions of black physicality, he calls himself "burrheaded" and "liverlipped" (10). To mimic white distrust of blacks, he terms himself a "dirty nigger" with "disgusting," "dirty money" (16). On another occasion, he suggests that white women imagine black men as hypersexual, as "artificial penises" (25). Harry's language works to foreground the depth of their racial and, by extension, social, cultural, and ideological differences. But his sarcasm, obnoxiousness, and cynicism also mask his emotional pain as well as his own anxieties and insecurities.

The verbal exchanges between Harry and Kathy dramatize a major storyline in *Speak Now*: how a black man and a white woman can come to love one another despite the racial anxieties to which they cling as part of their memories of living in the United States and which the conditions in France continue to perpetuate, if not exacerbate. Kathy's anxieties are more extreme than Harry's. Hailing from a privileged family that owns a lucrative tobacco business, she initially believes that the social obstacles between her and Harry are insurmountable. Harry's constant badgering of Kathy about her prejudices insinuates in her mind that he "hates" her and everything she represents (35). For this reason, she is stunned by his offer to marry her, his sympathetic strategy for enabling her to avoid her conservative father's indignation at having a pregnant, unwed daughter. "At the proper intervals prescribed by French law, you'll get letters—in French—demanding that you return to friend hubby's bed and board," Harry says, in detailing the plan to Kathy. "After six months of silence on your part, or better still, a bitter and indignant refusal from you, hubby then divorces you. A copy of which bill of divorcement will in due course be delivered to you. Then you marry some nice Robert E. Reb, and you, he, and *l'enfant de la patrie* live happily forever after" (35).

When Kathy confesses to Ahmad her reluctance to marry Harry, we see the depth of her anxiety: "She felt a certain surge of panic, as though they—Fats, Ahmad, the world—were tightening a noose about her neck. A noose that simultaneously bound her to Harry—to that—nigger, she thought viciously, and sat there, trembling with both shock and shame" (55). The discomfort she feels around Harry's friends, who question her motives, and in the society at large, which condemns interracial marriage, reveals her internal struggle. While she tries to demonstrate to all that she is willing to interact with, and even love, a black man, her racial presumptions and prejudices are frequently offensive, underscoring how far she has to go before she can truly understand blacks and the problem of racism.

Only after Kathy jealously observes an entranced white girl kiss Harry at the end of one of his performances at Le Blue Note does she realize the extent of her love for him, "in spite of [his] being black" (71). Jazz music often serves as a sexual interlocutor between Harry and Kathy.[15] Only at this time does she begin to envision herself spending the rest of her life as his wife. And only at this time does she have the audacity to say to him, "You're mine" (60). But as they grow closer, a series of events tests her faith in the power of love to overcome circumstances that work to pry them apart.

For example, a letter from her father demanding that she return to the United States because she has been living in Paris for two years reminds her of the legacy of white privilege and racism from which she came, and which continues to haunt her. Perhaps she is not destined to love Harry, she wonders; perhaps she should be thinking in this fashion: "I—I'm a white Southerner. A—a bigot. Prejudiced. I—hate Negroes! I—I despise them!" (120) Moreover, Ouija, Ahmad's seventeen-year-old daughter whose "absolutely stunning physical beauty" rivals Kathy's, is openly attracted to Harry and seems capable of stealing him from her (91). In fact, whenever Kathy and Harry argue about the impossibility of their relationship, she suggests that he and Ouija are meant for each other and should get married; she tells him, "Harry—after I—I'm out of your life—marry Ouija. Do. Please do. She—she's perfect for you. And I—I do so want you to be happy!" (119). Closer to the end of the novel, though, it becomes clear that Ouija is no longer a true threat because we see Harry imagining life in which he and Kathy tour Italy and Geneva (176).

Another example includes Harry's intermittent limp, the consequence of a war injury, which manifests the tensions both within Harry and between him and Kathy. It flares up after an argument with Kathy, who has just agreed to marry Harry even as she warns him not to "touch" or "kiss" her (38). In response, he complains that she has yet to learn a major lesson: his former attraction to Fleur probably means that he would not desire a white woman whose sexual fear and distrust of blacks recur in startling and consistently offensive ways. Indeed, as time goes on, the more she hurts his feelings, the more he limps.[16]

Speak Now ultimately portrays Kathy as an emotionally unstable and psychologically weak white woman who hails from a privileged family. On the other hand, Harry often comes across as an unlikely partner in love: a black man who has been wounded during his service in the Vietnam War. Harry's spiritual callousness, though, belies the deeper core of insecurities that developed alongside his resilience.

VICTIM'S GUILT AND THE "POLITICS" OF INTERRACIAL LOVE

Constantly, Harry stresses the social disadvantages that African-descended people have historically faced and that he encounters on a daily basis. Yet such racial views are quite complex and controversial, especially as they pertain to the notion of victim's guilt, an idea that arises during Harry's visit with Kathy to Ahmad's house. There he meets Raoul, one of the heroes of the student agitation for "Maoism, Trotskyism, anarchy, free love, student control of the great centers of learning, the elimination of examinations" (90). Though belonging to a privileged, educated class, Raoul expresses an aversion to the kind of "rich, liberal bourgeois" attitudes that he feels Kathy, Harry, and the Zahibuine family embody. Harry's spirited engagement with Raoul constitutes one of the most intriguing arguments in the novel on the issues of class, race, and politics.

Raoul and Harry stand for two different schools of thought. In terms of class, Raoul believes in the Marxist-based reformation of societies so that the haves and the have-nots can coexist on a level playing field. He argues that a specifically proletarian revolution could "make it possible for the sons of workers to enter the Sorbonne," the flagship university in Paris (131). The philosophical paradigm shifts this revolution entails would include ending the "racism, capitalism, bigotry, [and] religion" responsible for the social problems Raoul notices. It would also include bringing in "true Communism, the heroic Communism of Mao, instead of that quasi-capitalist *merde* of Moscow" (131). In contrast, Harry questions the premise of a working-class revolution. He suggests that intellectual elites—or their descendants, including Raoul—are hypocritical for identifying political movements with the working class, while expecting that their leaders would not come from this very class.

In terms of race, Raoul believes in the efficacy of Negritude, a 1930s anticolonialist movement of French-speaking black writers, intellectuals, and politicians led by Léopold Sédar Senghor, Aimé Césaire, Léon Damas, and Paulette Nardal.[17] Harry considers movements like Negritude interchangeable "*merde*" because they have not been as successful as initially expected. He tells Raoul, "I grant you that there is a fine excess of feces in our corrupt bourgeois society as well. But substituting one variety of *merde* for another doesn't help anything" (95). When Raoul criticizes Harry for fighting in the Vietnam War on behalf of America, despite its oppression of blacks, we learn that Harry refuses the black pride and commitment to black political causes that, ironically, Raoul, a white man, supports. For Harry, the "biological accident" of race is not enough to warrant his political affiliation with blacks. Nor does it trump the common humanity that he shares with all, regardless of racial difference. While the construction of race has undeniably led to the denigration of darker-skinned people around the world, Harry blames blacks (the victims) as well as whites (the victimizers) for its consequences.

It is worth quoting Harry at length here to reveal the passion with which he asserts the notion that victims are guilty for their own victimization:

> "I believe," Harry went on quietly, "that every crime is to some extent a contract between victim and criminal. Accepted by the victim. For nothing, *mon gars*, can happen to a man that he won't *permit* to happen. By which I mean, if one is prepared to pay the price necessary to maintain one's integrity, one's dignity, one's humanity, one can never be robbed of them. At worst, all one can be robbed of is life, which, without these things is nothing, *en tout cas*. So while I do not absolve the lordly white race of its unspeakable inhumanity towards every other variety of mankind that differs from it even slightly—the Opium Wars and the Sepoy Mutiny come readily to mind—I find that the black man bears a burden of guilt only a little less heavy. For if my people had *ever* learned not to decimate one another in insanely ferocious tribal wars, if it had occurred to any of them that whatever one might do with an enemy captive of one's own race, it was *not* permissible, say, to sell him to a white slaver—" (97)

Harry implies that blacks are partially responsible not only for their own internalized sense of inferiority, but also for literally having been oppressed. They were enslaved because they sold out their racial brothers and sisters to white enslavers.[18]

Harry goes on to suggest that since just as many blacks, if not more, refused to die for their freedom as those who revolted against slavery means that the African diaspora descends from a race complicit in its own persecution, or that they did not wholeheartedly believe they should be willing to die in their fight for freedom. The history of racial oppression that blacks have suffered, Harry concludes, should not distract us from realizing the extent to which their own misdeeds have worsened their predicament; he says, "We have always been a fratricidal people" (99). Provocative, to say the least, Harry substantiates his pessimism by pointing to the hypocrisy and double standards that are rampant in his own racial community. The fact that "our younger idiots," such as the separatist Black Panther Party, "are on record as demanding their own version of the segregation we were fighting against in the first place" compels him even to lament, "I am not proud of being black" (100).

Obviously, Harry lacks credibility as he casts doubt on the motives and benefits of both class- and race-based political mobilization. He consistently embodies the very antiblack prejudice that he finds so repugnant in whites and fellow blacks. Even Kathy realizes this point, exclaiming to Harry, "You're a racist!" (107). His own cynicism, which runs so deep that it dissuades him from committing to any kind of political activism, arises from a genuine disbelief in the efficacy of black political discourse, ranging from the racial separatism suggested above to the kind of Christian ethic of nonviolent protest that Martin Luther King Jr. once espoused.

At the end of *Speak Now*, when a French policeman clubs Harry across the head for being intimate with a white woman, Harry's pessimistic vision of racial progress is confirmed. Contrary to Paris's history of being a racial utopia for black expatriates since the mid-nineteenth century, the violence that eventually originates from this triangle of the officer and the interracial couple occurs in the context of a racial-political maelstrom that puts Harry and Kathy's marriage to the test.[19] This maelstrom is the culmination of several events that *Speak Now* depicts by referring faithfully to the student-engineered political upheaval in Paris, which occurred while Yerby was writing the novel in 1968. By the mid-sixties, Yerby had embraced the comprehensive research that makes the historical accuracy of *Speak Now* possible.[20] In this respect, the novel is a remarkable document about French educational and political history.

The novel broaches the subject of the student uprising when we learn that in 1968, Daniel Cohn-Bendit led a protest against the University of Nanterre's prohibition of young men sleeping in the dormitory rooms of their girlfriends. The next uprising, led again by Cohn-Bendit, but also involving Raoul, is a more substantive, if increasingly anarchic, rebellion against the academic and larger social, cultural, and economic conventions of Paris that have maintained the inequities between the haves and the have-nots. This protest forces the closing of the Sorbonne.

The battle escalates in the streets of Paris. Approximately ten thousand student *enragés* hurl pavement stones and use deadly slingshots as they engage in an all-out war with three thousand officers of the *Compagnies Républicaines de Sécurité* (Republican Security Companies or CRS), "the meanest, roughest, most brutal riot cops" beating them back with clubs and tear-gas grenades (127). The abduction of the directors of the Renault

Automobile Factory at Cléon by the *Confédération Française et Démocratique du Travail* (French Democratic Federation of Labor) exemplifies the spreading of emboldened revolutionary spirit throughout France. When the French government prohibits Cohn-Bendit from returning to the country after a trip to Germany, the students grow further incensed. They become more sophisticated organizers, recruiting protesters from Paris's working-class factory districts. At the same time, the CRS and other police forces close ranks behind the French government's attempt to suppress the revolution.

As the students and the government prepare for the inevitable showdown, the political unrest begins to affect the lives of Harry and Kathy in material and psychological ways. At this juncture, their willingness to talk at length about the political condition of France deepens their relationship. He remains skeptical of political action: "[The students] believe in the possibility of improving society, in the perfectibility of man. Don't know, can't even see, that what's wrong with any system—Marxism, Leninism, Stalinism, Trotskyism, Maoism, Castroism, capitalism, socialism, democracy, Negritude, Black Power, Apartheid, the Church—is that ultimately they have to be run not by angels, but by men" (135). In short, the popular deification of political leaders distracts us from their all-too-human susceptibility to corruption and egotism. This vulnerability convinces Harry that a political movement often springs from specious motives and ideological confusion. For this reason, he remains skeptical of the growing student rebellion in France and is willing to go to great lengths to prevent it from tearing him and Kathy asunder.

For instance, when Harry and Kathy decide to spend their honeymoon away from Paris, they travel to Nice, France, then eventually to Geneva, Switzerland. At the Geneva airport, they encounter a white man from the American South who scolds Kathy upon learning that she has married a black man. He then provides her with a free first-class ticket back to the United States. Harry learns that she has failed to rebuff the white man, seemingly due to her own lingering anxieties and doubts. Once again, he becomes frustrated and abandons her at the airport, leading to their *de facto* divorce.

Kathy does not spend much time in New York; she returns to Paris to seek out Harry and resurrect their marriage, even though the area remains dangerous. When she finally tracks down Harry and discovers Ouija at his apartment, she flees into the hazardous city streets. After rejecting the tempting seventeen-year-old girl because he remains in love with his wife, Harry races into the streets and searches for Kathy. He ends up finding Kathy injured and bloodied, and together they experience the fateful racial intersection of love and politics:

[Harry] ran faster than he'd ever run before in his life. He forgot his bad leg. His limp disappeared. He got there, bent, clawed her into his arms, rolled away from that massive, murderous curve blade that was scooping up tree trunks, packing cases, overturned cars, sewer gratings, stone benches—and all the thousand, thousand odds and ends the *enragés* had used to build their barricade—as though they weighed nothing at all, and showering them down again like broken toys.

It missed him by centimeters. He came up right, bore her away from there, crooning,

"Kathy. Baby girl. My baby. 'S all right now. Now we've got it made! Now—"

"Ouija," she said. "Oh, Harry, how could you? I hate you! I hate—"

But he bent and stopped her mouth with his own.

One-half second later, the CRS man's *matraque* caught him diagonally across the face and sent him down. From where he lay, looking up into that beet-red face, he knew suddenly, coldly, absolutely that the liberal, conciliatory, non-violent concepts he'd had preached at him all his life were nonsense, absurdities, that Whitey is universal; and that the planet Earth is too small for the white race and the black together. That one of the two of them had to get off. (208–9)

Overcoming his physical and emotional injuries (his limp), his love renewed because of Kathy's return to Paris, Harry enters the heat of a violent political battle, knowing that his dark skin has already fooled the rioters into thinking that he is one of the African students. Some students indeed look like the African members of *Les Katangais* and the Arab members of El Fatah, whose notoriety as "mercenary assassins" and "terrorists," respectively, gives the student revolt a discernibly racial and potentially criminal edge in the eyes of the police (6, 138). Consequently, the police's attempt to quell the uprising, but also to keep the African and Arab militants on their radar, ends up harming students caught in the crossfire.

In his search for Kathy, Harry stumbles into this bloody, violent mess, where his skin confuses the police and puts him in danger of arrest, which ultimately occurs. But the attack on Harry by a CRS officer and his fellows is complex, for two reasons. First, the initial response by the officer focuses on Harry's apparent role in miscegenation: "'*Parce que*,' he said, '*je n'aime pas les nègres, moi*. And *un nègre* with a pretty little blonde like you, even less. *Même quand la blonde* is a foreigner like you, *petite*. I find that sort of thing *dégoûtante*'" (209). Second, the subsequent response by the group mistakes

Harry's retaliation against the officer as part of the more systematic, racial violence against the political order: "An army of security men were upon him. Their *matraques* made a forest, shutting out the firelight," beating him "along with another even dozen bleeding, battered hulks of both sexes into quiescence" (210). Then they toss Harry into the large black police van and take him away, all while rebuffing Kathy's attempt to come along. Despite almost getting killed in this conflict, Harry and Kathy remain committed to each other and even grow stronger in love. Her subsequent admission to the American Consul that she is married to a black man; Harry's longstanding resistance to the overtures and sexual convenience of Ouija; and their mutual willingness to raise Kathy's soon-to-be-born child together, all consummate the progression of their relationship from suspicion to trust, from anxiety to security.

• • •

At the outset of *Speak Now*, in "A Note to the Reader," Yerby asks, "When a man and a woman of different races decide to join their lives, their fortunes, and their sacred honors, who . . . has the right or the arrogance to decide which of them misses, and which cegenates, as it were?" (vii). By bifurcating "miscegenation" into two words, "misses" and his neologism "cegenates," he underscores that the novel explores how the idea of miscegenation has informed anxious conceptions of cohabitation, sexual relations, marriage, and procreation between blacks and whites in the century after American slavery. The novel's student rebellion subplot at the same time exemplifies that racial politics has long been a key theme in Yerby's novels, contrary to his controversial claim that the "race problem" was never his theme of choice. It is true that this theme was associated with the special brand of racial realism—to which he had an aversion—that Richard Wright and his generation of African American writers promoted. It is also true that several of the novels Yerby published prior to *Speak Now* feature African-descended people in minor roles, which for many readers meant that the discussions of race and racism they found in his fiction held minimal political value. Revisiting this novel is the perfect starting point for broadening and revising these claims, which should enable us to deepen our understanding of Yerby's life and legacy.

NOTES

1. All parenthetical references to *Speak Now* correspond to the pagination in Frank Yerby, *Speak Now: A Modern Novel* (Dial Press, 1969).

2. Yerby could have been alluding to the real-life "Fatah," which Yasser Arafat, then leader of a Palestinian guerilla movement in Cairo, Egypt, created in the late 1950s as a nationalist organization for the liberation of Palestine.

3. For an aggregation of Yerby's commercial success, please see the following noteworthy sustained treatments of his life and work: namely, Bruce A. Glasrud and Laurie Champion, "'The Fishes and the Poet's Hands': Frank Yerby, a Black Author in White America," *Journal of American and Comparative Cultures* 23.4 (2000); Darwin Turner, "Frank Yerby: Golden Debunker," *Black Books Bulletin* 1.3 (Spring/Summer 1972); Hoyt A. Fuller, "Famous Writer Faces a Challenge," *Ebony* June 1966; Maryemma Graham, "Frank Yerby, King of the Costume Novel," *Essence* 6.6 (1975); Jack B. Moore, "The Guilt of the Victim: Racial Themes in Some Frank Yerby Novels," *Journal of Popular Culture* 8.4 (Spring 1975); Phyllis Klotman, "A Harrowing Experience: Frank Yerby's First Novel to Film," *CLA Journal* 31.2 (December 1987); and James L. Hill, "The Anti-Heroic Hero in Frank Yerby's Historical Novels," in *Perspectives of Black Popular Culture*, edited by Harry B. Shaw (Bowling Green, Ohio: Bowling Green State U Popular P, 1990).

4. Yerby was born on September 16, 1915, and Wright on September 4, 1908.

5. Note that Yerby dedicates *Speak Now* to Bontemps. Despite Yerby's vexed relationship to the racial-aesthetic principles of the Chicago Renaissance, he nonetheless was part of that intellectual community, at least for a brief period.

6. These words are taken from Wright's unpublished, working draft of an introduction to Whit Burnett's compilation of stories about African American life, initially entitled *The Violent Conflict* and in 1971 appearing as *Black Hands on a White Face*.

7. Frank Yerby, letter to Michel Fabre, in Richard Wright Collection, Schomburg Center for Research in Black Culture, The New York Public Library (April 1, 1963).

8. See Carla Cappetti, *Writing Chicago: Modernism, Ethnography, and the Novel* (New York: Columbia UP, 1993): 187–94. For information about the Chicago Renaissance, see Robert Bone, "Richard Wright and the Chicago Renaissance," *Callaloo*, vol. 9, no. 28, 1986; Cheryl Lester, "A Response to Lawrence Rodgers," *The Langston Hughes Review*, vol. 14, no. 1 & 2, 1996; Lawrence R. Rodgers, "Richard Wright, Frank Marshall Davis and the Chicago Renaissance"; Deborah Barnes, "'I'd Rather Be a Lamppost in Chicago': Richard Wright and the Chicago Renaissance of African American Literature"; Theodore Mason Mason Jr., "A Response to Deborah Barnes' 'I'd Rather Be a Lamppost in Chicago': Richard Wright and the Chicago Renaissance of African American Literature"; and Cappetti, *Writing Chicago: Modernism, Ethnography, and the Novel*.

9. The reviews of *The Foxes of Harrow* illustrate the distaste critics expressed over the discrepancy between this novel and African American novels that focused on African American experiences. But they did so obliquely, through critiques of the formal infelicities and thematic lifelessness: one reviewer said that *The Foxes of Harrow* "never catches the faintest flutter of the breath of life" and "is badly proofread and replete with unorthodox punctuation" (H. W. Wilson 914).

10. For more information, see Gene Andrew Jarrett, *Deans and Truants: Race and Realism in African American Literature* (Philadelphia: The U of Pennsylvania P, 2006).

11. In the postwar 1940s, Ann Petry's *Country Place* (1947), Zora Neale Hurston's *Seraph on the Suwanee* (1947), Willard Motley's *Knock on Any Door* (1947), and Yerby's *The Foxes of*

Harrow, The Vixens (1947), *The Golden Hawk* (1948), and *Pride's Castle* (1949) demonstrated that the avoidance of racial realism in African American literature could make an author's own racial identity incidental.

12. The critical reception of *The Foxes of Harrow*, along with his other novels of the 1940s, was lukewarm at best. One reviewer said that *The Foxes of Harrow* "never catches the faintest flutter of the breath of life" and "is badly proofread and replete with unorthodox punctuation." Another critic said that "literary standards are irrelevant to [*The Vixens'*] high sheen and jet propulsion." For another critic, *The Golden Hawk*'s "roaring prose belongs in a cartoon balloon, rather than between the corners of a full-price novel." Finally, another critic lamented that "an appropriate, albeit probably characteristic, vulgarity pervades [*Pride's Castle's*] expression of nineteenth-century tastelessness."

13. See "Masses, not 'Intellectuals,' Support Harlem's Book Stores, Survey Shows," *The Pittsburgh Courier*, 20 April 1946.

14. However, her Vietnamese nationality did not go over well with Harry's parents after the war (*Speak Now* 79). It is worth noting that the Georgia police view her as "white" when Harry brings her home with him, further illustrating the social construction and contingency of identity.

15. For examples of the role jazz plays as a sexual intermediary between Harry and Kathy, see *Speak Now* 43, 55, and 157.

16. For examples of her recurring anxieties over black sexuality, see *Speak Now* 24, 68. For the connection between Harry's limp and his emotional pain, see 38 and 203.

17. In his book *Discours sur le colonialisme*, first published in 1955 by Editions Présence Africaine and later translated by Joan Pinkham as *Discourse on Colonialism*, Aimé Césaire defines Negritude in the following way: "Our struggle was a struggle against alienation. That struggle gave birth to Negritude. Because Antilles were ashamed of being Negroes, they searched for all sorts of euphemisms for Negro: they would say a man of color, a dark-complexioned man, and other idiocies like that" (89).

18. Edward P. Jones's *The Known World* emphasizes this very subject.

19. For more information about the role of Paris in African American history, see Tyler Edward Stovall, *Paris Noir: African Americans in the City of Light*, Houghton Mifflin, 1996 and Michel Fabre, *From Harlem to Paris: Black American Writers in France, 1840–1980*, U of Illinois P, 1991.

20. Although the novel does not cover the aftermath of the student revolution in France, it is important to note here that it was not in vain. Edgar Faure, then the Minister of Education, enacted a series of educational reforms that addressed the students' concerns. For more information, see Daniel Singer, *Prelude To Revolution: France in May 1968*, South End P, 2002; Alain Touraine, *The May Movement*, Irvington Publishers, 1979; Mark Kurlansky, *1968: The Year That Rocked The World*, Ballantine, 2004.

BIBLIOGRAPHY

Bone, Robert. *The Negro Novel in America*. Yale UP, 1958.
Brown, Lloyd L. "Which Way for the Negro Writer?" *Masses and Mainstream*, vol. 4, no. 3, 1951, pp. 60–61.

Brown, Lloyd L. "Which Way for the Negro Writer?: II." *Masses and Mainstream*, vol. 4, no. 4, 1951, pp. 54.

Brown, Sterling, Arthur Paul Davis, and Ulysses Lee, editors. *The Negro Caravan*. Dryden Press, 1941.

Cappetti, Carla. *Writing Chicago: Modernism, Ethnography, and the Novel*. Columbia UP, 1993.

Césaire, Aimé. *Discourse on Colonialism*. Trans. Joan Pinkham. Monthly Review Press, 1972.

Ellison, Ralph. "That Same Pain, That Same Pleasure: An Interview." *Shadow and Act*. Vintage International, 1995, pp. 24–44.

Fabre, Michel. *Richard Wright: Books and Writers*. UP of Mississippi, 1990.

H. W. Wilson Company. *Book Review Digest*. H. W. Wilson Company.

Jarrett, Gene Andrew. *Deans and Truants: Race and Realism in African American Literature*. U of Pennsylvania P, 2006.

Parker, Jeffrey D. "Frank Yerby." *Afro-American Writers, 1940–1955*, edited by Trudier Harris and Thadious M. Davis. Gale Research, 1988. p. 227.

Teutsch, Matthew. "'Our Women . . . are Ladies': Frank Yerby's Deconstruction of White Southern Womanhood in *Speak Now*." *College Language Association Journal*, vol. 60, no. 3, 2018, pp. 334–47.

Wright, Richard. "Blueprint for Negro Writing." *New Challenge*, vol. 2, no. 2, 1937, pp. 53–65.

Yerby, Frank. "How and Why I Write the Costume Novel." *Harper's*, Oct. 1959, pp. 145–50.

Yerby, Frank. Letter to Michel Fabre. Richard Wright Collection, Schomburg Center for Research in Black Culture, The New York Public Library (April 1, 1963).

Yerby, Frank. *Speak Now: A Modern Novel*. Dial Press, 1969.

FINDING THE "NECESSARY ANGUISH"

Frank Yerby's "The Tents of Shem"

STEPHANIE BROWN

THE WORK OF FRANK YERBY, SO LONG NEGLECTED OR MALIGNED, IS UN-dergoing a significant critical reappraisal, as this essay collection demonstrates. While Yerby's short stories have drawn some attention, especially his first major publication, the 1944 O. Henry award–winning "Health Card," most of the recent focus has been on Yerby's first novel, *The Foxes of Harrow*, published in 1946 and justly deemed a fascinating and groundbreaking work.[1] Yerby's debut, in its tale of an Irish immigrant who marries a wealthy Creole and founds a plantation he believes (erroneously) will be the seat of a future Southern dynasty, offers an intriguing revision of the plantation novel's familiar narrative as well as an array of black secondary characters who transcend the models presupposed by the genre. A bestseller and the first novel by an African American writer to be adapted into a major Hollywood film, *Foxes* and its sequel, *The Vixens*, gave Yerby an entrée into popular fiction, allowing him to become one of the most popular African American writers of the twentieth century.

Yerby published more than 30 additional novels over the subsequent four decades, but scholars have not accorded most of them more than cursory consideration. In general, critics have been content to summarize Yerby's oeuvre by claiming that after unsuccessful attempts to publish "This Is My Own," a protest novel, Yerby shifted his focus for the next twenty years to "costume novels," featuring dashing white male characters (and their beautiful sex partners) in exotic settings. Critics continue by noting that in 1969, then long resident in Madrid, Yerby suddenly produced *Speak Now*, a novel centered on the story of a black American expatriate musician who falls in love with a white southern heiress. Two years later, Yerby's *The*

Dahomean appeared; it tells the story of an enslaved African chief's son and is widely considered Yerby's most significant work. Some critics mention that between 1946 and 1969 Yerby produced a second "protest" novel, "The Tents of Shem," which was twice rejected by publishers, first in 1963 and then again in 1969. The connection between Yerby's first unpublished protest novel and his second, however, has never been explored. I argue that "Tents" plays a crucial role in the evolution of Yerby's work. Specifically, it both harks back to the concerns and themes preoccupying the pre-publication Yerby and looks ahead to the substantial shift in the latter part of his career. "The Tents of Shem" creates a bridge between early and late Yerby, one that helps to show both the continuity and the development of his politics and his art.

Complicating an analysis of this nature is that fact that little but the title is known about Yerby's first unpublished novel, "This Is My Own." The manuscript no longer exists, possibly having been destroyed by Yerby himself.[2] Similarly, there is little consensus about the manuscript's content or the reason it went unpublished. James L. Hill describes the novel as "a protest story about a Northern black steel worker turned professional boxer" that publishers "rejected . . . but not without encouragement" (391), while Laurie Champion and Bruce Glasrud observe that "white publishing houses thought it too incendiary" (16). Yerby himself, as Gene Andrew Jarrett notes, described his protagonist in a letter to a reader as "a Negro PhD" and insisted that the novel was anathema to publishers because "the book buying public—which is 99 percent white" simply did not believe in the existence of "fine, well-educated, clean, intelligent, moral Negroes" (qtd. in Jarrett 149). In fact, Yerby told the same reader, his editors "suggested that [he] have [the protagonist] quit school in his early high school days and become a prizefighter" (qtd. in Jarrett 149).

Correspondence between Yerby and his agent Muriel Fuller indicates that the novel underwent numerous revisions in response to editors' suggestions. Yerby himself describes cutting "quite literally with scissors—hunks of manuscript." Consisting, according to Yerby, of "ninety one thousand words" written in "slightly over seven weeks," the book contained, in Yerby's own estimation, "clichés, sloppy writing, and technical imperfections." Yet over the course of his correspondence with Muriel Fuller, it also emerges that Yerby altered his characters and plot substantially as well. Bucklin Moon of Doubleday, Edward Aswell of Harper's, and Fuller herself all made suggestions that Yerby apparently took, including eschewing graphic representations of racial violence; "deleting Henry's [the protagonist's] photographic memory, and making his school career more plausible by letting him be less of a paragon"; and excising a final thirty-five pages set in Africa and England (Letter to Fuller [3 January 1944]). Additionally, Yerby's first wife, Flora, told Fuller in a letter that she had "been through [the manuscript] and removed all the flowery phrases" (Letter [5 January 1944]). Specifically, Yerby later told Fuller, he had excised

> all far-fetched, melodramatic incidents: The old woman being tossed off the Street car in Atlanta (the fact that I saw this happen does not make it more believable), Henry's fight with the Hillbillies in Gary, and his fight with the MPs in the Southern camp were deleted. Miss Curtiss' opinions in the second chapter, the long stagey dialogue about racial problems at Professor Cokk's house also were cut out. (Letter to Fuller [1 March 1944])

Despite the many revisions, Edward Aswell nevertheless passed a second time on "This Is My Own." Two years later, Dial Press published *The Foxes of Harrow*. Its success proved a strong inducement to Yerby to produce novels throughout the 1950s that adhered more or less closely to the formula he had established in his debut, even as he moved with his family to Europe, first settling in France and then, after divorcing Flora, moving to Madrid in 1956 with his second wife, Blanquita. There, by the 1960s, James L. Hill notes that Yerby "became noticeably concerned about the critical reception of his novels" which, Hill argues, "also spawned his interest in writing about contemporary issues" ("Frank Garvin Yerby," 401). The result of his rediscovered desire to write a contemporary story with political relevance was "The Tents of Shem," a novel set in 1963 but with its roots in Yerby's life and work in the 1940s. Most critics and biographers of Yerby have mentioned "Tents," usually noting, as Hill does, that while "neither Yerby nor his publishers ever indicated why [it] was not published," it is likely that "Yerby's editors decided that the novel lacked the popular appeal of his previous novels and would damage his noncontroversial image." Yerby himself alludes to this assessment in a "Note to the Reader" he wrote in 1969 following his final revision of the earlier manuscript; it reads, in part, "Why was THE TENTS OF SHEM not published in 1963? . . . Say that there were persons then connected with the writer by ties of both business and friendship who succeeded in convincing him, against his own better judgment, that the publication of this novel would be damaging to his public image . . . and advised him to burn it, or, if he could not overcome a writer's perverse love for the misbegotten children of his psyche, to store it away in the remotest attic he could find" ("Tents," unnumbered reader's note). Critics also often follow Hill's lead in suggesting that "The Tents of Shem" "influenced his writing of his two most important novels, *Speak Now* and *The Dahomean*" (401). However, no one has looked closely at the manuscript itself. Doing so provides an entirely new trajectory for Yerby's career. The manuscript is the pivot around which Yerby's career as a novelist turned. Like "This Is My Own," whose rejection led Yerby to rethink the protest genre and embark upon a series of successful "costume novels," "The Tents of Shem" changed the direction of his work. It offered him a space in which to articulate his own ambivalence about race politics in the United States, ultimately resulting in his addressing race more overtly than in his previous novels.

Like "This Is My Own," "Tents" was rejected twice, this time by Yerby's established publisher, Dial Press, first in 1963 and again in 1969. Unlike "This Is My Own," which Yerby dismissed after the publication of *Foxes* as "a conventional social protest novel" that he "would be ashamed to write now," "Tents" remained one of Yerby's favorite efforts (Carter 14). In a handwritten note on the title page of the revised manuscript, Yerby even intones, "it remains the very best I've <u>ever</u> done." Similar to "This Is My Own," "Tents" also features a well-educated and articulate African American, Dred Scott Johnson, at the center of its narrative. However, Yerby entwines Johnson's story with that of Marvin Ellis, a handsome white "romantic lead" much more typical of his successful "formula" fiction. Ultimately, Dred Johnson and Marvin Ellis function as figures for the complexities of the Civil Rights movement in the United States, which Yerby told Hoyt A. Fuller in a 1966 *Ebony* interview that he followed closely from his expatriate vantage point, at least in part so that he could explain events to European friends (188).[3] Together, these characters also pave the way for the appearance in 1969 of Harry Forbes in *Speak Now*, Yerby's first true black protagonist and, I would argue, possibly the long-delayed successor to Henry of "This Is My Own," the "paragon" Yerby described to Fuller as "intelligent, educated—no 'Bigger Thomas' in any sense of the word . . . myself" (Letter to Fuller [25 November 1943]). Indeed, a contemporary review of *Speak Now* describes Harry as "a cultivated, erudite and disenchanted nomad who has trenchant opinions on matters humane, from French cab drivers to the fall of the Roman empire and the Sorbonne rebellion" (*New York Times*, 30 November 1969).

"Tents" opens with what will be the driver for the plot, a discussion of the exclusivity of the small, upper-middle-class New York town in which the novel is set. Marvin, a former star football player and war hero who is now the principal of the local high school, gives Millicent Merriweather, the newly hired English teacher with whom he ultimately has an extramarital affair, an overview of "Hazelhorne," whose history dates to the Revolutionary War era and whose design is the legacy of a fictitious Thomas Hepplewhite. According to Marvin, Hepplewhite (the name is clearly meant to evoke the eighteenth-century English furniture designer George Hepplewhite, underscoring the town's WASP origins and bona fides) intended the town to stand as an indictment of all things "urban": "'Notice how the streets of Hazelhorne curve gently, making letter S's most of time?' Marvin asks. 'Adds to the beauty, but it exposes our yards much more than a rectilinear city plan would have'" ("Tents," 15). Such exposure, Marvin suggests, demands that the inhabitants adhere to specific standards in order to maintain the placid façade of the community. Part of this order includes policing the occupants of Hazelhorne, and Marvin notes that he most recently voted to exclude a "celebrated painter" because "along with his indisputable genius went a propensity for strong drink and riotous living, which included taking sunbaths stark naked" (15). Yet, it is also clear that the real "urban" threat Hazelhorne perceives is one of identity, not behavior. When Hepplewhite designed the town, "he had in mind a certain sort of people" (13). "Does a man have the right to choose his neighbors?" Marvin rhetorically asks. He answers his own question stating, "Frankly, I don't know. I do know that a homogenous, harmonious community like ours is a very pleasant place to live" (14).

Marvin is called upon to spearhead an attempt to drive Dred Johnson's family out of Hazelhorne through strategies ranging from buying him out to blackmailing him. The situation offers an obverse mirror of Yerby's own experience some twenty years before the era in which the novel is set, at a time when restrictive housing covenants were still being used legally for racial segregation.[4] In a 1946 profile in the *Afro-American*, Michael Carter describes Valley Stream, Long Island, where Yerby and his family lived at the time. Carter describes the house as "a little six-room plus sun parlor and dinette, red oak frame house that like all the other little middle-class houses on the Island," and he continues by taking readers on a tour of the town, highlighting the segregation apparent underneath the "red oak frame" façades: "As you leave the railroad station, you are bound to notice the anti-Semitic slogans carefully worded-in over the advertising placards in the waiting rooms. They are obviously written by unhurried hands. One of them says, 'Rout the Jews,' and another says, 'And the n—s too.'" (14).

The article, which appeared just as *The Foxes of Harrow* climbed the bestseller list, notes that the other residents of Valley Stream did not begin to ignore or mistreat Yerby and his family until they realized that they were not white; furthermore, James Hill remarks, "after the writer deposited $150,000 in a local bank [following the publication of *Foxes*], the Yerbys became the community's favorite citizens" (391). This information, of course, could only have come from Yerby himself, and the presentation of the incident serves both to highlight the absurdity of the community's racism and to underscore Yerby's own relative indifference to its ramifications. Carter highlights Yerby's relative indifference: "Yerby is not unmoved by [his neighbors' attitudes] but it doesn't annoy him and he doesn't discuss it" (14). Yerby directly addresses, in fact, the question of why he chose Valley Stream over the urban environment of Harlem, remarking that he "didn't move to Harlem because [he didn't] like ugliness [or] any slum area" (Carter, 14).

Yet, for all of Yerby's insistence at this juncture in his career that he was "not exposed to the kind of life that would enable [him] to produce a good protest novel" (Carter, 14), two decades later Yerby nevertheless anchored the plot and title of his first modern novel in an all-white community desperate to retain what Marvin muses are modern-day "tents of Shem," in which "we take our ease . . . while compelling [Canaan] to hew our wood and draw our water" ("Tents," 121).[5] Functionally, the novel consists of two intertwined plotlines, both centering on moral dilemmas faced by Marvin, the white protagonist. In the first, Marvin initiates, consummates, and then ends a sexual relationship with Millicent "Merry" Merriweather, who is beautiful and intellectually accomplished, "the only Ph.D. on the faculty [at the high school], and the only authentically lovely woman in all of Hazelhorne" (4). In the second moral dilemma, Marvin attempts first to intimidate and then to blackmail Dred, but finally he is forced to face his racist assumptions and renounce his plan to drive the Johnsons from Hazelhorne. The novel wraps one plot in the other, as Marvin combines an out-of-town trip aimed at digging up dirt on Dred with a rendezvous with Merry. Yerby ends the narrative abruptly with the newly enlightened Marvin's sudden death in a car wreck in which Merry, now engaged to another man after losing Marvin's baby in a miscarriage brought on by near-fatal pneumonia, is also killed.

Yerby's editor at Dial, Bob Cornfield, rejected the novel, arguing in a letter that it was "split in its effect." "There are almost two novels here," Cornfield writes, "one small, defined, startling and sure, yet not completed, and a bigger work, more indefinite in intent, thus perhaps greater in ambition and method." For Cornfield, the book was "an uneasy mixture of the realistic and the almost apocalyptic. The moral plains," he concludes, "are too various for a certain consistency of vision to be held, at least for me" (Letter [22 January 1970]).

Yerby's response, a week later, was scathing. He accused Cornfield of judging the novel according to his own "puritanical concepts of sexual morality" and remarked that Cornfield's inability to grant Yerby's characters "the weight or impress" they deserved was "neither Marvin's fault nor [Yerby's], but rather [Cornfield's]." Yerby concludes by indicting Cornfield's views, "to me, your comments about the last half of the book tell me less about my novel than they do about *you*" (Letter to Cornfield [29 January 1970]).

Leaving aside all questions of "morality," Yerby argues the book is about "a poor, sad, mixed-up slob who was a reluctant son of a bitch" who ultimately "accepts defeat" (Letter to Cornfield [30 January 1970]). In this context, the two narratives Cornfield identifies in fact work in tandem rather than at cross-purposes. What Cornfield sees as "inconsistency" makes sense if one considers "The Tents of Shem" as an opportunity for Yerby (and the reader) to explore the ramifications of moral and intellectual certainty in the context of a complicated personal and political issues like the reality of mid-twentieth century American racism. To be too sure of one's stance on race, the novel ultimately concludes, is to lack the "necessary anguish" to experience full humanity, in the phrasing of the character of Foster Dillon, a wealthy white attorney who is one of the few to refuse to support the campaign against the Johnsons. For Marvin, acknowledging his "anguish," which entails recognizing the anguish of others as well, marks both his liberation and his destruction.

In both his extramarital affair and his campaign to discredit Dred Johnson, Marvin begins from a position of certainty about the rightness of his inclinations. He rationalizes his desire for Merry as the logical result of the inability of his wife, Dee, to maintain her original standards of beauty. Marvin remarks, after spending time with Merry, that he sees Dee

> with the furious, merciless clarity of contrast. Her hair, which over the years had retreated from taffy blonde to mousy brown, now liberally streaked with grey, hung about her shoulders in one of those long-ish bobs that only a teenager could afford to wear, and not even all teenagers, at that. It was characteristic of Dee's rather painful honesty that her hair remained both unbleached and unretouched. *And of her taste,* he thought wryly, *that she doesn't realize a woman of forty-three shouldn't wear it that way.*
>
> He dropped his gaze to what was visible of her body, which, since the jersey knit clung to her, was rather a bit too much. She had gained close to forty pounds since their marriage. (24)

Marvin's relationship with Merry, in which she professes her helplessness to deny her "dumb beast, bitch-kitty of a body" and her attraction to an older man who calls her "Infant," threatens to upend his family's happiness and his social position in Hazelhorne, yet he never seriously considers not pursuing a relationship cast as inevitable (290).[6] Marvin's desire for Merry is apparently shared by virtually every other man in Hazelhorne, thus sanctioning his extramarital affair. From the recently widowed football coach to the lawyer Dee hires to document Marvin's infidelity for divorce proceedings, men fawn over Merry. Indeed, even Dred remarks to Marvin, in front of his wife, "my guess is that . . . you laid that pretty English teacher. My comment on that is, if you didn't, you were a goddamned fool" (302). In this sense, the town condones Marvin's adultery even more comprehensively than his racism. While his extramarital affair does not lead him to physical harm, his obsessive pursuit of negative information about Dred, whose Harvard degrees, wartime service and apparent wealth all mark him as one of Yerby's "paragons," leads Marvin to physical danger. He persists because, as he sees it, he has no other choice but to try to dissuade the Johnsons from living in Hazelhorne. "Few men's liberalism survives their fortieth birthday," he tells Dee. "When a man has acquired a wife, children, a mortgage—even a certain status in the community, the amount and degree of pure altruism he can afford becomes sharply reduced" (111). Dee agrees with Marvin, in contrast to Merry, who bemoans the fact that his political convictions show that "the same man with the mind of a poet can also have such a bargain basement soul" (127). His certainty that he must drive the Johnsons out, however, is also based on the "absolutely indefensible, but not—let's face it!—untenable atavism" of his bedrock aversion to the figure of the interracial couple evoked by his encountering Manny, Dred's handsome, mixed-race son, and picturing an African American man dating his own daughter, Anne, as Manny ultimately does (112).[7] In both cases, Marvin's convictions about his own actions are driven by desires and fears, but he perceives them as based in logic, rationality, and "common sense." As he puts it to Samson Myers, the realtor who sells the Johnsons their house in Hazelhorne, "I can't deal with causes . . . the facts are headaches enough" (162). Interracial relationships, Marvin tells Anne as he counsels her to forget about Manny, are simply doomed to fail, regardless of love, courage, and noble intentions, no matter who the participants are and no matter where they live.[8] In his conflict with Dred, Marvin has, as he later tells Colonel Carson, Dred's former commanding officer, "run head on into the world's oldest conflict: between what is right, and what is expedient"—and initially he believes he knows which side he is on (221).

Dred Johnson is, of course, the catalyst for Marvin's evolution from smugness to self-loathing, the engine of his journey from "son of a bitch" (a category into which he is initially placed by both Carson and Myers) to chastened spouse and citizen. Yet because Marvin and Dred are both figures for Yerby's own philosophical ambivalence, they are less foils than counterparts.[9] Marvin meets Dred for the first time while defending him from an attack by violent white teenagers. Entering their house so that Dred's wife, Beth, a nurse, can dress the wound he has sustained, Marvin looks around at their furniture—"a good bit more expensive and even more tasteful than his own"—and books—"everywhere . . . [i]n three languages"—and quickly realizes that "he could easily be persuaded to like them" (81). Yet he returns to offer Dred a large sum for his house on behalf of the homeowners' association because they fear that real estate values will drop in the wake of an "invasion" by African American buyers. Dred refuses, as Marvin says he expected all along, and the conversation quickly turns from economics to "miscegenation":

> "Wait," Dred Johnson said. "Are you, personally, still opposed to our living here?"
> "Yes," Marvin said. "And with even better reasons than before. You'd better take that boy of yours in hand, Johnson!" (187)

Beth objects forcefully, defending Manny and observing that historically, interracial sexual relationships were more often instigated by whites than blacks, as evidenced by "the fact that American Negroes are at least eighty percent a mulatto race."

> "Beth, Baby," Dred said; "let's drop the subject, shall we? Or at least, this aspect of the subject?"
> "Why?" Beth said. "When it's this aspect of the subject that all the rest are based on—that is the cause of all the rest?" (188).

Beth, described by Yerby as "the best black woman character I've ever written," points unerringly to the heart of Marvin's objections, but he and Dred nevertheless continue to compare their perspectives on race (Hill, "An Interview" 238). Echoing Yerby's own observations twenty years earlier, Dred notes that although he finds Hazelhorne's "culturial [sic] level rather disappointing," he refuses "to live in ghettos, or in any surroundings inferior to [his] personal standing" (189). He then explains that having "built America . . . with our brawn, our sweat" and having "died for it, more or less willingly, in every war," African Americans have every right to live "any place [they] goddamn well please, as long as it's within the confines of the land that was conceived in liberty and dedicated to the proposition that all men are created equal." If whites attempt to stand in the way, Dred observes wryly, then "you have to maintain the dubious contention . . . that the Declaration of Independence was written upon toilet paper for tail wiping purposes" (191).

Ultimately, Marvin agrees with Dred's logic but maintains "all his carefully thought out objections, based not on the Negro's right to equality, which he didn't question, but his readiness for it, which he did" (193). Dred objects that "readiness" is a matter of opportunity but says that "for [his] own selfish reasons" he will see to it that "whatever Negroes may come here [Hazelhorne] are decent, upstanding, and, if possible, outstanding folk." Though he initially agrees to Dred's proposition, when Beth mentions that Manny is "out with your daughter, sure as shooting," Marvin returns to his original intransigence (194).

The remainder of the novel tracks Marvin's attempts to discredit Dred, initially as part of the campaign to force him to move and then, when Marvin's son Bob strikes and seriously injures Manny, in an attempt to persuade Dred not to bring charges. Marvin first contacts Dred's former commanding officer, Colonel Carson, then makes a pilgrimage to Dred's (and Yerby's) home town of Augusta, Georgia. There he learns that one of Dred's commanding officers considers him a hero for having saved his life under enemy fire while another officer deems him a criminal, based on an accusation of dealing in contraband goods while stationed in France. Unable to reconcile the two versions of Dred's history, Marvin finds himself wondering again about the role played in his life of "necessary anguish . . . of which, it would seem, Dred Johnson had already had his share" (280). In Augusta, as Marvin prepares to return to New York, he stops at a diner for lunch and sees five young African Americans stage a peaceful protest:

> There were five of them: two boys and three girls. They were better dressed than any Negroes he had seen since he had come South. The boys wore neat, dark business suits, vests, white shirts, ties. The girls were variously clad in sweaters and skirts, a simple wool dress, a two piece—all subdued, all very well cut. Their kinky hair had been straightened then coiffed with considerable art. They wore no jewelry. Very little makeup. What they wore was something else—something, Marvin thought achingly, that has almost disappeared from

the Western World. Call it dedication. Purpose. But, Sweet Suffering Christ, look at them! Look at them and know— (280–81)

A crowd of whites attack the young men and women, and Marvin realizes, at last, what his own position looks like from the outside: "their faces wearing that expression by which you know them everywhere: that hard, set, quiet look of perfect certitude, that absence of all doubt, that lack of—Foster's phrase smashed back into his brain—of necessary anguish" (282). Marvin watches as the whites "drag the black youngsters out of the diner, smash them to the sidewalk outside, ring them round about, kicking." As the protesters practice passive resistance, he sees the "girls' faces bloody, young, slender, lovely female bodies being kicked" and feels compelled to defend them; seeing "Anne there in their place, being ringed about, kicked into unconsciousness," he accepts "once and for all and forever their humanity, and thereby, his own" (282).

Marvin jumps into the fray, and after the ensuing fight, in which he is far outnumbered, Marvin is arrested, fined, and released.[10] Interviewed by a local reporter before he leaves town, Marvin gives a statement in which he both reverses his earlier "pragmatic" appraisal of racism as an unpleasant but inexorable fact of mid-twentieth-century life and echoes Dred's evocation of the Declaration of Independence:

> Look at them and know—that they're going to win. That they can't lose. They've got it made, friend. Because we can't fight them. Because behind them is everything America stands for, all the pretty words in all the Fourth of July speeches ever made. One nation, under God, indivisible. Self evident truths: Life—to live as best they know how; liberty—even to drink a goddamned coke and eat a gutbusting sandwich at a greasy lunchcounter; and the pursuit of happiness, however they define happiness. And don't ask me about my stupid sister! She can marry anybody she goddamn well pleases . . . (286)

Having conflated Anne with the black female activists, Marvin is now free to recognize the absurdity of his earlier insistence that she and Manny split, and his final statement, alluding to the apocryphal sister of racist discourse, thoroughly contradicts his earlier stance on interracial relationships. Marvin returns to Hazelhorne determined to articulate his new understanding of his position as a white man in a racist country and world. "I, individually, don't want to wear my pale skin as a badge of dishonor," he tells Dee, "which is what it is, really—" (286). Marvin then goes on to chronicle the atrocities committed by whites throughout history, clearly illustrating his profound political and philosophical shift. He demonstrates a new ability to think beyond the local concerns that have thus far preoccupied him, expanding outwards to think about the global ramifications of a belief in white supremacy:

> What color were the men who exterminated the Caribe Indians? The Chibchas? Who dragged black men across half the world to make them slaves? Committed upon them, upon their women, every unspeakable barbarity conceivable? Who blew Hindus from the mouths of cannon in their own land? Who murdered Chinese by the thousands in order to enforce the right to sell them the opium that was turning them into witless sots? Where are the Iriquois [sic] today, Dee? The Blackfeet, the Senecas, the Cherokees, the Comanche, the— God, the list is endless! . . . When in all of human history has the white man not been the scourge of earth? . . . I shudder at the day when they'll rise up and ring us about. When to save our colorless hides we'll have to kill and kill again until this blasted planet remains a barren hunk of radioactive rock. (293)

In his final encounter with Dred, Marvin plans to tell him that he no longer intends to try to blackmail him, but Dred first announces that he has been reassigned to Geneva and then begins to talk before Marvin has the chance to speak. Dred admits that the information Marvin has uncovered is true and that he stole and sold military goods on the black market. To give Marvin context, however, he describes the torment of his early life and the psychological effects of systemic racism on African Americans, believing that Marvin will at least try to understand. He tells the newly receptive Marvin that he has always known that he was capable of doubt, no matter how "smug" he appeared to be. "Things claw at your guts, too," he tells Marvin.[11]

> "You have your share of—"
> "Necessary anguish?" Marvin said.
> "Yes. . . . And it's the essential quality of a civilized man. That whatever he does, he can't be *sure*." (302)

Dred explains his own discovery of the "necessary anguish" as arising from his realization that he had been conditioned by a racist society not only to hate whites, but also to hate himself. He describes his attitude in the war as nearly suicidal and his criminal activities as something he justified as "getting back some of Grandpappy's unpaid wages" (308). All of this changed, he says, when he found himself in an unexpected firefight and fought ferociously for the first time, drawing the attention of Colonel Carson, the man whose life he saved and who, Dred says "gave me back my pride." Under Carson's command, Dred tells Marvin, he also served alongside a southerner who took pleasure in making racist comments but then died saving Dred's life later. If Carson gave him pride, Dred insists, the southerner, Gene, gave him a "capacity for compassion, pity, love.... I won't let any son of a bitch ruin that, rack me back into hate again" (353). Marvin finally reveals that he never intended to blackmail Dred, and Beth, overcome with relief, kisses Marvin in a final gesture of forgiveness.

Marvin's experience in Augusta, which marks the turning point in his attitude toward the Johnsons, inspires Manny to move South to work as a civil rights activist. In his final conversation with Dred, Marvin learns the story of Manny's conception and adoption. The result of Dred's relationship with a German woman, who cared neither for Dred nor, ultimately, for their son, Manny comes to live with Dred and Beth, who embraces him fully. By the novel's end, Manny and Anne are divided, Anne attending a single-sex school in Massachusetts and Manny newly involved with a woman he describes as "not quite as black as Mom [Beth], but almost" (339). Marvin, who has reconciled with Dee, has his final encounter with Merry who tells him that she has miscarried and now intends to marry Colonel Carson. Driving back with her while thinking to himself that the future he sees ahead, "oversupplied now with that necessary anguish," will consist of "liv[ing] out his life in the state of quiet desperation," Marvin suddenly realizes that another car is about to run him off the road (350). In the ensuing crash, both Marvin and Merry die.

The novel's sudden end reveals a different Yerby than the one who penned either "This Is My Own" or *Speak Now*. While the first novel can no longer be read, Yerby's letters to Muriel Fuller indicate that his final revision of the manuscript ended "with Henry embarking for Africa" (Letter [1 March 1944]). Similarly, *Speak Now* ends with Harry and Kathy's reconciliation and their realization that "it was going to work" because "the knowledge that admission of failure to a world that confidently expected and freely predicted that failure didn't even exist as an alternative for them" (191–92). Especially if one interprets Harry and Kathy's relationship as a metaphor for the history and future of American race relations, as Matthew Teutsch does, the contrast is stark between their recognition of the role of love and humility in overcoming racism and Marvin's resigned acceptance of the same discovery.[12] Yet it is clear that the earlier manuscript grapples with some of the same questions that make *Speak Now* a groundbreaking book.

Ultimately, a close examination of "The Tents of Shem" reveals a Yerby prepared to readdress the issues of race that motivated his first novel, "This Is My Own," through the prism of experiences that affected him directly at the time. Yet he was not ready to use a contested but finally successful interracial sexual relationship as a figure for American race relations. The final "apocalyptic" ending underscores the destructive capacity of Marvin's newly overturned worldview—he has acquired the "necessary anguish" at last to embrace a future in which he will recognize his principles and try to live by them, but his newfound ambivalence shatters the man he thought he was. In the end, Marvin represents a generation that must disappear to clear a space for the next, including the youthful protesters, or Manny and Anne, or, finally, *Speak Now*'s Harry and Kathy. In the same way, the unpublished "Tents" marks a transitional moment in Yerby's prose and a space in which he found a new and productive direction. As the final postscript in his letter to editor Bob Cornfield observed, "I'll finish *The Dahomean* soon" (Letter [January 30 1970]).

NOTES

1. See, for example, Gene Andrew Jarrett's "'For Endless Generations': Myth, Dynasty, and Frank Yerby's *The Foxes of Harrow*" (*The Southern Literary Journal* 39:1, 2006) and *Deans and Truants: Race and Realism in African American Literature* (U of Pennsylvania P, 2011); Stephanie Brown's *The Postwar African-American Novel: Protest and Discontent, 1945–1950* (Jackson, UP of Mississippi, 2011); John C. Charles's *Abandoning the Black Hero: Sympathy and Privacy in the Postwar African American White-Life Novel* (Rutgers UP, 2012); and Veronica Watson's *Souls of White Folks: African American Writers Theorize Whiteness* (Jackson: UP of Mississippi, 2013).

2. Several critics, including Laurie Champion, Bruce A. Glasrud, and John C. Charles, suggest that Yerby burned the manuscript. This assumption seems to be rooted in a 1944 letter Yerby sent to Muriel Fuller, who had tried and failed to place the book with Harper and Brothers, in which he asks (presumably rhetorically) if he now "should send it to Atlantic Monthly Press—or quietly burn it?" (Letter [25 March 1944]).

3. In the same interview, Yerby noted acerbically that while he could not play an active role in the Civil Rights movement because he feared that militants faced violence and he was "a coward," nevertheless he remained committed to visiting and understanding the United States: "I love my country. Unfortunately, my country doesn't love me enough to let me live in it" (Fuller, 188).

4. Restrictive housing covenants have a long and ignoble twentieth-century American history. Used extensively in the 1920s and 1930s, covenants aimed at excluding potential

residents on the basis of race, ethnicity, or even, in some cases, a working-class background, were finally ruled unconstitutional in 1948, while discriminatory practices in housing were precluded more comprehensively in the Fair Housing Act of 1968. See, for example, Richard R.W. Brooks and Carol M. Rose's *Saving the Neighborhood: Racially Restrictive Covenants, Laws and Social Norms* (Harvard UP, 2013.)

5. The reference is to the biblical story, told in Genesis, of the fate of Noah's three sons, Shem, Ham, and Japheth, and the "curse of Canaan," the son of Ham, as a result of Ham's "discovery" of Noah's nakedness while the latter lay drunk in his tent. Noah called upon God to "enlarge Japheth/and let him dwell in the tents of Shem/and let Canaan be his servant" (Genesis 9:27), a prophecy seen as being fulfilled by the subduing of the land of Canaan by the Israelites described in 1 Kings 9:20–21. The "curse of Ham," a misnomer that also relies on a possible mistranslation of "Ham" as "black," was sometimes used as a biblical justification for American slavery.

6. The overtones of incest in the novel are hard to ignore. Merry tells Marvin that she feels "all kinds of quasi-incestious [sic] feelings—I adored my father, and he left us; I worshipped my brother, and he went with Dad" (127). Marv's preferred nickname for Merry is "Infant," a moniker that echoes "Babygirl," Harry Forbes's usual term for Kathy Nichols, his much younger lover, in *Speak Now*. "Babygirl" is also what Marvin sometimes calls his teenage daughter, Anne. For her part, Anne rebukes her father when he refers to himself as "old," telling him "I think you're kind of all right. All the girls in my class get the giggles when you walk by. Makes me feel great. I wouldn't want to have the kind of fathers they've got" (103). Later, as Dred Johnson's son Manny, to whom Anne has been attracted and whom Marvin's son Robert has brutally attacked, lies in the hospital badly injured, Anne tells Marvin, who has just explained to her that he intends to send her away to a boarding school so that she can never see Manny again, that he is "still a little old living doll" (251). Given that Manny is near death, the implied positioning of Marvin as a "living" successor for her affections is discomfiting.

7. Anne's name is, of course, no accident. In the Harlem of the 1920s, "Miss Anne" was a term applied to a "voluntary Negro," a white woman interested in African American culture, African American lovers, or both. See Carla Kaplan's comprehensive history *Miss Anne in Harlem: The White Women of the Harlem Renaissance* (Harper, 2013). Harry, in *Speak Now*, refers to Kathy repeatedly as "Miss Anne," as well, employing the term more in its original sense to designate an arrogant or condescending white woman.

8. Marvin bolsters his lecture with improbable anecdotes illustrating the obstacles to Anne's relationship with Manny, including a story about a white southern friend and his Jamaican wife who are unable to find acceptance even in Greenwich Village and end up suffering from alcoholism and in a mental institution, respectively; and a tale about an African chieftain who "was disposed by his own tribe when he returned from his studies at Oxford with an English bride" (249). He also delivers an impromptu lecture on French attitudes, claiming that Manny's light skin would make him a target of French police prejudiced not against African Americans but against Algerians. Like most Yerby heroes, Marvin expatiates freely on many subjects; here; however, his words have to be reconsidered in the context of Harry and Kathy's decision to remain together in *Speak Now*, where they will presumably settle in France and produce children Kathy explicitly hopes will look like

Ouija, the young Algerian woman after whom Kathy announces she wishes to name her first daughter.

9. *Speak Now*'s Harry Forbes brings Dred and Marvin together, combining Dred's southern childhood and expatriate experience with Marvin's sexual and artistic prowess. For example, Harry's skill as a clarinetist wins Kathy's admiration and love in a scene that echoes "Tents," in which Merry is awestruck by a reading of Marvin's poetry and subsequently reveals her own desire. In both cases, the artistic work was created for another woman (Harry plays an original composition, "Fugue for Fleur," written for his late wife; Marvin's poems were originally dedicated to Dee) but is powerful enough to transcend its original context. All three also share military experience overseas and war wounds: Marvin and Dred in World War II and Harry in Vietnam.

10. It is tempting to speculate that the fight between Marvin and the white supremacists in Augusta reflects "Henry's fight with the Hillbillies in Gary," an excised portion of "This Is My Own," though of course this is unknown.

11. The metaphor of doubt as "things clawing at one's guts" is literalized in Marvin's war wound, in which his abdomen was cut open by flak and surgeons were forced to drastically reduce the size of his stomach to save his life; as a result, Marvin suffers from an inability to eat normally and from stomach pain.

12. See Teutsch "'Our Women . . . are Ladies': Frank Yerby's Deconstruction of White Southern Womanhood in *Speak Now*."

BIBLIOGRAPHY

Carter, Michael. "Meet Frank 'Foxes of Harrow' Yerby." *The Afro American*. 2 March 1944. 14.

Fuller, Hoyt A. "Famous Writer Faces a Challenge." *Ebony*, June 1966, pp. 188–94.

Glasrud, Bruce A., and Laurie Champion. "'The Fishes and the Poet's Hands': Frank Yerby, A Black Author in White America." *Journal of American and Contemporary Cultures*, vol. 23, 2000, pp. 15–22.

Hill, James L. "Frank Garvin Yerby." *Writers of the Black Chicago Renaissance*, edited by Steven C. Tracy, U of Illinois P, 2011, pp. 386–412.

Hill, James L. "An Interview with Frank Garvin Yerby." *Resources for American Literary Study*, vol. 21, no. 2, 1995, pp. 206–39.

Jarrett, Gene Andrew. *Deans and Truants: Race and Realism in African-American Literature*. U of Pennsylvania P, 2011.

Teutsch, Matthew. "'Our Women . . . are Ladies': Frank Yerby's Deconstruction of White Southern Womanhood in *Speak Now*." *CLA Journal*, vol. 60, no. 3, 2017, pp. 334–47.

Yerby, Frank. *Speak Now*. Dial Press, 1969.

Yerby, Frank. "The Tents of Shem." Unpublished manuscript. Collins-Callaway Library Archives and Special Collections. Paine College, Augusta, GA

A CAMUS FOR THE COMMON FOLK

Yerby, Religion, and Existentialism

ANDERSON ROUSE

W. E. B. DU BOIS WROTE "A LITANY OF DEATH" IN RESPONSE TO THE 1906 Atlanta race riots. In the poem, he implores God to punish the violent white mob who attacked and killed African Americans in Atlanta. He asks, "How long shall the mounting flood of innocent blood roar in Thine ears . . . for vengeance" and pleads that God would "pile the pale frenzy of blood-crazed brutes, who do such deeds, high on Thine Altar" (51). Central to Du Bois's poem is a search for meaning in black suffering. He demands that God explain "*What meaneth this? Tell us the plan; give us the sign*," and begs that he would "sit no longer blind . . . deaf to our prayer and dumb to our dumb suffering" (52). Du Bois's struggle to explain black suffering and alienation, caused by racism and discrimination, was a central concern shared by African American authors in the twentieth century.

After the end of World War II, black writers and thinkers, from Richard Wright to bell hooks, influenced by French existentialists like Albert Camus and Jean-Paul Sartre, adapted existentialism as a way to explain and respond to the African American experience. It would, however, be a mistake to view black existentialism as solely derived from European thought; as philosopher Lewis Gordon contends, when describing black existentialism, "it would . . . be fallacious to assume that that influence functions as the cause instead of the opportunity" (*Existentia Africana* 9). As Gordon asserts, "nihilism gnaws at black existence," and he argues that this question of existence, in defiance of dehumanization and racism, could be expressed, as Albert Camus does in *The Myth of Sisyphus*, by asking, "Why go on?" (9). Explaining the impetus for these kinds of questions about meaning, Gordon suggests that "if one is nearly everywhere told that one is not fully a human being, but one finds oneself struggling constantly with human responsibilities . . . the moment of theoretical reflection demands engagements with such idiosyncrasy" (28). This demand to engage with such idiosyncrasy drives much of the work of postwar black writers, including the novels of Frank Yerby.

In his novels, Frank Yerby displays a sophisticated awareness of philosophical ideas, especially absurdism, and theological questions, despite his insistence that his novels could not be "reduce[ed] to a morality play" (Hill, "Interview," 212), and even though he argued that "if a novelist . . . wants to preach he should go on the pulpit" (Cross 6). While Yerby is justly described as the "King of the Costume Novel" and "prince of the pulpsters," his novels are not mere escapist fiction (Bone 176). Critics such as Bernard W. Bell, in *The Afro-American Novel and Its Tradition*, largely dismiss Yerby's contributions, describing him as "a highly talented and popular creator of historical romances with white heroes that are primarily designed for pure entertainment" (336–37), and Yerby acknowledged, in an 1966 interview with Hoyt Fuller, that his novels were "written with the 'middleclass housewife mentality in mind,'" emphasizing the need to "let people escape once in a while" (192). Other critics have taken Yerby more seriously. As early as 1953, for example, Carl Milton Hughes, in *The Negro Novelist, 1940–1950*, suggests that "even though Yerby's books are designed for sheer entertainment, several serious passages appear" (158). Hughes notes Yerby's evolution as an author, observing that "there emerges slowly his development from a merely competent writer of historical narrative to a serious student of labor issues involved during the [eighteen] nineties as appears in his treatment of strikes in *Pride's Castle*" (275). This focus on class and labor also appears in Yerby's other novels. Darwin T. Turner, in his seminal work, "Frank Yerby as Debunker," argues that scholars of the late 1960s dismissed Yerby because "he has refused to fit comfortably into any of the cherished stereotypes" of African American authors (569). Turner contends that Yerby's most significant cultural contribution is that "he has debunked historical myths relentlessly," describing him as "an entertaining debunker of historical myths" (572, 577). Stephanie Brown, in *The Postwar African American Novel*, reaches a similar conclusion, arguing that Yerby uses "the power of fiction to reshape historical fact in the minds of the general public" (73).

Yerby, in addition to using fiction to debunk historical myth, also develops arguments about religion—that religion is invented "nonsense," and, therefore, not worth killing or dying for; that God, if he exists, is cruel, careless, or distant; and that morality need not hew to an *a priori* standard. As

Turner argues, "ideas—bitter ironies, caustic debunkings, painful gropings for meanings—writhe behind the soap-opera façade of [Yerby's] fiction" (570). The experiences of Yerby's protagonists reveal that "man's life is a joke played by a merciless and senile deity" (Turner 571). Yerby, through his answers to the problems of evil and suffering, expresses a version of what scholars have referred to as "black existentialism." As Lewis Gordon succinctly defines the term, "black existentialism explores the problems of existence generated by the complex history of black peoples" ("Introduction," 123). In particular, Yerby's work reflects the influence of absurdism. Literary scholar Esther Merle Jackson, in a 1962 essay in *Phylon*, argues that "the absurd sensibility is an acute consciousness of human consciousness of human crisis: it celebrates man's desperate struggle to order the moral universe, without recourse to powers outside of himself" (359). Like Camus in *The Myth of Sisyphus*, Yerby, in his novels, advances the argument that embracing absurdity is the best response to the problem of existence. Like Camus, who describes the absurd as a "divorce between man and his life, the actor and his setting," the "confrontation between the human need and the unreasonable silence of the world," Yerby emphasizes the feeling of disconnection men and women feel in a universe seemingly without meaning (6, 28). The alienation and abandonment expressed in Yerby's novels reflect the novelist's own experience, since he, to an even greater degree than other postwar black writers, struggled to find his own place. As an expatriate and as an African American novelist who seemingly eschewed political or social issues, Yerby was "an outsider, if not an anomaly, in postwar African American fiction" (Łuzack 74). Moreover, Yerby, as an African American, reflected the absurdity of the experiences of black Americans. As Jackson argues, "the shape of human suffering" reflects the "actual condition of the Negro: his alienation from the larger community, his isolation within abstract walls, his loss of freedom, and his legacy of despair" and, therefore, she contends, "he has served as a prototype of . . . 'the absurd'" (359). Yerby, then, responded to religious belief and voiced a philosophical response to human suffering (though, not specifically African American suffering) that was shaped by absurdist thought.

Other black authors of the postwar period wrestled with similar themes. Will Thomas's *God Is for White Folks* (1947) characterizes God as unconcerned with African Americans; in particular, Thomas argues that "God won't do anything for Negroes but keep them fooled" (4). Richard Wright, in his autobiography *Black Boy* (1945), explains that African Americans are "pulled toward emotional belief" but reject religion because, like Wright, they believe that "none of it was true and that nothing would happen" (102). Wright, in *Black Boy*, *Native Son*, and *The Outsider*, James Baldwin, in *Just Above My Head*, Ralph Ellison, in *Invisible Man*, and Toni Morrison in *The Bluest Eye* all grapple with the problem of black existence. For example, through Hall Montana, a character in *Just Above My Head*, Baldwin argues that there "ain't nothing up the road but us" (500). Montana's statement is an expression of Baldwin's belief, as Goyland Williams contends, "that man must be his own savior" (44). Just as Yerby questioned religious traditions, Baldwin, disillusioned by the cognitive dissonance created by Christianity's "claims to being a religion based on love" while justifying oppression and ignoring class and racial discrimination, began to "think . . . without the filter of religion" (Lapenson 201). African American writers and thinkers, though influenced by existentialism intellectually and, in Wright's case, personally, adapted existential thought to their realities shaped by their own social and historical contexts. In particular, Wright, as Nina Kressner Cobb suggests, found that the freedom obtained by rejecting the "tyranny of convention" (Gibson 344) left him with a "terrifying sense of isolation" (Cobb 374). Lewis Gordon argues that the question "What is to be done in a world of nearly a universal sense of superiority to, if not a universal hatred of, black folk? . . . animates a great deal of the theoretical dimension of black intellectual productions" ("Introduction" 1). Not all postwar black authors were comfortable with existentialism's influence; Arna Bontemps, for example, dismissed Wright's *The Outsider*, his novel which most clearly reflects existential thought, as a "roll in the hay with existentialism" (15). Yerby, as "debunker," challenges religious belief and its attempts to impose meaning on the universe and engages with the ideas of existentialism.

The foundation of existentialism, and, more specifically, absurdism is the acceptance of a nonexistent God. As Sartre explained, "the existentialist . . . finds it extremely embarrassing that God does not exist, for there disappears with Him all possibility of finding values in an intelligible heaven" and therefore, man is "condemned to be free" (294–95). Denying the existence of eternity and the Christian afterlife, Camus insisted that since there was "no superhuman happiness, no eternity outside of the curve of the days," one must accept death and delight in life: "stone, flesh, stars, and those truths the hands can touch" (*Nuptials* 90). Reflecting the French philosopher's rejection of religious belief as a necessary foundation for realizing and responding to the absurd, Yerby rejects religious belief throughout his novels. The novelist attacks religious bigotry, describes all religions as "nonsense," and debunks the Christian Bible, most notably through *Judas, My Brother*.

Yerby is forthright in his criticism of organized religion, particularly Christianity, characterizing religion as a pretext for intolerance and cruelty and condemning hypocritical religious leaders. He most clearly makes the criticisms in *The Golden Hawk*, *The Saracen Blade*, *An Odor of Sanctity*, and *Tobias and the Angel*. In Yerby's 1948 novel, *The Golden Hawk*, set in the late seventeenth century (largely in the Spanish colony of New Granada), the novelist uses a fictionalized version of the Spanish Inquisition to condemn religious bigotry. The Inquisition wreaks havoc on families and individuals throughout the novel. Most of the crew of *The Seaflower*, captained by Kit Gerado, suffers at the hands of the Inquisition. The nobleman Don Luis (Kit's father) also had Kit's mother, Jeanne, tortured by the Inquisition for refusing to tell Don Luis where Kit fled to after her son had attempted to choke Don Luis for whipping her, inspiring Kit to seek revenge against the nobleman. Yerby suggests in this novel that religious and political leaders are evil when they excuse cruelty in the name of religious principle.

Yerby also portrays the consequences of religious intolerance in *The Saracen Blade* (1952). Set during the early thirteenth century in Italy, France, and Jerusalem, Yerby puts religious conflict—between Christian Europeans and Muslim Saracens, Catholics and Albigensians, and Jews and Christians—at the forefront of the novel. Pietro, the son of a blacksmith born on the same day and in the same town as the Emperor Frederick II, is raised and educated in multiethnic and pluralistic Sicily. Pietro's father, Donati, was close friends with a Jewish merchant, Isaac ben Ibrahim, leading Donati to question his own prejudices and realize that if "Isaac was kind and good . . . was it not possible that other Jews . . . were good people?" (15). Pietro, raised by ben Ibrahim and taught by Christian priests, Muslim imams, and Jewish rabbis, criticizes the use of religious dogma to justify injustice, since he was "confused" that Christians should scorn Jews and slaughter Saracens "in the name of Jesus" and that "to his Moslem friends, women existed only as vehicles to serve their pleasure" (21). Frederick II, who befriends Pietro after he saves the emperor from being gored by a boar, echoes Pietro's views of religion. Explaining his desire for revenge against Pope Innocent III, who had denied him his crown, Frederick declares that "Cope and Miter can cover villainy as well as any other dress" (27).

Convinced that religion is no justification for violence or bigotry, Pietro exemplifies religious tolerance. When he joins the knight Gautier on the crusade against the Albigensians (1209–1229), he declares, "I will slay no man because he does not believe what I believe" (98). Later in the novel, Pietro describes Muslims as "warriors who love God as much as we [Christians] though we call Him by another name" (117). Yerby, through his protagonist in *The Saracen Blade*, condemns organized religion since it promotes intolerance, and commends religious toleration.

Yerby's 1965 novel, *An Odor of Sanctity*, also condemns religious belief as a justification for intolerance. Set in Muslim Spain in the ninth century, Yerby uses the setting, medieval Europe, and the interactions between Christians (both Catholic and Eastern Orthodox), Muslims, Jews, and atheists to reexamine the same issues he explored in *The Saracen Blade*. The novel's protagonist, Alaric Teudisson—or Aizun ibn al Qutiyya, as the Moors called him—is seemingly touched by the hand of God. With the face of an angel and a booming voice, he receives visions of a martyred saint, Saint Fredegunda, hears voices, and seems to work miracles. Alaric, or San Alarico as he comes to be known, however, is no religious fanatic, instead describing himself as a "freethinker" who believes that Muslims, Jews, and Christians all worship the same God.

Alaric's religious skepticism, and his career as a saint, began early after receiving a vision of a slaughtered saint, dripping with gore, while he was being seduced by a castle maid. Alaric, in frenzied horror, contemplates what he has seen, thinking that if "[God] let them nail his own Son to a tree, between two thieves ... to Him, a woman's arms or her [breasts]" were nothing (4). Reeling at his vision, Alaric queries God, asking, "Do You truly love death and anchorite saints who sit in their own excretion, devoured by vermin to the greater glory of Your Name? Is the odor of sanctity anything more than a foul smell? Or is it You we worship or filth or pain?" (4) After Alaric cries out from the horrors he has seen, his mother rushes into his bedroom and, smelling the cheap perfume of the serving girl, declares him a saint, a recipient of a divine vision. Later, reflecting on this first time he was called a saint, Alaric observes that his "poor mother confused a whore's scent with the odor of sanctity" (236). In the eyes of young Alaric, what humans called holy, the smell of ascetic monks, the scent of corruption and rot associated with a "dead saint," was in reality filthy and tawdry. Through Alaric, Yerby highlights the idea that religion corrupts humanity's ideas of good and evil.

Yerby's criticism of religious faith and religious leaders is most clearly displayed in *The Serpent and the Staff* and *Tobias and the Angel*. He depicts Vardigan Childers, the Calvinist uncle of Duncan Childers and the protagonist of *The Serpent and the Staff*, and L'Amour McSimple Fearsome, a "lady preacher" in *Tobias and the Angel*, who is a thinly veiled caricature of Aimee Semple McPherson, a Pentecostal evangelist and founder of the

Foursquare Church in Los Angeles. Yerby portrays organized religion as unloving and hypocritical. Vardigan Childers, in *The Serpent and the Staff*, embodies Yerby's criticism of religion. Duncan's pious grandmother, Minna Bouvoir, describes Vardigan and the whole Childers family as "Scotch Presbyterian . . . tight-fisted, dour, unloving," observing that "somehow they manage to make even virtue seem an evil" (24). Minna reserves special criticism for the Reverend Vardigan Childers, painting him as "beyond [her] comprehension" in his ability to make "a loathsomeness of such simple, pleasant things: like dancing; like boys and girls bathing together in the bayou" (24). She even goes as far as to diagnose Vardigan with "a sickness of the mind" (24). Duncan shares his grandmother's opinion of Vardigan, telling the minister that "the doctrine of predestination that only the elect are saved and only Presbyterians and damned few of them are among the elect and maybe there's nobody among the elect but you Uncle Vard sitting on the right Hand of God" (310–11). Vardigan, like Yerby's other representatives of religion gone awry, is intolerant, unloving, and perhaps most damningly in Yerby's mind, self-righteously judgmental of life's pleasures, which he deems sinful.

In *Tobias and the Angel*, Tobias becomes L'Amour's paramour in order to increase his wealth, since, as Angie explains, "bringing salvation is a lucrative business" (103). Angie comments that the "first rule in any evangelist's handbook" is to "pry the sucker . . . loose from his ready cash" (103). Yerby, through Angie, mocks the religious ecstasy that permeated revivals in the late nineteenth and early twentieth centuries, recounting that, after L'Amour

> preached the greatest sermon of her entire career . . . sinners fell out . . . in mounds, piled atop one another in layers three to five sinners deep, all of them jerking, screaming, foaming at the mouth, talking in tongues, a prey to a religious ecstasy so great that fully fifteen female sinners conceived *pro obra et gracia* of well—if not the Holy Ghost— at least of volunteers working in his spiritual behalf. (107)

Yerby's L'Amour is drunken, greedy, and lecherous and, like Aimee Semple McPherson, who was accused of disappearing with a lover to a resort town, she has Tobias stay at a small town in Mexico to keep him out of the reach of female converts. Yerby uses the character of L'Amour to lampoon the hypocrisy of religious leaders who are only concerned with financial and personal gain and sexual gratification. Throughout Yerby's novels, religious leaders, like L'Amour McSimple Fearsome and Vardigan Childers, in *The*

Serpent and the Staff (with the possible exception of Alaric, the protagonist of *An Odor of Sanctity* who becomes a saint) are discredited, either because of their hypocrisy or because they, in Yerby's mind, condemn laudable things while praising undesirable actions and characteristics.

In addition to attacking religious intolerance and religious leaders, Yerby describes religions as fictions created to give meaning to an otherwise meaningless existence, echoing Camus's characterizations of religious belief. Yerby's condemnation of religious intolerance is closely linked to his view of religions. This connection is best demonstrated in *An Odor of Sanctity*. Since Alaric believes that all religions were invented, he concludes that religious intolerance is wrong, since "to discriminate between the nonsense of one or another faith was an impossibility; that all were false, and all were true," a finding shared by his friend, Saadyah, who declares that "all religions are but superstitious nonsense" (434, 488). Additionally, since religion, according to Alaric, was invented to give meaning to life, "any faith that denies life becomes a perversion and a vice" (497).

As James L. Hill observes, in *An Odor of Sanctity*, by "combining the traditional anti-heroic elements of the picaro and the modern image of the fictional saint, Yerby creates the image of a character dedicated not so much to the supernatural god as to what remains of the sacred in the ravaged human community" (5). Religion, as presented by Yerby in this novel, reflects existentialist thought: it is an answer to the cruel reality of meaningless human existence, imbuing lives with meaning and affirming human life. This answer to existence, in absurdist thought, is not an answer at all, but is instead a form of "philosophical suicide"; as Camus argued, hope, especially religious hope, was the antithesis of truly living, since "hope . . . is tantamount to resignation" (*Selected Essays* 90). Alaric echoes Soren Kierkegaard's view of faith when he argues that faith should be life-affirming, not life-denying.

Alaric is not the only Yerby protagonist to argue that religion is nonsense. Raised in a religiously pluralist environment, Pietro, in *The Saracen Blade*, comes to view Christianity, Judaism, and Islam as "so much arrant nonsense" (19). Pietro, surrounded by conflicting religious ideas, becomes "amused . . . that grown men could not even agree upon which days were holy, much less in their interpretation of God" (20). Needless to say, Pietro, by thirteen, sees himself as "half a heretic" (21). Yerby argues through his novels that studying religion from a comparative perspective results in the end of religious belief. In *Devilseed* (1984), one of his characters, the college-educated playboy, Stanford Duclos, reflects after visiting a Chinese temple, that "the one sure result of the comparative study of religion was that you inevitably lost your

belief in any one of them because no other discipline made more cruelly clear
... what utter nonsense they all were" (273). In his novels Yerby articulates
his belief that all religions are "nonsense." Yerby's debunking of religion is
foundational to his development of existentialist ideas.

This description of religions as "nonsense" also appears in *Tobias and the Angel*. Angie, the protagonist's guardian angel, or perhaps his alter ego, rejects the idea that there even is good and evil, at least as humans understand it. He argues that religions are all "nonsense," invented to give human life meaning and dignity. Angie, in a sort of postmodernist approach to religious belief, also contends that all religions are equally true and false, like Alaric in *An Odor of Sanctity*. Angie declares that "everything some poor bastid really believes ... even great wickednesses 'n stupidities [are] so" (179). He argues that all religions are "bloody nonsense" and asserts that all religions—in particular, Christianity and Hinduism—are the same (180). He doubles down, asserting that religions are "myths one 'n all. Compendiums o' the dreams 'n racial/tribal memories o' th' naked ape. Walls built around his littleness 'n his fears. Props fer his feeble pride" (50). Angie reaches the same conclusion that Yerby protagonists like Alaric reach: since religion is invented, religious intolerance is inexcusable. He argues that "everything ye poor mixed-up bastids [humans] believe is so" and that "ye've no right to reject th' other fella's bloody nonsense, deny him the right to believe it, or try to convert him to yers" (181). Yerby, through Angie, urges religious tolerance, even though he suggests that belief has power. Significantly, Angie himself is perhaps merely a figment of Tobias's imagination, even though he has agency in the story.

For Yerby's protagonists—and for the author himself—religion was more than just harmless nonsense; instead, it could be used to justify intolerance (a point clearly made in *Tobias and the Angel*, *An Odor of Sanctity*, *The Golden Hawk*, and *The Saracen Blade*), and stop innovation. Pietro, in *The Saracen Blade*, comes to see religious belief as a barrier to progress, declaring that "faith stops thinking, and thought is the root of life without which we become beasts, faith is surrender and dependence and becoming children again, it is refusing to accept the unimaginable variety of truth and the unwillingness to permit another his variant. Faith stops progress" (232). Yerby also portrays religious belief as the antithesis of reason and progress in *The Serpent and the Staff*. Duncan, the protagonist, is "dedicated to rationality," and due to that dedication, he rejects religion. Reflecting on an encounter with his uncle, the Presbyterian minister Vardigan Childers, Duncan asserts that "the religious man is not so much irrational as antirational. He hates logic. Tackle him with that weapon, and you don't even dent his armor" (147). Yerby, like Camus, describes faith as a kind of "philosophical suicide" that prevents humans from facing the true reality of their existence.

Yerby's clearest statement about religion is his 1968 novel, *Judas, My Brother*. Displaying his role as "debunker," Yerby presents "a demythologized account of the beginnings of Christianity" (*Judas* 6). He informs the reader that the novel focuses primarily on two "controversial" questions: "whether any man truly has the right to believe fanciful and childish nonsense; and whether any organization has the right to impose, by almost imperial fiat, belief in things that simply are not so" (6). This novel crystallizes Yerby's rejection of religion as an answer to the problem of existence.

Judas, My Brother traces the life of Nathan Bar Yehudah, the son of a member of the Sanhedrin, who comes into contact with biblical characters from Jesus (Yeshu'a ha Notzri) to Judas Iscariot (Jehudah Ish Kriyoth). Throughout the novel, which is littered with citations, Yerby debunks the Christian Bible. Through pages of endnotes, Yerby engages with the scholarly debate—as it stood in the late 1960s—over the factuality of the Gospels. For example, he contends that Jesus was born in Nazareth, not Bethlehem, that Herod the Great died before Yeshu'a was born, that the miracle of turning water into wine was the result of a trick played by Nathan, that the feeding of the five thousand was done through Uncle Hezron's generosity rather than by divine intervention, that there was no such place as Gethsemane, and that Jesus never appeared to the disciples after his death. Nathan, in an aside addressing the presumably largely Christian audience, asserts that "your whole Christian tradition is a subtle distortion of the way things really were" (270). This kind of debunking also appears in *Tobias and the Angel* when Angie (the "angel") assaults the idea of a historical Jesus, arguing that "them rum old sods called Essenes, who was always a washin' the hide right off their own bones, made him up. Got sick'n tired o' waitin' round for their 'Teacher of Righteousness' to put in an appearance and bash the bloody Romans" (18). Later, Angie declares that Jesus was "only a figment of the Essenes' diseased 'n disordered imaginations," and he argues that "the New Testament is an Essenes' forgery" (37, 140). Yerby, through Nathan, also argues that religion distorts reality. Nathan laments that "once [humankind] finds [Jesus], and see his rude, rare, contours—like some monster's from the sea—they throw him back again, putting in his place the image of a plaster doll, polychromed and bright" (281). In *Judas, My Brother*, Yerby elaborates on the absurdist rejection of religion as a false solution for humanity's suffering and emphasizes that religion obscures the truth. By debunking and criticizing religious beliefs and religious leaders, Yerby performs a kind of revolt against religion, an important step on the path towards recognizing and responding to the absurd.

As part of his revolt against religious belief, Yerby uses his novels to question the existence and characteristics of God. He argues that God was created to give human life meaning (an idea that reflects existentialist philosophy) and, that if a deity did exist, he or she would be evil, since it allowed human suffering. In *A Woman Called Fancy* (1951), Yerby's first novel to feature a female protagonist, the novelist uses a cynical snake-oil salesman, Wyche Weathers, to make this point. Wyche recites a kind of natural and moral history of humanity, arguing that "the whole history of man . . . has been made up of his efforts to raise himself up from the ape he was into something approaching the angels" (48). He asserts that man conceived of God because "something in that awful, blind cosmos had to care about him, so he invented God" (49). This idea—that humankind invented God to give life meaning—appears in Yerby's later work as well. In *An Odor of Sanctity* Alaric asserts that the Greeks' and Romans' "warring, capricious, idle, mischievous, ribald, and cruel gods" made more sense than "Christian or Muslim belief" since "they gibed perfectly with the senseless world he knew and suffered" (360). He reaches the conclusion that "there is nothing more invincible in this world . . . than the will to believe. And the more idiotic the belief, the stronger it is held (400). Alaric argues that God is invented to provide meaning in a meaningless world. He declares that since "we . . . are born knowing we must die," humans "are continually condemned to reinvent God. A meaningful God for a meaningless universe" (405). Alaric explains that "of all Creation man bears the heaviest burden: the knowledge of his own approaching death. And since he finds . . . the destruction of so perfect a masterpiece . . . intolerable, he hath been compelled throughout creation to invent gods" (438). Yerby's characters, reflecting the influence of absurdist thought on the novelist, argue that humans invented God to give their lives meaning.

Yerby's novels also suggest that God is uncaring or even malicious and demonic. Fancy, in *A Woman Called Fancy*, comes to believe that God is either uncaring or irrelevant. Near the end of the book, after Fancy's husband, Court Brantley, is accused of murdering his mistress, Fancy pleads with God to save his life, declaring, "if You let her drag him down to death after her, what good are You, God?" (501). While Court is eventually found innocent, Fancy expresses the viewpoint that God does not care about humankind and leaves them to their own devices. In *The Saracen Blade*, Yerby explores the idea that random chance and absurdity, rather than divine decree, controls the fates of men and women, and that God, unable or unwilling to intervene, only watches from afar without interfering. Pietro, watching hawks down birds that were baked into a pastry at a nobleman's feast, reflects that "people were all little birds, playthings of fate, fools of destiny," and like those birds, "they plunged blindly through life and things happened to them—without rhyme or reason—and in heaven God laughed" (126). Roget, Gautier's Albigensian uncle, joins Pietro in his quiet assault on the idea of divine providence. Roget, who lost his faith in the Church after participating in the Fourth Crusade, tells his nephew, "I wonder if God ever has spoken to man—or even if there is a God at all" (135). Later, facing death by drowning or by Arab arrows, Pietro remains unconvinced of divine intervention, musing that "faith has never brought any man deliverance in human history unless it happened to coincide at that moment with the mysterious workings of the will of a very capricious God" (233). Like Camus, who contends that "the world is beautiful, and outside there is no salvation," Yerby, through Pietro, expresses skepticism about salvation and providence (*Nuptials* 103).

As in *The Saracen Blade*, characters in *The Serpent and the Staff* believe God is unconcerned with human affairs—or altogether irrelevant. Calico, the protagonist's prostitute-turned-paramour, rejects the idea of divine intervention, declaring "fat lot of good [God] ever did me. . . . I taught myself to read and write as a little girl. I even kept myself clean. . . . I grew and I was pretty. So my mother sold me a man who ran a cathouse" (84). Later in the book, as she dies during childbirth, Calico proclaims, "[God] doesn't care. We're like cockroaches to Him. That is, if He even remembers we're here" (113). Calico is not alone in asserting that God is uninterested in the lives of humans. Luvinia, an African American woman, asserts that God specifically ignored African Americans, observing that "hit 'pears to me your white folks' God just don't hear no niggers' prayers" (101). Through Luvinia, Yerby expresses views of God and Christianity similar to those of black authors such as Will Thomas, James Baldwin, and Richard Wright and theologians such as William R. Jones, who in *Is God a White Racist?* (1973) claims that "black Christianity was a form of misreligion that fulfilled a vital role in keeping blacks oppressed" (xv). This idea expressed by Luvinia—that God is unable to or uninterested in preventing human suffering—appears throughout Yerby's novels. In *Devilseed*, Mireille Duclos, the prostitute-turned-madame-turned-grand-dame protagonist, who throughout the book suffers sexual and physical violence, declares, "What God let happen to me doesn't incline my heart toward piety" (100).

Beyond portraying God as unconcerned with human pain and suffering, Yerby's novels also imply that God may be malicious or evil. In *An Odor of Sanctity*, Zoë, who is an adherent of Eastern Orthodoxy, ben Ezra's slave, and Alaric's first lover, scorns Alaric's guilt for his brother's death, which he blamed on his decision to engage in sexual activity with her. Zoë denies his belief that his brother Ataulf had died because he had "sinned." She states, "methinks I like not this God you serve. To punish one man's sins, he takes another's life" (96). Like ben Solomon, Zoë redefines sin and challenges Alaric's view of God. Zoë then accuses Alaric of not being Christian, asking him if he "worship[ped] some Gothic pagan god" since "God . . . pardons sins, and slays no man" (96). Yerby, through Zoë and ben Ezra, challenges the idea of a vengeful God and tries to define good and evil according to human relationships, rather than through divine decree.

Throughout *An Odor of Sanctity*, the protagonist's friend Saadyah ben Sahl describes God as uncaring, capricious, and cruel, since evil exists and God does not punish it. Alaric befriends Saadyah ben Sahl, an atheist Jew and the son of Alaric's employer in Toledo, the merchant Hasdai ben Sahl, at the urging of Saadyah's sister, Ruth, and his father. Alaric, the "saint" and a Christian firmly convinced of God's existence and goodness, debates with Saadyah. At the beginning, Alaric believes "that God lives. And though we cannot comprehend His ways, we must so order our little span beneath His sun that life shall have meaning, dignity, and grace, by fearing Him and keeping His commandments" (228).

Eventually, Saadyah sets out to instruct Alaric in the "devil's catechism" and challenges his beliefs. Saadyah acts as a stand-in for Yerby, a voice of reason, supported by the rarely heard authorial voice. After Alaric reacts in horror to discovering that his friend is an atheist, Saadyah answers that as a Jew, he has had "too much experience of that guidance and that protection" to turn to God for comfort or protection: he has "been enslaved by the Egyptians, captured by the Babylonians," and "treated with tender loving care by you Goths"; he mentions the persecution of Christians as well (247). Saadyah, like other characters in Yerby's historical novels, dismisses the idea of divine control after being confronted by suffering and evil. Saadyah goes as far as to call Alaric a "devil-worshiper," since he believes in a God who would punish humans for exercising their free will (247). Saadyah encourages Alaric, haunted by the suicide of his betrothed (which he believes he caused), to "[rid] him[self] of his monstrous God" (260). He declares that God "delightest in cruelty, in pain; and the piteous screams echoing unending doom" (265). Saadyah prefers atheism to worshiping a deity who delights in cruelty, arguing that he would prefer not to have any god in his "private heaven," reasoning that "before I'd see it peopled, throned, and ruled by a monster, I'll see it empty!" (265). Saadyah describes God as monstrous, delighting in the torment of men and women.

In *Judas, My Brother*, Nathan, the protagonist, also comes to believe the God is uncaring, evil, or nonexistent. After his wife, Helvetia, is raped by patricians and commits suicide, Nathan attacks his wife's abusers, but their slaves beat him senseless. His uncle, Hezron, rescues Nathan and returns him to Judea. While recovering at the Essene monastery in Qumran, Nathan ponders if God ever visited man and composes a poem in which he declares that, though he "cry in the daytime," God "hearest not" (86–87). While at Qumran, Nathan comes to the conclusion that either God is a "Monster," if he used "poor sinless chaste pure kind good Helvi" to punish him for his sins, or that God does not exist, believing that "it was less repugnant morally not to believe in God at all than it was to worship an absentee landlord of a deity on one hand . . . or Satan's own fiendish twin on the other" (92). Nathan argues, "If you insist upon retaining all three concepts: man's freedom and God's total knowledge, and limitless power, then you *must* dethrone YHWH and put black Samael-Satanas in his place, for a deity that can act and won't . . . and then metes out a punishment so awful that no sin . . . is commensurate with it . . . is Evil's pristine self!" (93). Later in the novel, Nathan declares that he "prefer[s] atheism to demonolatry" (135).

Nathan, like characters in other Yerby novels, portrays God as either useless, demonic, or monstrous. He describes God as both a "little grimacing posturing useless imaginary God" and an "eyeless, faceless, blind, three-headed, son-sacrificing cannibalistic monster of a god" (431, 439). Nathan ties his definition of sin to his view of God, declaring that sin cannot be "what is offensive to God" because based on what God "permits to happen daily in His world . . . absolutely nothing whatsoever offends Him, no matter how fiendishly cruel or nauseously vile" (199). He continues, asking his audience to "permit [him] . . . to pay your God the respect of disbelief for . . . in the moral sense he is . . . irrelevant; and, at worst, a monster. And . . . demon worship is a sin" (199). He concludes by defining sin as "any relationship, any act, which involves the humiliation, the wounding of a human soul" (199). Nathan is not the only character in *Judas, My Brother*, to describe God as a monster; the decurion Telemarchos, the husband of the prostitute-turned-disciple Shelomith, deplores "this invisible faceless eyeless blind monster of a God of yours" (212).

As in *Judas, My Brother, An Odor of Sanctity,* and *The Saracen Blade,* Yerby characterizes God as monstrous and uncaring in *Tobias and the Angel.* Facing the death of his wife, Anne, Angie calls God a "cruel monster" and, after Angie's wife dies in childbirth, the narrator states, "you might have heard his fellow Angels weep" for there is "only one Celestial Being who doesn't. Who's forgot how. The Auld Cuss. Alias God" (200, 271). This causes Angie to restate his claim that God "don't give a damn" about anybody but himself (313). As in his other novels, Yerby challenges the idea of a loving God, as Angie, rebuking Tobias, declares that "ye invent a lovin' merciful Father and a five year drought comes along 'n half a continent dies o' thirst 'n hunger" (50). To explain why evil exists, despite the existence, as Tobias believes of a loving God, Angie proposes that God and Satan "are joined hip 'n thigh," in order to explain "plagues, crimes, mass murders, abysmal bestiality, cities fire bombed, atomized, helpless babes 'wasted,' people whose noses ye don't like gassed, others whose camouflage job displeases you lynched" (58–59). Angie's alternative theology tries to find an answer to the problem of evil by proposing that God and Satan are one. Yerby uses *Tobias and the Angel* to advance the idea that God, if he exists, is uncaring or cruel.

Angie also holds that God, or "th' Auld Cuss," is limited by "Random Chance" and the "Absurdity Factor." God, according to Angie, is confounded by humans, asserting that "it's ye humans what have got Him buffaloed," since "when Night 'n Chaos gave birth to Him they forgot—or weren't able—to give Him control over Random Chance 'n the Absurdity Factor" (21). Nevertheless, Angie tells Tobias to avoid Nancy, a prostitute, because "the Laws of th' Universe is fixed" since "th' Auld Cuss is a Presbyterian," and "He believes in predestination" (28). Tobias chooses to ignore Angie, and as a result, Nancy dies after being gang raped. Yerby criticizes the idea of free will. Angie declares that God is "self-limitin', which means He hangs up His all-knowingness, 'n His total power long enough to grant ye poor humans freedom o' will, which works out to havin' th' freedom to get yerselves fried" (35). Angie believes that free will and the absurd limit divine power, even though humans face destruction for exercising their free will. Yerby's novels assert that God is a human construct, designed to give human life meaning or, if he were to exist, that God is powerless, unconcerned with human suffering, or monstrously evil.

Beyond challenging religious belief and religious leaders and questioning the existence and nature of God, Yerby also directly engages with the philosophy of absurdism. Absurdism asserts that "the creation of an ethic must be, in fact the responsibility of the individual," a project that many of

Yerby's protagonists embrace by suggesting their own definitions of right and wrong (Jackson 369). In *A Woman Called Fancy*, Yerby explores ethics and morality. When Fancy inquires of her employer Wyche Weathers if it is wrong for her to want to be with Court Brantley, even if he could not or would not marry her, Wyche answers her query by declaring that "anything that exalts that dignity of yours . . . is good" and "anything that debases it—is bad" (49). In *An Odor of Sanctity*, the Jewish merchant Solomon ben Ezra offers a similar definition for sin. He argues that "to violate another. To force one's will, one's greeds, one's angers, one's lust—and, good fathers, one's dogmas and one's cant—upon one another is the stuff of sin" (77). To ben Ezra, coercion makes an action wrong, while mutuality makes an action morally acceptable. Mirelle Duclos in *Devilseed* reflects a similar definition of good and evil. She embraces a kind of hedonism, explaining to her friend and lover, Paquita, that "if I enjoyed it, it was good. If I didn't, it was bad" (69). Good acts, in Yerby's novels, are enjoyable, mutual, and promote human dignity. This definition of good and evil is rooted in Yerby's engagement with absurdist thought; like Camus, who argues that life is only truly enjoyable after one has accepted death and been "stripped of all hope" of an afterlife gained by good deeds or faith, Yerby emphasizes that enjoyment of life is the only true good (*Selected Essays* 90). No longer limited by external ethical constraints, his protagonists can find freedom, a key part of absurdism, as Jackson points out: "the absurd view attempts to recover for man the principle of freedom" (366).

Yerby's novels also reflect existentialism's influence when his characters question the meaning of human existence. Faced with the tragedy of absurdity, his protagonists respond by embracing life and refusing to surrender through physical or philosophical suicide. Despite "this desire for unity, this longing to solve, this need for clarity and cohesion"—in short, a hunger for meaning—Yerby's protagonists (in particular, Duncan in *The Serpent and the Staff* and Harry in *Speak Now*) recognize that they cannot "know whether this world has a meaning that transcends it" (Camus, *The Myth* 51). They conclude that, if there is a meaning, it is unknowable, so they continue to live and seek to enjoy life in spite of this alienation and absurdity. The absurd, the "universe of infinite human possibility," depends on an individual's "reflection upon the significance of his own life" (Jackson 359–60). Duncan Childers, the atheist protagonist of *The Serpent and the Staff*, argues "the good or ill that one does is equally meaningless. As meaningless as a cockroach . . . if a man's life is only a lightning flash in the eternity of time, he owes it to himself to flash gloriously" (218). Childers advances the idea that since men and women's lives are meaningless, humans should embrace life fully. In *Speak Now* (1969),

Harry Forbes shares Childers's existentialist vision. As Harry explains to Kathy Nichols, a down-on-her-luck tobacco heiress from Durham, North Carolina, whom he offered to marry in order to legitimize a child she has conceived out of wedlock, "it makes no sense, which makes it right. A part of the pattern of the universe. My two-bit contribution to the galloping insanity the world's dying of. A nice, fat, assbackwards bit of absurdity" (38). Ewa Łuczak observes that "as in Camus's system, the absurd is a key term in Harry's philosophical vocabulary" (108). She contends that Harry, like Camus's Sisyphus, in deciding to marry Kathy at the end of the novel, "refuses to surrender in face of what looks like senseless action" (112). Both Harry and Duncan embrace the tragedy of the absurd and respond by living life.

Yerby reflects the influences of absurdism throughout his oeuvre. He develops three main contentions. First, he argues that religion is nonsense, an attempt to give meaning to a meaningless universe and recommends, rather than religious belief, embracing absurdity and, as Camus instructed, "imagin[ing] Sisyphus happy" (Camus, *Myth*, 123). Second, Yerby asserts that God, at least the God of Christianity, is either cruel, unconcerned with humanity, or nonexistent. Finally, he contends that right and wrong depend on the situation, rather than on an established moral code; right actions promote human dignity and give pleasure, while wrong actions debase humans, are unpleasurable, and result from coercion. While Yerby does not engage directly with the central arguments of black existentialism per se and seldom focuses on black suffering in particular, his challenges to the ability of religious belief in response to morality, his insistence that religions are invented, and his criticism of religiously based ideas of morality all reflect his embrace of existentialist ideas. Yerby's novels explain and propagate absurdist ideas throughout. Rather than just being the "prince of the pulpsters," Yerby is popular philosopher for the masses, a Camus for the common folk.

BIBLIOGRAPHY

Baldwin, James. *Just Above My Head*. Dial Press, 1979.
Bell, Bernard W. *The Afro-American Novel and Its Tradition*. U of Massachusetts P, 1987.
Bone, Robert. *The Negro Novel in America*. Yale UP, 1958.
Bontemps, Arna. "Three Portraits of the Negro." *The Saturday Review*, 28 March, 1953, pp. 15–16.
Brown, Stephanie. *The Postwar African American Novel: Protest and Discontent, 1945–1950*. UP of Mississippi, 2011.
Camus, Albert. "Nuptials at Tipasa." *Lyrical and Critical Essays*, edited by Philip Thody, translated by Ellen Conroy Kennedy, Knopf, 1968, pp. 65–72.

Camus, Albert. *The Myth of Sisyphus, and Other Essays*. Translated by Justin O'Brien. Vintage Books, 1991.

Camus, Albert. *Selected Essays and Notebooks*. Edited and translated by Philip Thody, Penguin, 1970.

Cobb, Nina Kressner. "Richard Wright: Exile and Existentialism." *Phylon*, vol. 40, no. 4, 1979, pp. 362–74.

Cross, Leslie. "At 35, Frank Yerby Has 7 Best-Sellers," *The Decatur Herald*, June 27, 1952, p. 6.

Du Bois, W. E. Burghardt, "A Litany of Atlanta." *The Book of American Negro Poetry: Chosen and Edited with an Essay on the Negro's Creative Genius*, edited by James Weldon Johnson, Harcourt, Brace, 1922, pp. 49–54.

Fuller, Hoyt W., "Famous Writer Faces a Challenge." *Ebony*, vol. 21, no. 8, June 1966, pp. 188–94.

Gibson, Donald B. "Richard Wright and the Tyranny of Convention." *CLA Journal*, vol. 12, no. 4, 1969, pp. 344–57.

Gordon, Lewis R. "Black Existentialism." *Encyclopedia of Black Studies*, edited by Molegi Kete Asante and Ama Mazama. SAGE Publications, 2005.

Gordon, Lewis R. *Existentia Africana: Understanding Africana Existential Thought*. Routledge, 2000.

Gordon, Lewis R. "Introduction." *Existence in Black: An Anthology of Black Existential Philosophy*, edited by Lewis R. Gordon. Routledge, 1996, pp. 1-10.

Hill, James L. "The Agnostic Musings of African American Popular Novelist Frank Garvin Yerby." *Forum on Public Policy*, Winter, 2008, pp. 1–9.

Hill, James L. "An Interview with Frank Garvin Yerby." *Resources for American Literary Study* vol. 21, no. 2, 1995, pp. 206-39.

Hughes, Carl Milton. *The Negro Novelist, 1940–1950*, Citadel Press, 1953.

Jackson, Esther Merle Jackson. "The American Negro and the Image of the Absurd." *Phylon*, vol. 23, no. 4, Fourth Quarter, 1962, pp. 359–71.

Jones, William R., *Is God a White Racist? A Preamble to Black Theology*. Beacon Press, 1973.

Lapenson, Bruce. "Race and Existential Commitment in James Baldwin." *Philosophy and Literature*, vol. 37, no. 1, 2013, pp. 199–209.

Łuczak, Ewa. *How Their Living outside America Affected Five African American Authors: Toward a Theory of Expatriate Literature*. Edward Mellen Press, 2010.

Sartre, Jean-Paul. "Existentialism is a Humanism." *Existentialism, From Dostoevsky to Sartre*, edited by Walter Kaufmann, Meridian Books, 1957, pp. 287–311.

Thomas, Will. *God Is for White Folks*. Creative Press, 1947.

Turner, Darwin T. "Frank Yerby as Debunker." *The Massachusetts Review*, vol. 9, no. 3, 1968, pp. 569–77.

Williams, Goyland. *An Existential Reflection on Suffering in James Baldwin's* Just Above My Head *and Toni Morrison's* The Bluest Eye. 2014. University of Kansas, MA thesis.

Wright, Richard. *Black Boy: A Record of Childhood and Youth*. Harper Collins, 1945.

Yerby, Frank. *Devilseed*. Doubleday, 1984.

Yerby, Frank. *The Foxes of Harrow*. Dial Press, 1946.

Yerby, Frank. *The Golden Hawk*. Dial Press, 1948.

Yerby, Frank. *A Women Called Fancy*. Dial Press, 1951.

Yerby, Frank. *Judas, My Brother: The Story of the Thirteenth Apostle*. Dial Press, 1968.
Yerby, Frank. *An Odor of Sanctity: A Novel of Medieval Moorish Spain*. Dial Press, 1965.
Yerby, Frank. *The Saracen Blade*. Dial Press, 1952.
Yerby, Frank. *The Serpent and the Staff*. Dell, 1958.
Yerby, Frank. *Speak Now: A Modern Novel*. Dial Press, 1969.

ACKNOWLEDGMENTS

IN A PROJECT SUCH AS THIS, THERE ARE MANY PEOPLE TO THANK. FIRST and foremost, I must thank the contributors, many of whom have been doing research and scholarship on Frank Yerby for a number of years. Scholars such as Darwin Turner, James L. Hill, and Maryemma Graham have done important work on Yerby, beginning in the 1960s and continuing to the present. I want to thank Jonathan Penton and Rosalyn Spencer at *Unlikely Stories* for publishing an early piece that I wrote on the myth of white southern womanhood in Yerby's short stories and novels. I'm grateful to Paine College for celebrating Yerby's legacy and for commemorating the centennial of his birth. My wife, Melissa helped me copyedit this collection. Finally, I thank the staff at the University Press of Mississippi because of the work they did to get this collection into your hands.

CONTRIBUTORS

Catherine L. Adams was an assistant professor of English and the former chair of the Humanities Department at Paine College. She is currently an assistant professor of English at Allen University. She earned her BA in English from Johnson C. Smith University, her MA in African American Studies from Temple University, and her PhD in Afro-American Studies from the University of Massachusetts Amherst. From 2012 to 2016, she directed cohorts of Yerby Scholars—students at Paine who were engaged in primary and secondary research regarding the life and literary contributions of the prolific Frank G. Yerby.

Stephanie Brown is the associate dean for academic affairs and an associate professor of English at the Ohio State University at Newark. She is the author of *The Postwar African-American Novel: Protest and Discontent, 1945–1950* (2013, UP of Mississippi) and the editor, with Eva Tettenborn, of *Engaging Tradition, Making It New: Essays on Teaching Recent African American Literature* (2008, Cambridge Scholars Press). She has also written numerous articles on African American literature and culture. Her current book project is a study of the discourses of labor and work in American historical and speculative fiction.

Gene Andrew Jarrett is Seryl Kushner Dean of the College of Arts and Science and Professor of English at New York University. He specializes in African American literary and intellectual history from the eighteenth century to the present. He is the author of two scholarly books, most recently *Representing the Race: A New Political History of African American Literature* (New York UP, 2011). He is the editor of eight books on African American literature and literary criticism, the latest being the two-volume *Wiley Blackwell Anthology of African American Literature*; in addition, he is the founding editor-in-chief of the African American Studies module for Oxford Bibliographies Online, published by Oxford University Press.

Among his many honors and achievements, Jarrett has received fellowships from Harvard University's Radcliffe Institute for Advanced Study and from the American Council of Learned Societies.

John Wharton Lowe is Barbara Methvin Distinguished Professor of English at the University of Georgia. He has authored or edited nine books, including, most recently, *Calypso Magnolia: The Crosscurrents of Caribbean and Southern Literature* (UNC Press), which won the 2017 C. Hugh Holman Award as the best book in Southern Studies. He has two edited books forthcoming: *Approaches to Teaching Gaines's "The Autobiography of Miss Jane Pittman" and Other Works* (MLA; coedited with Herman Beavers); and *Summoning Our Saints: The Poetry and Prose of Brenda Marie Osbey* (Lexington Books). He is currently writing the authorized biography of Ernest Gaines.

Guirdex Massé, PhD, is an assistant professor in the Department of English and Foreign Languages at Augusta University. An interdisciplinary scholar of African American and African Diaspora literatures and cultures, his research explores the ways in which racial and cultural identities, as well as notions of citizenship and freedom, emerge from the transnational encounters of black writers, intellectuals, and artists. He is currently working on a manuscript that examines the participation of James Baldwin, Richard Wright, George Lamming, Léopold Sédar Senghor, Jacques Stéphen Alexis, and Aimé Césaire at the First International Congress of Black Writers and Artists (1956).

Anderson Rouse is a doctoral candidate in United States history at the University of North Carolina, Greensboro. His research focuses on religion, race, and gender in the urbanizing and industrializing South of the twentieth century. His dissertation will explore the relationship between the careers and teachings of evangelists in the post–Civil War South and politics and society in the region.

Matthew Teutsch is the director of the Lillian E. Smith Center at Piedmont College. He has written on authors such as Frank Yerby, Ernest J. Gaines, William Faulkner, Lyle Saxon, Catharine Maria Sedgwick, and others, and his publications have appeared in *CLA Journal*, *MELUS*, *Mississippi Quarterly*, and *Studies in the Literary Imagination*. He is a regular contributor to *Black Perspectives*, the African American Intellectual History Society's blog, and *Teaching United States History*. He also works with the Society of Nineteenth-Century Americanists' podcast. His research focuses on African American, southern, and nineteenth-century American literature. He maintains *Interminable Rambling*, a blog about literature, composition, culture, and pedagogy.

Donna-lyn Washington is currently an adjunct lecturer of English at Kingsborough Community College in Brooklyn, where she utilizes popular culture in her pedagogy. She is currently under contract with University Press of Mississippi to edit the book *John Jennings: Conversations*, in a series showcasing significant contributors to the genre of comics. Her position as senior editor at *ReviewFix*, a popular-culture website, has allowed her to interview people from a variety of industries. She has contributed entries to *The Encyclopedia of Black Comics* and has an MA in English from Brooklyn College.

Veronica T. Watson is professor of English and director of the Graduate Program in Literature and Criticism at Indiana University of Pennsylvania. Her publications include *The Souls of White Folk: African American Writers Theorize Whiteness*; *Unveiling Whiteness in the 21st Century: Global Manifestations, Transdisciplinary Interventions* (coeditor); "Through the Valley of the Shadow of Death"; "Theorizing White Racial Trauma and its Remedies" (coauthor), and other articles. Watson teaches nineteenth- and twentieth-century African American literature; southern American literature; civil rights literature; black feminism; and critical race and critical whiteness studies. She is currently working on a collection of short fiction by Frank Yerby.

INDEX

Absalom, Absalom! (Faulkner), 104n2, 106, 111, 120, 121
absurdism, ix, 164–66, 177–79
Algren, Nelson, 108

Baldwin, James, vii, viii–ix, xiii, 8, 27, 45, 70, 166, 174
Bell, Bernard W., 164
Benton's Row (Yerby), 52–54, 67
Bernard, Emily, 65
Best Short Stories by Black Writers, 1897–1967, The (Hughes), viii–ix, 8, 72
Black Arts Movement, vii, 132, 134
Black Boy (Wright), 58, 165–66
"Blueprint for Negro Writing" (Wright), 38, 130
Bone, Robert, viii, 3, 11, 32, 34, 37–38, 44, 89, 129, 144n8
Bontemps, Arna, viii, 8, 29, 30, 37–39, 112, 130, 144n5, 166
Book of the Month Club, 57, 129
Braudel, Fernand, 114
Breen, Joseph, 92
Breity, Harvey, 57, 58–59
Brown, Lloyd L., 132
Brown, Stephanie, 3, 54–55, 57, 59–60, 66n1, 95, 160n1, 164

Camus, Albert, xii, 163, 165–66, 170–71, 174, 178–79
Carr, Greg, 6
Carter, James, 68
Carter, Michael, 151–52

Challenge, 23n30, 28–31, 38
Champion, Laurie, x, 3, 11, 13, 54, 144n3, 148, 160n2
Charles, John C. (John Charles Williamson), x, 56, 92, 93, 102, 160nn1–2
Chesnutt, Charles, x
Chicago Renaissance, vii, xi, 28, 36–39, 129–30, 144n5
Chicago School of Sociology, 36–37, 130
Christianity, 140, 160–68, 170–75, 179
Circum-Caribbean, xii, 109, 124, 125n7
Civil War, 49–52, 55, 91, 92, 106, 134
Clarke, Henrik, 8, 74
Common Ground, 52–53, 74
Conroy, Jack, 37, 39, 44–45
Cornfield, Bob, 4, 152–53, 160
Courage, Richard, 32, 34, 37–38
Crawford, Ruth B., 14–15, 23nn29–32
Crews, Harry, 48
Crowther, Bosley, 89–90

Dahomean, The (Yerby), viii, xii, 63–64, 69, 106, 125n9, 134, 148, 150, 160
Darkness at Ingraham's Crest, A (Yerby), viii, 106, 134
Devilseed (Yerby), 170–71, 174, 178
DeLoughrey, Elizabeth, 116
Double V Campaign, 76–77
Du Bois, W. E. B., 6–7, 10, 22n16, 32–34, 49–50, 65, 76–77, 111, 163
Dunbar, Paul Laurence, x, 22n16
Dunham, Katherine, 37, 108, 112

Ebony Magazine, 21n10, 69–70, 144n3, 150
Ellison, Ralph, viii–ix, 27, 132, 166
existentialism, ix, 35, 63, 115, 163, 165–66, 170–71, 178–79

Fabre, Michel, 44, 130–31, 145n19
Fairoaks (Yerby), 134
Fast, Howard, 48–51
Faulkner, William, 64, 106, 111, 112, 120, 121, 125n10
"Fire and Cloud" (Wright), 40, 85n5, 130
Fisk University, vii, 8, 14, 16–18, 20, 23n25, 23n36, 28–29, 36, 47
Floodtide (Yerby), 9
Foner, Eric, 50
Ford, Nick Aaron, 50
Foxes of Harrow, The (film), xi–xii, 12, 17, 89–105, 147
Foxes of Harrow, The (Yerby), viii, ix, 9, 27, 36, 39–40, 44, 48–49, 51, 54–57, 60, 64, 67, 85n4, 89–105, 106, 109, 118, 125n10, 129, 131, 133–34, 144n9, 145n12, 147, 149, 151–52, 160n1
Freud, Sigmund, 121–22
Fuller, Hoyt, 21n10, 144n3, 150, 159, 160n3, 164
Fuller, Muriel, 72, 107, 148–49, 150, 159, 160n2

Georgia Writers Hall of Fame, 48
Gillian (Yerby), viii
Glasrud, Bruce, x, 3, 11, 13, 54, 144n3, 148, 160n2
Gloster, Hugh M., 9, 44
Golden Hawk, The (Yerby), ix, x, xii, 9, 54, 106–26, 145n12, 167, 171
Gone with the Wind (film), xii, 90, 106
Gone with the Wind (Mitchell), xii, 27, 54–55, 89, 91, 104n2, 106, 125n8
Gordon, Lewis, 163–66
Graham, Maryemma, x, 3, 4, 11, 21n4, 69, 84, 144n3
Gray, Emma C. W., 4, 14–16, 23n23, 23n31, 23n36

Green, Martin, 112–13
Griffin's Way (Yerby), 134

Hail the Conquering Hero (Yerby), 123–24
Haines Institute, 3, 14, 21n2, 23n26, 47
Hanna, Mark G., 108
Harlem Renaissance, xi, 28–32, 130–31
"Health Card" (Yerby), vii, viii–ix, 6, 8, 12, 13–14, 19, 22n21, 23n25, 40–43, 54, 70, 72–74, 83, 104n1, 106, 130, 131, 147
"Helicopter, The" (Yerby), 72, 86n8
Hill, James L., vii, ix–x, 3, 4, 8, 11, 21n4, 21n10, 22n12, 70, 84, 89, 144n3, 148, 151–52, 170
Himes, Chester, vii, 8, 27, 44, 130
"Homecoming, The" (Yerby), 13–14, 16–17, 22n21, 70, 74–77, 83
hooks, bell, 163
"How and Why I Write the Costume Novel" (Yerby), 59, 60, 61, 69, 80–81, 86n10, 92, 108, 134
Hughes, Carl Milton, 164
Hughes, Langston, viii, ix, xiii, 8, 29–30, 32–33, 45, 54, 56, 57, 61, 66–67, 70, 72, 87
Hurston, Zora Neale, 30, 35, 44, 46, 70, 79–80, 112, 144

"Ignoble Victory" (Yerby), 59–60, 66n1

Jackson, Blyden, ix, 49, 51, 90–91
Jackson, Lawrence P., 11, 28, 31
James, C. L. R., 64–65, 110, 117–18, 123
James, Jennifer, 71–72, 83
Jameson, Fredric, 114
Jarrett, Gene Andrew, vii, x, 3, 11, 43, 64–65, 94, 104n5, 125n10, 144n10, 148, 160n1
Jarrett, Thomas D., 9
Jerng, Mark C., x, 55, 60, 95–96
Johnson, James Weldon, 29–30, 112
Johnson, Kathryn, 60
Judas, My Brother (Yerby), 124, 166, 172–73, 176–77

King, Stephen, xii
Klotman, Phyllis R., 93, 95, 144n3

Laney, Lucy C., 14, 21n2, 23n26
Linkon, Sherry Lee, 7
Locke, Alain, 31, 51–54, 56, 66
"Long Black Song" (Wright), 12–13
Long Dream, The (Wright), 34–35
Loving v. Virginia, 128
Lukács, Georg, 124
Lupack, Barbara Tepa, 90
Lyon, Bill, 44–45, 47, 48

manhood, 42, 70, 72, 81, 83
Martin, George R. R., xii
masculinity, xi, 56, 69–70, 72, 78, 80, 81, 83
Match, Richard, 48–49, 51, 90
"Matter for a Book" (Hughes), viii
McHenry, Elizabeth, xi, 48, 60–61, 64, 67
McKenzie's Hundred (Yerby), 129
McMillan, Terry, 60–61
McPherson, Aimee Semple, 168–69
Millender, Mallory, 22n15, 68–69, 72
"Miss Anne," 161n7
Mitchell, Margaret, xii, 27, 55, 89, 104n2, 106
Morgan, Stacy I., 31
Morrison, Toni, x, 166
Mullen, Thomas, xii

Native Son (Wright), 45, 57–58, 166
"necessary anguish," 156–58
New Anvil, 37, 39, 44–45
New Negro Renaissance. *See* Harlem Renaissance
New York Times, 58, 60, 89–90

Odor of Sanctity, An (Yerby), 133, 167, 168, 169–71, 173, 175–76
Old Gods Laugh, The (Yerby), 123–24, 133
Outsider, The (Wright), 166

Paine College, vii, xi, 3–9, 11–26, 28–29, 47, 68–69

Pitts, Lucius H., 4
Pride's Castle (Yerby), 9, 145n11, 145n12, 164

racial realism, 71, 80, 84, 129, 131–32, 143, 145
Radway, Janice, xi, 57–58, 113
Ramon, Marie Christina, x
Rampersad, Arnold, 58
Reconstruction, 49–50, 55, 59, 66n1, 80–81, 91
Rediker, Marcus, 109, 111–12, 115, 116
restrictive housing covenants, 151, 160

"Salute to the Flag" (Yerby), 13–14, 19
Saracen Blade, The (Yerby), viii, ix, x, 54, 167–68, 170–71, 173–74, 177
Sartre, Jean-Paul, 163, 166
"Schoolhouse of Compere Antoine, The" (Yerby), 70, 80, 83, 88
Schuyler, George, x, 91
Scott, Julius S., Jr., 4
Séjour, Victor, 121
Selznick, David O., xii, 91
Serpent and the Staff, The (Yerby), 9, 134, 168–69, 174
Smethurst, James, 22n16
social realism, 31–40
South Side Writers Group, 38–39
Speak Now (Yerby), vii, viii, x, xi, xii, 9, 18, 48, 61–63, 67, 69, 85n4, 86n8, 106, 108, 127–46, 147, 150, 159–60, 161n6, 161n8, 178
Stahl, John M., 90, 91–92, 95
Strauss, Helen, 70, 72, 85n3
"Supper for Louie" (Yerby) 70, 78–80

"tents of Shem" (Genesis), 161n5
"Tents of Shem, The" (Yerby), xii, 148–60
Teutsch, Matthew, 129, 159–60, 162n12
Thieme, John, 115
"This Is My Own" (Yerby), xii, 43, 106, 131, 148–50, 159, 162n10
Thomas, Will, 165, 174

"Thunder of God, The" (Yerby), 37, 39, 40, 41–42, 44–45
Tobias and the Angel (Yerby), viii, 167–69, 171–72, 177
Trouillot, Michel-Rolph, 119
Tuchock, Wanda, 90, 91–92, 95
Turner, Darwin, viii, ix, xiii, 3, 9–10, 22n12, 25, 63–64, 67, 93, 105, 115, 116–17, 126, 144n3, 164–65, 180

Vixens, The (Yerby), viii, 9, 50–51, 60, 107, 109, 133–34, 147

Walker, Grace, 28–29
Watson, Veronica, 3, 160n1
Webster, Harvey Curtis, 52–53
West, Dorothy, xiii, 23n30, 28–31, 38
Western: A Saga of the Great Plains (Yerby), 9
White, Walter, 91
"White Magnolias" (Yerby), 22n21, 40, 42

Williams, Roscoe, 4
Winfrey, Oprah, 64
Woman Called Fancy, A (Yerby), 9–10, 173, 178
Woodward, Isaac, 75
Wright, Richard, vii, viii–xi, xiii, 8, 12–13, 27, 32, 34–38, 40, 42–44, 57–58, 70, 85n5, 89, 90, 129–33, 142, 144n4, 163, 165–66, 174

Yerby, Blanquita (née Calle-Perez), 149
Yerby, Flora (née Williams), 107, 149
Yerby, Frank. *See individual titles of works*
Yerby, Jacques, 86n10
Yerby, Rufus Garvin, vii, 8, 47, 84n1
Yerby, Wilhelmina Ethel Smythe, vii, 8, 47, 84n1
Yerby Scholars, 6, 8, 11–12, 14, 16–20, 23n27, 24n38, 24n40

Zanuck, Darryl, 91

www.ingramcontent.com/pod-product-compliance
Lightning Source LLC
Chambersburg PA
CBHW030624230426
43661CB00053B/2128